DEFIANT GEOGRAPHIES

ILLUMINATIONS CULTURAL FORMATIONS OF THE AMERICAS

John Beverley and Sara Castro-Klarén, Editors

DEFIANT GEOGRAPHIES

RACE & URBAN SPACE IN 1920s RIO DE JANEIRO

LORRAINE LEU

UNIVERSITY OF PITTSBURGH PRESS

A portion of chapter 3 is reprinted from "Urbanization, Ruination, and Refusal: Racialized Geographies in 1920s Rio de Janeiro," *Journal of Latin American Cultural Studies* 25, no. 1 (2016): 19–34. A portion of chapter 4 is reprinted from "Eradicating Blackness from the Ideal City: Urbanization, Global Spectacle, and Brazil's Centenary," in *Urban Latin America: Images, Words, Flows, and the Built Environment*, edited by Bianca Freire-Medeiros and Julia O'Donnell, 190–209 (New York: Routledge, 2018).

Published by the University of Pittsburgh Press, Pittsburgh, Pa., 15260

Manufactured in the United States of America
Printed on acid-free paper
10 9 8 7 6 5 4 3 2 1

Cataloging-in-Publication data is available from the Library of Congress

ISBN 13: 978-0-8229-4600-7
ISBN 10: 0-8229-4600-9

Cover art: "Demolition on Train Street," Augusto Malta, n.d., G. Ermakoff Archive.
Cover design: Alex Wolfe

For Robin and Eva . . . my all

CONTENTS

ACKNOWLEDGMENTS

A NUMBER OF YEARS AGO I was browsing in a secondhand book fair in the Largo da Carioca in downtown Rio, when I spotted a lavishly illustrated publication on Morro do Castelo (Nonato and Santos 2000). Fascinated by its evocative images, I realized that I was standing barely a couple of blocks away from the spot where a vibrant hillside community of over four thousand people had once lived, worked, and played. Moreover, that neighborhood had been the site on which the city was founded. Despite its historical importance and architectural treasures, the municipal and federal governments had leveled it to make space for the country's first mega-event—the Rio de Janeiro World Fair of 1922. I dipped into that book often over the next few years as I thought about the factors that must have motivated such a decision, and its impact on residents' lives. It was not until my first full year at the University of Texas at Austin in 2012 that I had the opportunity to turn my curiosity into a book project. Charles Hale, the then director of the Lozano Long Institute of Latin American Studies (LLILAS), invited a colleague and me to organize a faculty seminar on urban Brazil. Over the course of a semester a group of UT Brazilianists from half a dozen disciplines received a course release to meet once a week, discuss readings, and talk about our work. I have never learned so much in such a short time as I did there, and I am grateful to all who participated for that. I am particularly indebted to Charlie Hale for the opportunity and for all his encouragement for this project. His support also enabled me to get a year's research leave to write the book, so it really would not have emerged without his help.

Defiant Geographies would certainly never have taken shape without the intellectual, emotional, and general moral support provided by my husband and colleague, Robin Moore. I have run many of the ideas for this work past him, and every time I feel a profound admiration for his clarity of thinking, mental agility, and creativity. I also greatly admire his own work and the contributions he has made to thinking race and culture in the Hispanic Caribbean. I feel incredibly fortunate to have him as my most productive interlocutor. His practical support has also been invaluable, especially as our daughter Eva was born shortly before I began at UT. At home he has been happy to frequently take on more than his share of responsibilities and parenting in order to make time for me to work on this project. His unruffled, reassuring manner in all things also makes our professional and personal life run a remarkably smooth course. This book is dedicated to him for all this and so much more, as well as to our most precious collaboration, our beautiful daughter, Eva.

I would also like to thank colleagues, former colleagues, and those who have at some point formed a part of UT's Latin Americanist intellectual community. For all of the advice, reading suggestions, pearls of wisdom, general support, and camaraderie, thank you to Jossiana Arroyo-Martínez, Jason Borge, Luis Cárcamo-Huechante, Bianca Freire-Medeiros, Juliet Hooker, Fernando Lara, Ana Flávia Magalhães Pinto, Gabriela Polit, Sônia Roncador, and Christen Smith. It was my good fortune on arrival at UT to have as chairs of my two home departments the dynamic and visionary Charlie Hale (LLILAS) and Jill Robbins (Spanish and Portuguese). They played key roles in my appointment, my first years here, and continue to cheerlead for me from afar. I am pleased that I continue to count on the rock-solid support of my current chairs, Jossiana Arroyo-Martínez, Jorge Pérez, and Virginia Garrard. Thanks are also owed to Richard Flores, senior associate dean in the College of Liberal Arts, who facilitated my period of research leave that was crucial to writing the book. We UT Latin Americanists are a lucky lot to have access to the Benson Library on our campus and I am repeatedly astounded by the extent of the material held there. My colleagues at the Benson are the most patient and willing anywhere, and I especially want to mention AJ Johnson and Linda Gill, who impress me with their knowledge and whose willingness to help I deeply appreciate. My graduate students have indulged me in discussing some of the ideas in the book and offered valuable feedback. Several of them have provided research assistance that helped keep the project moving at various moments when I really needed it. Thank you, Ricardo Correa, Charles Wight, Alida Perrine, Angela Tapia, Daniela Meirelles, Célia Cordeiro, and Catalina Iannone. I am indebted to the brilliant Sara McTarnaghan (LLILAS class of 2015 and now at the Urban Institute in Washington), with whom I coauthored a conference paper on Vila Autódromo, some of which appears in the epilogue of this book.

Via email, WhatsApp, Skype, and in happy reunions at conference venues around the world, I continue to count on sustaining conversations about work and life from a group of dear friends who are former colleagues at the University of Bristol. David Brookshaw, Jo Crow, Ruth Glynn, and Catherine O'Rawe, thank you for your support and love across the miles. My dear Jo deserves special mention for her willingness to travel across the Atlantic about every eighteen months so we can catch up in person. I also want to thank my colleagues Maite Conde at the University of Cambridge and Peter Wade at the University of Manchester for weighing in at different points along this journey. In the United States, Amy Chazkel, Michael Conniff, and Brodwyn Fischer pointed me in the direction of material and offered reading suggestions. Additionally, I wish to thank friends and colleagues in Brazil and staff at the Biblioteca Nacional and the Arquivo Geral da Cidade do Rio de Janeiro for all their assistance. Thanks are also owed to the series editors, John Beverley and Sara Castro-Klarén, and the team at the University of Pittsburgh Press, especially Josh Shanholtzer, Amy Sherma, and Alex Wolfe.

Finally, I don't even know how to begin to thank my father, Philip Leu, who lives in our family home in Trinidad, but whom I hold close in my heart every day, for all that he has contributed to this and every project that I carry out. His pride in my every undertaking makes me feel that anything is possible, and so each successfully completed project owes something to him. His life has been an enduring example of hard work and self-sacrifice for my late mother, Bernice, and for us children, and so much of what we all are today is because of them.

DEFIANT GEOGRAPHIES

Figure I.1. "Discussing the Problem," *O Malho*, July 29, 1905. Biblioteca Nacional Digital Brasil.

INTRODUCTION

IN A CARTOON in a Rio de Janeiro satirical magazine (fig. I.1), two black city dwellers chat in vernacular Portuguese about the infamous urban reforms that took place under Mayor Francisco Pereira Passos between 1903 and 1906. Their conversation touches on key aspects of the relationship between people of color, the government, and the modernizing spaces of the city:

> "The government's knocking down houses; Mister Passos too. Mister Oswaldo from the hygiene department, he's shutting down everything that don't smell good . . . Tell me, where are we supposed to live?"
>
> "Well, I hear the experts been talking 'bout workers' housing problems."
>
> "To hell with the experts! You don't make a house with words, or letters on a page. By the time they sort this out we'll be in a fine mess!"
>
> "Well, there's no way I'm living on the streets. When I have nowhere to lay down my bundle I'll make some noise and force the government to put a roof over my head . . ."
>
> "That's easy for you to say, you don't have a wife and children . . ."
>
> "Then be like me—don't have any! Nobody can make us! This is a free republic."

The magazine's cartoonist imagines a discussion in which the humble black worker on the left criticizes city and state officials for their inaction in the face of the housing crisis that they have aggravated in a frenzy of demolition related to the reforms. The places that he occupies in the city are being eliminated in the name of hygiene—a social cleansing that also targets a highly visible black presence downtown. The character on the right is represented as a *malandro,* an Afro-descendant street hustler and dandy who typically avoided not only the oppressive menial work available to the black population after abolition but also the responsibilities of family in difficult living conditions. The characters articulate two modes of resistance to the spatial order proposed by the urbanization project. The worker verbally counters and condemns the violence of his negation as a citizen. He is conscious of his inscription by the reformers as superfluous to modernity—he is not the ideal worker that the state has in mind in its eulogizing discourse on labor, so there is little point waiting for the authorities to meet his needs. He also understands his inscription as an obstacle to modernity because he is racially signified as unhygienic. The *malandro* proposes to demand housing from the government using potentially violent protest if necessary. He will occupy the streets and show his dissent for their proposed model of the city, using his body to impose his own spatial practices on the capital. He mobilizes the racialization that produces him as unruly and criminal, but imagines himself as a citizen in a "free republic" when he threatens disorder to the modernizing project. His character implicitly critiques the bourgeois norms idealized by reforms that make black families homeless and make it difficult for the black population to survive and socially reproduce.

Both characters demonstrate a clear political consciousness in their practices of refusal and resistance in the face of the racialized violence of the urbanizing city. They wage their struggle for survival in the context of a genocidal and "topocidal" (Porteous 1989) national project intent on eliminating blackness and annihilating the places in which people of color resided. In fighting for a place to live they fight for their existence. In disputing and claiming territory they create what I call "defiant geographies," interventions into space that can challenge geographies of domination, even if momentarily. I also conceptualize the spaces produced by such practices as "deviant," in the sense that they deviated from those sanctioned by dominant social groups and were spaces in which oppressive laws often were flouted, or social norms contravened. They were, therefore, frequently criminalized and demonized—the targets of police persecution and the moralizing force of official discourse. This defiance is a fundamental characteristic of Rio's black geographies. According to Katherine McKittrick and Clyde Woods, "Black geographies disclose how the racialized production of space is made possible in the explicit demarcations of the spaces of *les damnés* as invisible/forgettable at the same time as the invisible/forgettable is producing space—always, and in all sorts of ways" (2007, 4). Defiance is therefore the creative capacity to invent and adapt spatial practices that persistently introduced black bodies and subjectivities into prohibited spaces. The spaces of the reformed city are therefore produced by coloniality's structures of racial domination, but also by people considered nonwhite or "less than white" talking back, gazing back, and taking back. The dispute over territory plays out in the ideal models of urbanity that the state, the city, and its elites seek to impose and the ways in which black and blackened subjects use their own decolonizing spatial logics to introduce alternative ways of being in and understanding the city.

This book is about how "race makes space." The brevity of this formulation from Don Mitchell (2000) of the interrelationships between racialization and the production of space belies the many ways in which the two are mutually constituted. Mitchell's aphorism has been the impulse underlying my reading of one of the most important moments in Brazil's urban history. My analysis focuses on the next hugely ambitious project that followed the Passos reforms and that sought to continue its work of Europeanization and erasure. This project was momentous for a number of reasons. First of all, it was designed to commemorate the centenary of Brazil's independence from Portugal in 1922. Because of this the reforms were deeply intertwined with the process of envisioning not just the capital city but also the nation of the future. They therefore offer us privileged insights into the relationship between the production of space, modernization, and the creation of a national imaginary. Secondly, the scheme involved razing to the ground an entire hillside in the middle of downtown Rio within a couple of years, with the technology available in 1920s Brazil. Additionally, the culmination of the plan was the construction of a mini-city containing sumptuous pavilions and palaces to function as the site of an international exposition—the first world fair hosted by a Latin American nation. Considering the monumentality of this endeavor it is curious that a significant body of scholarship on the subject has not emerged.[1] Mitchell explores his pithy statement using apartheid South Africa as a site for his analysis, which means that there are few subtleties or hidden agendas to unearth in the exploration of race as a geographical project in his case study (2000, 250–55). The challenge of this book has been to unpack how race makes space in a country with one of the largest populations of color in the world, but where race injustice has been notoriously obscured in powerful national discourses of racial harmony and color blindness. In unraveling these dynamics I highlight how urbanization functions as a technology of racial oppression and how racialized subjects defy the implantation of dominant spatial orders. Ultimately, I make an intervention in a body of scholarship on Brazil's urban development that has been overwhelmingly focused on class.

The exposition city that was to symbolize Brazil's progress, its cosmopolitanism, and its bright, white future required a great leap of the imagination. Three decades of Republican rule had been somewhat underwhelming in terms of meeting the state's modernizing goals (Motta 1992, 26). By 1922, although urbanization, industrialization, and modernization were under way, Brazil remained predominantly rural. In 1920 70 percent of the country's employed males were engaged in agriculture, land ownership patterns were neocolonial, and a landed oligarchy continued to wield power (Burns 1980, 373–74). The end of the First World War had brought recession to Brazil's economy. The 1920s therefore began in a climate of economic uncertainty, and a souring relationship between the government of President Epitácio Pessoa (1919–1922) and the military. After the presidential elections of 1922, when the candidate endorsed by the army lost, a group of junior officers revolted at Copacabana in Rio de Janeiro against power sharing in the Republican government between privileged elites from the states of São Paulo and Minas Gerais. The revolt failed, but signaled a more generalized protest against a decadent republic from emerging urban middle-class groups. In the same centennial year the Communist Party of Brazil was founded with a radical agenda for political and social change (Burns 1980, 360, 383, 385–87). Despite or perhaps because of all this the government pressed on with its ambitious plans to celebrate the centenary and create an exposition city that would demonstrate the country's advances.

THE CASTELO NEIGHBORHOOD

A grand gesture was necessary for the production of this ideal space. It came in the form of destruction on a monumental scale of an entire hillside community in the city center. Morro do Castelo, or Castelo Hill, was the site where the colonial city was founded in 1565, and the area was a treasure trove of architectural history and an important site of collective memory. Yet it was flattened in precisely the year that Brazil was celebrating a hundred years of its independence. Clearly, the meanings of that space had become so degraded that it was considered incompatible with the modernizing impulse of the 1920s nation. Castelo's illustrious beginning belies its inglorious end. It began as a foundational space that symbolized imperial power at its most official. The Portuguese relocated the city to this hillside, strategically overlooking Guanabara Bay and away from the swampland at the mouth of the bay. The hilly terrain was seen as advantageous for military defense, and the colonizers imposed an architecture of power on the land, which included a fortress, the seat of government, a church, and a prison. The viceroy's residence and those of the other highest-ranking dignitaries in the colony were situated there. It was a site from which the Portuguese sought to impose their civilizing mission across a vast, newly claimed territory. By the end of the sixteenth century, however, with swamps being drained at the mouth of the bay and a growing population needing more water and easier access to goods, the hillside began to be abandoned for the reclaimed land below (Nonato and Santos 2000, 60–67). Castelo began its own descent, from a space of colonial authority and domination to a space stigmatized as degraded and criminal by the postabolition period.

The Passos reforms had targeted part of the hillside for demolition to make way for one of the crown jewels of the scheme, the construction of a Parisian-style boulevard—the Avenida Central. A contemporary newspaper report offers us a glimpse of the ruthless determination to modernize the city and eliminate spaces and bodies that stood in the way. In January 1905 city officials served an eviction notice to inhabitants of a rooming house on Castelo, giving them a mere eight days to vacate the property. In fact, the authorities eventually ejected the residents and demolished the building even before the scant period of notice had expired (*Correio da Manhã*, January 5, 1905; *Correio da Manhã*, January 11, 1905). The housing crisis that was created by the extensive demolition of collective housing and the ongoing arrival of new immigrants was felt acutely in those already overcrowded tenements left standing downtown (Vaz 1994). Some of the newly homeless who left the city went to nearby suburbs if they had sufficient resources. However, the majority sought out a space in remaining rooming houses, or swelled the ranks of those finding shelter in hillside communities or in recently configured favelas. The number of collective residences decreased in the districts of Santa Rita and São José that were vital to the city's commerce and services (the latter the district in which Castelo was located). However, in nearby downtown districts their number had actually increased by 1919, demonstrating that in the main residents did not abandon the central areas of the city as a result of the reforms (Pechman and Fritsch 1985, 76, 180). These densely occupied dwellings defied attempts to alter the occupation of space in the capital. Despite the increasingly difficult living conditions produced by this demand, for ordinary people survival depended on their proximity to the central zone (Abreu 1986, 48). Castelo lost one of its slopes during that urbanization initiative, but the rest of the hill was left intact until 1920, when demolition work began to make way for the world fair. Until then it remained as a site of tension or disruption in relation to the modernizing project. Those who occupied these hillsides downtown bore the stigma of illegality. The chronicler Luiz Edmundo describes the Morro de Santo Antônio (which was adjacent to Castelo and itself flattened from 1952) as being inhabited by criminal types, the unemployed, and the destitute (1957, 147).

This reputation of hillside neighborhoods appears to have been exaggerated, at least in the case of Castelo, as Cláudia Quelhas Paixão argues. Working with district police logs between 1916 and 1922, she finds that out of a total of 426 incidents involving *castelenses,* or residents of Castelo, the latter appear as the offenders in only 104 cases. Of these, the most common problems between residents involved petty theft and physical aggression in their overcrowded living spaces. Significantly, two of the most commonly reported incidents overall, accidents and traffic accidents, indicate that residents were victims of the city's modernization rather than threats to it. Paixão notes that the majority of reported accidents took place in 1921 and 1922 as a result of demolition work on the hill (2008, 155). She concludes that public discourse helped to project the neighborhood as an unsanitary site of criminals and layabouts in order to justify its removal (33).

Data collected in 1908 by a life insurance company provides evidence of residents who were involved in the informal economy that was profoundly criminalized by the 1890 Penal Code. The neighborhood was also famous for its fearless capoeira fighters. However, the insurance data also lists professionals such as architects, engineers, and teachers among its residents (*Almanaque Laemmert* 1908, iv). Paixão also mines the police logs to find professions such as domestic servant, stevedore, vendor, tailor, carpenter, bricklayer, soldier, and corner-store owner. Nor was housing unregulated in Castelo, although (as discussed in chapter 3) there were informal dwellings in the neighborhood. City officials had previously inspected the tenement building mentioned above whose residents were given the eight-day eviction notice, and reported that it conformed to building codes and regulations. Many tenements were owned by prominent members of the Republican elite and were inspected and regulated by the city (Directoria Geral de Saúde Pública 1906). In fact, the government owned several properties on Castelo Hill where they housed retired military personnel and their families. This did not prevent public discourse from producing the neighborhood as a degenerate space of illegality. Interestingly, one rooming house on the Rua do Castelo belonged to the father of the writer Olavo Bilac, one of the most strenuous critics in the press of the persistence of the "barbarous" customs of the poor in the modernizing city center (see Fridman and Moraes 1999).

Contemporary chronicles offer a glimpse into the racialized landscape of Castelo close to the time of its destruction.[2] Castelo had a significant Italian, and to a lesser extent, Portuguese immigrant population. In fact, the writer and art critic Gonzaga Duque, writing under the pen name Américo Fluminense, observed that Italians were in the majority by the time of the Passos reforms, and that the neighborhood's historically largely black population had dwindled significantly (Fluminense 1905, 45–46).[3] Despite this demographic change, Castelo persisted in the urban imaginary as a black space. A 1911 political cartoon, for example, identifies Castelo as a place of capoeira fighters, *mulatas*, and carnival revelers.[4] It appears that public perception continued to associate the hillside with black social "types"; for example, "candomblé priests, ex-slaves and *capoeiras*" (Stuckenbruck 1996, 56), even after the demographic shift. Despite the diminished demographic presence of Afro-descendants in the neighborhood by the early twentieth century, blackness continued to signify the space, and accounts of the time often produced white residents as black. The neighborhood acquired a racial script that gave certain meanings to the spatial and cultural practices of its inhabitants. Even when a grammar of racial difference is not explicit, the spaces of the poor in Brazil are often referenced with what Jaime Alves calls an "alternative vocabulary to delineate a social geography that has everything to do with race" (2012, 32). The descriptors that official public discourse and the press employed for Castelo were also used to characterize blackness: *backward, colonial, criminal, indolent, insanitary.* In this sense, if we understand Castelo as a "black space" in an urban imaginary, we can comprehend the vehemence and determination with which it was destroyed.

INVISIBILIZING BLACKNESS

In 1922 Brazil's ideal capital city could only be imagined via a mnemonic erasure of the history of slavery. A policy facilitating white European immigration supported the urbanization project that aimed to achieve this. Both initiatives were hopelessly optimistic in their attempts to eradicate blackness from the city, when around 60 percent of the country's population after the abolition of slavery was Afro-descendant (Tinhorão 1998, 264). In fact, newspaper chronicles in the late nineteenth and early twentieth century frequently complained that Rio's urban spaces had the appearance of an African street market—such was the presence of former slaves and their descendants on the streets (Moura 1983). Therefore, one of the main motivating factors in early twentieth-century public works was finding a solution to the overwhelming perception of Rio de Janeiro as a black city. In the state's modernizing vision there was no place for blackness—blackness as phenotype, and also as behaviors, sociabilities, subjectivities, and as certain ways of occupying space. The targets of the early twentieth-century urbanization projects were therefore people of color as well as poor European immigrants blackened by their occupation of the same spaces of the city as former slaves and their descendants.

Saidiya Hartman has argued that the ruling visual logic of plantation slavery was hypervisibility (1997, 36). She observes that the plantation was laid out so that the slave was the permanent object of the surveying gaze of the overseer. Black bodies had to be visible in order to be forcibly subordinated. The early Republican state and the municipal authorities of Rio demonstrated a keen interest in constraining and punishing black bodies, but not in training them for entry into the labor market. They considered the black population incapable of adapting to modernity. This is an idea that prevails in public discourse until at least the late 1940s. The report that accompanied a 1948 census on favelas in Rio's Federal District describes the black population as "inherently backward, lacking ambition and ill-adjusted to the social demands of modern life" (quoted in Valladares 2005, 65). Reforming black bodies and behaviors to support an emergent capitalist economy was therefore not on the official agenda. Instead, the state opted for reconfiguring its labor force through European immigration, which would also achieve the objective of whitening the population. The fantasy of total dominion over the black body that was reliant on its hypervisibility in the plantations gave way to a fantasy of eradicating blackness from the most valued spaces in the city. Hypervisibility gave way to its inverse: a logic of removal or invisibilization. Postabolition legal codes supported removal, criminalizing black cultural expression such as capoeira street fighting and dance, and black forms of sociability in public spaces, such as gatherings around the street vendor's stall, serenades, and the rowdy carnival revelry of the *cordões*.[5] The vagrancy law targeted occupations of the street with literal expulsion from the city—infractors were loaded into the holds of steam ships and dispatched to remote areas in the Amazon, Acre, and the island of Fernando de Noronha in the north of the country (Sevcenko 1993, 69–70; Carvalho 1999, 178–79).

Urban reform was a key tool of removal and invisibilization. As mayor, Pereira Passos was the first to conduct a radical social engineering experiment through public works that aimed to eliminate people like the characters in our opening cartoon from the city center. This was an extremely ambitious initiative and the mayor enjoyed unconstitutional powers to realize his goals and those of the federal government (Sevcenko 1993, 45–48). The reformers destroyed 1,600 buildings, made 20,000 people homeless, and incurred a huge debt in the process of remaking downtown Rio in the image of Haussmann's Paris (Rocha and Carvalho 1995, 77). The demolition frenzy constituted a violent attack on the city and its humblest inhabitants, making way for the construction of elegant avenues, monuments, and high cultural institutions (Abreu 1997, 59–67; Meade 1999, 84–94; Needell 1984, 400–403; Sevcenko 1993, 48–68). Contemporary newspaper commentators taken aback by the scale of the destruction complained that many demolished buildings were perfectly solid and had been unnecessarily destroyed. Ultimately, the reforms aimed to reorganize space so that the city center was reserved for the production and circulation of goods, the emerging areas of the south zone for the affluent, and the new suburban neighborhoods for the less well-off and the poor (Abreu 2003). Additionally, this ambitious urbanization scheme aimed to alter social and cultural uses of space. Public health and sanitation concerns were used to do away with popular forms of socialization and informal commerce, and inculcate the social and cultural values of the elites in the center of the city.[6]

This and subsequent violent modes of urbanization were inextricably bound up with race, though important studies of the Passos reforms have tended to analyze them primarily as attacks on the popular classes.[7] One reason for this, no doubt, is the significant degree of coexistence in spaces of the poor between Afro-descendants and poor whites, including recently arrived immigrants primarily from southern Europe, but also from places like Turkey and Syria.[8] They also shared overcrowded housing with internal migrants from Brazil's rural interior who frequently had Portuguese and some indigenous blood, occasionally with African heritage, too. The challenge of this book has been how to deal with a racially and ethnically diverse population thrown together in a densely occupied space without erasing difference by subsuming them all under the category of class. I explore the racialization of three of the groups that inhabited this dynamic landscape in the context of the centennial urbanization project, while also looking for traces of social and cultural practices that hint at racial or ethnic self-identifications in these spaces. Throughout this work I therefore examine official discourses of race and space, while gleaning clues as to the experiences of living in the city of Afro-descendants, poor southern European immigrants, and rural migrants from the interior. In this way, I explore the interdependence of race and geography in the production of spaces of the poor. This study therefore understands race as a structuring principle in analyzing space and sociocultural relations in a Brazilian city at a particular historical moment.

RACE AND MODERNITY

Marly Motta characterizes the history of Brazilian social thought in the twentieth century as an effort to understand and encourage modernity (1992, 8). In fact, blackness is what modernity imagines and constructs itself against, from the perspective of the state and dominant social groups. In the postabolition period social scientists such as Raimundo Nina Rodrigues (1862–1906) and Francisco José de Oliveira Viana (1883–1951) elaborated theses on the "problem of blackness" as an obstacle to progress and considered the possibilities offered by whitening. These two notions are fundamental to Republican thinking on modernization and have persisted in Brazilian development models in various forms to the present day. Scholarship on black Atlantic populations has engaged in considerable discussion of modernity's ambivalence toward black subjectivities (Gilroy 1993, 191), and the ways in which progress and nation building are underwritten by black oppression.[9] Critical race theory has drawn attention to how racist ideas are constitutive of a modern imagination, and the principles and practices of universality (Crenshaw et al. 1995). Richard Iton has observed that black experiences of modernity are of exclusion from meaningful participation in political life and civil society, while black populations served as raw material for the naturalization of modern social, political, and economic arrangements (2008, 17).

Political and legal theorist Denise Ferreira da Silva has commented that critical race theory approaches that focus heavily on presenting quantitative and qualitative evidence of social exclusion may not offer the most effective framework for understanding racial subjugation in a country like Brazil, in which racial democracy is such a powerful ideology. For her the problem with the focus on race-based exclusion is that "if one's race difference is not explicitly found to determine unfavorable social thoughts or actions, exclusionary ideas and behavior, it cannot be proven to be the ultimate cause of the ensuing harm to that person's rights." This means that denunciations of race injustice become difficult to articulate as such when they do not meet the criterion of "race invocation." In Brazil, she argues, race injustice occurs because blackness and whiteness indicate distinct kinds of modern subjects. The bodies and the spaces inhabited by people of color are signifiers of illegality, while white bodies and spaces of whiteness are produced to signify the notions of universal equality and freedom that underlie modern conceptions of the just and legal (2001, 426, 441).

This book examines an early moment in this naturalization of whiteness as the ideal outcome of modernization and urbanization. It also explores how blackness "haunts the dreams of ordered civilization" (Gilroy 1993, 191) articulated in a national project like the Centennial World Fair. I examine the community annihilated to make way for the exposition city, as well as the strategies for disappearing the nonwhite or less-than-white population deployed in the exhibition's imagined nation. This study seeks to establish a historical point of reference for the ongoing social pathologizing of raced bodies and spaces that places them outside legality and makes their removal entirely justified in order to maintain order and facilitate progress. Morro do Castelo in 1922, or Vila Autódromo nearly a century later—these two communities, decimated in the name of mega-event preparation, are not spaces of exception where laws are suspended to modernize and serve real estate speculation. They were already produced as illegal, and were therefore perceived as rightful victims of the deterritorialization and violence meted out by private/public consortia.

BLACKNESS AND WHITENESS IN BRAZIL

"Whether they consider me mulatto or black, I am forever condemned to be mistaken for the hired help. . . . Life is hard when you're not white" (Barreto [1915] 1961, 52–130). This condemnation of antiblack racism in early twentieth-century Brazil comes from the pages of the *Intimate Diary* of one of Brazil's most important writers. Afonso Henriques de Lima Barreto died in the year of the centennial, and he published withering critiques of the mayor, the city's well-off, and the demolition of Castelo in the press, especially the weekly magazine *Careta*.[10] Lima Barreto's accounts of the everyday humiliations he experienced as a man of color negotiating the spaces of light-skinned elites provide rare first-person glimpses of racial prejudice in Brazil at this time. The quote above underlines how a white gaze, and the discourses and representations that inform it, produce him as a racial other. As Lima Barreto notes, this gaze sometimes constructs him as mulatto and other times as black. According to this conception of race in Brazil, the author is able to alternately (or simultaneously) occupy two categories of raced being.

I do not draw attention to Lima Barreto's observation in order to argue for the supposed fluidity or ambiguity of racial classification in Brazil. To do so would suggest that race operates very differently from a binary system of white/black because of the many color descriptors that Brazilians use in racial speech and identification (Harris 1964, 1970). Many influential authors have disproven the notion that race relations, identifications, and forms of discrimination in Brazil are entirely different from similar phenomena in other countries such as the United States where a biracial model predominates (Silva 1985; Hasenbalg 1985; Skidmore 1993; Andrews 1991; Sheriff 2001).[11] Nevertheless, some scholars remain convinced that analyzing Brazilian race relations in terms of whiteness and blackness imposes a foreign, binary paradigm upon Brazil.[12]

In the 1990s Silva questioned analyses of Brazil in relation to the United States in which the latter's racial system is understood as a kind of universal model. For her the particularities of race in Brazil lay not in the much-discussed issue of racial ambiguity but in "the attempt to write race (black) consciousness against a (national) construction of race, which was produced against the idea of race separation. In Brazil, unlike the United States, neither culture nor social structure [is] organised around the idea of racial division" (1998, 213). Silva thus suggests that comparative possibilities between the two countries depend on acknowledging that the "intrinsically multiple quality of black subjectivity demands attention to the specific historical and discursive developments informing a society's strategies of racial subordination. However, because race has been the common discursive basis for worldwide subordination of nonwhites throughout the history of modernity, the study of any specific strategy of racial subordination must account for its placing in the global historical and discursive context in which the histories of modern societies and the biographies of racialised subjects have been written" (230).

Silva therefore argues that the US racial system should not be a default model against which we read race in Brazil. However, since racial oppression has been a mechanism of modernity the world over, national forms of subordination can be analyzed with reference to processes elsewhere. Such analyses should take account of a society's particular conditions. One of the most salient differences for her between the US and Brazilian racial systems is the absence of legal segregation in the latter that, as mentioned earlier, can make it difficult to hear denunciations of race injustice (2001, 426). Additionally, Brazil's discourse of racial mixing[13] has obfuscated the operation of race difference as a mechanism of exclusion, so that social, political, and economic disadvantage becomes the result of class difference. Therefore, the raced dimension of systemic and structural oppression is frequently silenced or rendered elusive (2001, 441, 427).

Despite the lack of segregation laws in Brazil, early twentieth-century urban reforms in the capital city explicitly aimed to whiten and Europeanize these spaces. Segregation has ultimately come about in practice, with over 70 percent of the country's urban black population living in self-constructed housing in the twenty-first century.[14] In this book I explore an important early moment in this racialization of space and how notions of whiteness and nonwhiteness informed spaces and imaginaries of the city. I am attentive to the particularities of time and place, grounding my study in a 1920s neighborhood whose past, present, and stymied future were profoundly influenced by assumptions born out of local, national, and global conceptions of race. I analyze these assumptions as they appeared in public discourse, visual forms, and as they materialized in the built environment and the ways that people occupied it. Because these are notions of race articulated in the press, in texts by nation builders, intellectuals, and social theorists, and in visions of the city by travelers, artists, or the official city photographer, they can only hint on occasion at what ordinary city dwellers made of the lived experience of race.

In 1920s Brazil, historian Paulina Alberto argues, the average Afro-descendant individual would not have identified publicly as "black," given the profoundly negative characteristics associated with the term; nor would they have joined explicitly race-based causes when faced with the urgent problems of hunger, poverty, and unemployment (2011, 5, 20). However, her study focuses on a vocal minority of black intellectuals who did publicly and proudly claim their African heritage. These claims were part of what Alberto terms a "conceptual agility" that denounced racial injustice while often endorsing national ideologies of racial harmony. She traces the moment when the notion of Brazil's flexible racial system gained acceptance as the 1870s, when both visitors and Brazilian thinkers remarked on the mixture between people of different colors as something unique in the Americas. Brazilian social theorists and abolitionists imagined this supposedly harmonious coexistence as an opportunity to assimilate and civilize the Afro-descended population (8–9). Alberto explores how black intellectuals often embraced the progressive potential of an ideology that equated racial mixture with social inclusion. As she argues, they strategically deployed notions of racial harmony as an ideal that they demanded be realized (10, 4). In this way, they strived to locate blackness centrally within Brazilian identity. It may seem incongruous that the Republican government pursued a policy of whitening while the country was beginning to emerge in the national and international consciousness as a site of racial tolerance and mixture. However, as Alberto explains, "Even as this ideology of 'whitening' envisioned the disappearance of nonwhite people, particularly those of African descent, it simultaneously cast Brazilians' willingness to intermix as evidence of their unique openness and enlightenment in racial matters" (10).

Alberto acknowledges that her study focuses on a small category of Brazilian society—educated, potentially upwardly mobile people of color writing in the black press (20). However, her examination of their interventions is important in demonstrating both their regional and historical specificities, as well as how race came to be understood nationally as primarily relations between whites and blacks (21, 5–8). As far as indigenous peoples were concerned, "foundational fictions" (Sommer 1993) in the mid-nineteenth century wrote them into the national narrative as a race disappearing because of war, sacrificial death, and miscegenation (Alberto 2011, 8).[15] As Alberto points out, the first national census of 1872 did not include a category for "Indians," only *caboclos*—those of part indigenous and part European ancestry. As discussed in chapter 1, the civilizing potential of the caboclo became an important topic of conversation among some social thinkers and in press representations in the first two decades of the twentieth century. Despite the chronic problems that nation builders ascribed to their character on account of racial mixing, it seemed that caboclos' distance from blackness made it possible to imagine them as a redeemable racial group.[16]

In addition to *caboclo*, people may have self-described or been described in Brazil's big cities in the 1920s as *crioulinha, preto retinto, cor escura, pardo-claro, mulata, branco sardento,* and many other variations on black or white.[17] Despite all of these subgroupings, blackness and whiteness remained fundamental to understandings of race in the capital. The color descriptors above come from the novel *Clara dos Anjos* that Lima Barreto completed in the year of the centenary and that appeared posthumously in 1948. Lilia Moritz Schwarcz describes the work as Lima Barreto's most insistent on detailing the race and color of the capital's residents (2017a). She notes that his prose lingers over its descriptions of dark skin in a way that was unusual for the time, given that writers, artists, and photographers tended to hold whiteness as the aesthetic norm, and alleged technical difficulties in representing brown and black subjects (2017a, 126, 127). In the novel, Clara, for instance, is a young woman who lives in the suburbs of Rio de Janeiro, part of a respectable family of modest means. Her father, the author tells us, is mixed race with lighter skin (*pardo-claro*), but "with bad hair, as people say" (36). Her mother is darker-skinned but has straight hair. Their daughter inherits her father's lighter skin and her mother's straight hair, and is brought up to believe that with the love of her parents and a good education she could be somebody in life. However, after her "seduction" by a *modinha* singer, Cassi Jones de Azevedo, Clara becomes pregnant. Cassi is from a white family that is better off economically and that has delusions of grandeur on account of a real or fabricated aristocratic English ancestor. Clara pays a visit to Cassi's mother and demands that he marry her: "Dona Salustiana was livid; the mulatto girl's interjection infuriated her. She looked her up and down, in a deliberate and unhurried way. Finally, she spat out, 'What did you say, you little *negra?*'" (103). In the space of a couple of sentences, Clara is both *mulatinha* and *negra*. Race talk may describe her as *mulatinha* because of her racial mixture, lighter skin, and straight hair. However, the white woman's gaze constructs her unambiguously as *negra* when reinforcing the racial hierarchy. Thus, despite all of the creative color codes of everyday speech, Clara experiences a moment much like Frantz Fanon's when he violently encounters the gaze that fixes him in white imaginations and splinters his body into racist stereotypes (Fanon 1967, 109–40). Just as Fanon is "burst apart" on the train in Paris (109), the white gaze destroys Clara's sense of self; she is unable to escape this gaze in the crowded space of the tram that carries her home: "Her upbringing, full of protective vigilance, had been misguided. She should have learned directly from her parents that her girlish and womanly virtue was besieged from all quarters, and she should have been taught this with real life examples, of course. . . . The tram was packed. She looked at all those men and women. . . . There was probably not a single person among them who was not indifferent to her plight. After all, she was just a little *mulata* and the daughter of a postman!" (104–5).

The novel ends with Clara's desperate utterance, "We are nothing in this life." As a result of Dona Salustiana's injurious racial slur, Clara experiences a second violation, what George Yancy describes as having one's body penetrated by the white gaze and then having that body returned in a distorted form (2008, 66). At this moment when Clara experiences her (non)being through others, she is trapped within what Fanon describes as a "crushing objecthood" (1967, 109). Fanon begins his essay with a realization akin to Clara's that racial marking destroys a sense of one's humanity and possibilities: "I came into the world imbued with the will to find a meaning in things, my spirit filled with the desire to attain to the source of the world, and then I found that I was an object in the midst of other objects. . . . All I wanted was to be a man among other men" (109–12).

The encounter with Cassi's mother occasions a similar trauma and revelation for Clara. Her upbringing has been all wrong and in vain. The insult reveals that "she was not 'just a girl' like all the others. According to her society's generally accepted beliefs, Clara was something much less" (104). In the tram, Clara looks back at the passengers and understands how they see her. They are indifferent to the disgrace that has befallen her because her body is already freighted ("battered down" in Fanon's words [112]) with the supposed deficiencies of her race. Racial descriptors and social niceties may construct her as mulatinha, but the gazes of those on the tram expose a violable negra who is sexually available to white men.

Lima Barreto's own experiences also underline the ways in which whiteness and blackness framed social interactions and relations. For the purpose of my analysis, whiteness and blackness are also important in terms of thinking about the production and negotiation of spaces of the city. While he may have been *mulato* in some social contexts, as the author points out in his diary, white society and those who police its boundaries are ultimately unequivocal about his blackness. His indictment, "Life is hard when you're not white," comes after an incident at a reception that he attends as a functionary of the Ministry of War. There were many "aristocratic young ladies" at the festivities, he notes, and no one else was required to produce an invitation, except for him ([1915] 1997, 31). Lima Barreto's qualification of his racial status—mulatto or black, or however "they" consider him—makes it clear that he is not self-identifying in a fluid way. These are descriptive terms that others assign to him. He may have been a mulatto to fellow intellectuals and those aware of his reputation as a writer.[18] However, he is an anonymous black man to the functionaries in a government office, and they subject him to exactly the same gaze that Cassi's mother directs toward Clara—deliberate and disdainful.

Lima Barreto deplores this objectification and it provokes a reflection on how the profits of slavery built that space, with its heraldic ornamentation and aristocratic pedigree. His musings contain an explicit homage to black resistance that is extraordinary for its time:

> I don't know how, but the image of a large plantation appeared before my eyes. . . . From the slave barracks, unaware of the warbling of birdsong, several hundred blacks emerged, in dense rows weighed down by captivity. Rows of black bodies fanning out, silent, humble, with the secret energy of a fiber piercing the earth. After penetrating a hundred meters it bursts out like a crystal-clear spring; the more it descends, the higher its temperature and pressure, and the more complex its composition. It returns to the face of the earth as a geyser. The lower it goes, the stronger it becomes, and there in the depths of the earth, it plots, revolts, disturbs, and erupts like a volcano . . . and there are no barons, viscounts, dukes, or kings that can divert it from its course. (27–29)

On another occasion, he reflects on how the same spatial practices that would be tolerated according to naturalized white privilege would be criminalized for him. When asked why he did not join his classmates at the polytechnic school in jumping the wall of a theater to gain free entry, he replies, "Well, you're all white; you're cheeky 'Polytechnic lads'. . . . But what about me? Poor me. A blackie. The police would arrest me first. I'd be the only one taken in" (Schwarcz 2017b, 122).[19] Lima Barreto, therefore, clearly understood his racial position as black or, as he put it in this section's opening quotation, *não ser branco*. He and his character Clara's accounts of being racially marked by the white gaze underline the relationality of blackness and whiteness. In my analysis I similarly frame race relations at this time through prisms of blackness and whiteness, with the understanding that these are markers of what is a complex epistemic field.[20] Distance from and proximity to blackness and whiteness determined life experiences, expectations, and opportunities.

Blackness in early twentieth-century Brazil was fundamentally a category of subordination, although descriptors, context, appearance, and class could differentially affect Afro-descendants' everyday negotiation of social relations. While whiteness was the ideal to which the ruling elites aspired, several scholars have explored the complicated racial status of poor white European immigrants as well. This group appears in my study as city dwellers who shared space in tenement buildings with former slaves and their descendants. They gossiped, socialized, argued, and fought with their black neighbors and coworkers, all the while resisting the discrimination that resulted from the less-than-ideal whiteness their poverty produced. Public discourse of the time often "blackened" poor white immigrants, constructing them with some of the descriptors used for the black population. In the broader context of the African diaspora Christina Sharpe uses the term "blackened" to describe those whose proximity to blackness and whose material conditions and circumstances position them as not properly white. They therefore have imposed upon them the same negative qualities projected onto black bodies (2010 190). In Brazilian scholarship, the phenomenon of blackening in the late nineteenth century and first decades of the twentieth is a well-established line of inquiry; for example, historians and literary scholars have analyzed the blackening of European immigrant workers in São Paulo (Andrews 1991); and of the Portuguese in Brazilian literature (Bletz 2010); how Italian immigrants were compelled to identify as "white" in order to distinguish themselves from Afro-descendants and avoid discrimination (Bletz 2010; Marques 1994; Lesser 2013); and the profound ambiguity of the relationship between southern European immigrants and modernity, with immigrants described with the same language used for blacks, such as *dirty* or *lazy* (Menezes 1996).

Defiant Geographies is a cultural studies project. It examines a wide variety of cultural texts and forms in order to understand what made a historically important, centrally located community disposable. I analyze primary sources to shed light on the politics of representing racialized space at a key moment in the history of nation formation. These sources include press articles, cartoons, lithographs, paintings, novels, chronicles, photographs, and more. The four chapters of this book all address themselves to unraveling the multifarious ways in which race makes space.

Chapter 1 explores how racialized subjects and spaces are produced discursively in official public and press discourse. One of the primary concerns of the Republican government that replaced the monarchy in 1889, the year after slavery was abolished, and that lasted until 1930 was the negative effects of race mixture on Brazil's population. Nation builders, social theorists, scientists, and pseudoscientists found hope for the country's future in the whitening thesis, which held that an infusion of white blood through immigration would eventually eliminate the country's black and mixed-race racial heritage. The implicit flip side of the whitening project was the creation of "racialized spaces of social death wherein Black lives are rendered less than fully human." I deliberately quote anthropologist Faye Harrison's (2014) assessment of police killings of black men and women across the United States today, despite obvious contextual differences, in order to highlight a long (and transnational) history of making life impossible for black people. In 1922, when the Brazilian government and dominant social groups asked themselves what kind of Brazil they desired for the next century, it was a Brazil without people of color. They refashioned parts of the capital city with that ideal in mind, and entrenched earlier reforms designed to distance undesirable sectors of the population from downtown in the name of emergent capitalist development. This moment in the city's and the country's urban histories matters greatly because this paradigm of development has resonated so strongly over the century that followed. This chapter builds on existing scholarship on race thinking in Brazil in the first decades of the twentieth century by exploring racial formation in tandem with urbanization. It considers how ideas about race become naturalized in thinking the city. The chapter also attempts to get at racialized meanings and experiences in relation to living in the city, but can only do so imperfectly, considering the available sources.[21] The latter are generally mediated accounts by city officials and in the pages of the press that sometimes offer glimpses of daily life and the struggle of black and blackened people to occupy the city.

Chapter 2 considers the role of visuality in the interdependent production of race and space. It traces pictorial representations of Castelo Hill at various historical moments in order to unpack the visions of social difference they produce. These portrayals include paintings, lithographs, political cartoons, and photographs from the nineteenth century until the time of the neighborhood's destruction. I go back in time before 1922 in my visual analysis in order to demonstrate the ways in which such material consistently construed Castelo as racialized space over time. These images mobilize ways of looking that help us to understand the spatial and cultural constructions of racialized others. The chapter frames the dynamics of these gazes in the context of their production and circulation, and the ideologies that informed their viewing. These intersections of vision, race, and modernity stage colonial and neocolonial power, reflecting and refracting sociospatial orders and hierarchies on the canvas or paper. They also point to the limits of such representations of authority and alterity, when a subject rendered mute by the artist or photographer speaks volumes by returning or countering the gaze, thereby resisting certain racialized meanings, or refusing to become an object of knowledge. Subjects' active, affective, and embodied engagement with the space they occupy in the image often escapes capture within modernity's authoritarian gaze, or exceeds representation.

This chapter therefore analyzes the drama of racialized visuality—the tension between attempts to fix difference as part of a national project based on the subjugation and elimination of certain groups, and the ways in which the latter often manage to undermine this official visual rhetoric. This defiant "looking back" affords glimpses of alternative experiences of modernity that hint at the reality of inhabiting eliminable racialized spaces.

Chapter 3 considers such alternative spatialities, using newspaper articles, chronicles, photographs, and an archived interview to imagine how residents engaged in mapping and remapping Castelo Hill based on their occupation of and territorial struggles over the neighborhood. It explores everyday life and social and cultural practices in a dynamic tangle of interethnic geographies, in which the spatial practices of different racialized individuals and groups meet, and sometimes clash. This chapter reconstructs *castelenses*, residents of Castelo, as geographical subjects who obstructed the dominant spatialities that the Republican and municipal governments wished to impose downtown. It also considers them as political subjects, not only when they denounced repressive policing, or participated in meetings and protests against the demolition, but in their everyday engagement in a racialized struggle to survive. To remember how castelenses lived, worked, celebrated, and fought is to recount stories that understand them as geohistorical agents. These people also made space in the city, with their street vendors' cries, their carnival clubs, their religious festivals, and their spaces of socialization in yards, on street corners, and around washtubs. They produced their own geographical knowledge that differentiated between micro-communities in the neighborhood and that challenged the homogenizing official imaginaries of the hill. This chapter weaves together strands of information mostly gleaned secondhand, which points to the limits of imagining how residents produced space with the available sources. However, I acknowledge different ways of inhabiting the city from the perspective of the racialized poor. These accounts seem particularly important in the context of the most recent initiatives in Brazil to annihilate communities that stand in the way of mega-events.

In chapter 4 I examine the spectacle of whitening staged by the government and the municipality in the miniature city constructed for the world fair of 1922–1923. This international event was Brazil's first "mega-event," and it presented an unprecedented opportunity to imagine into existence the ideal city of the future, a blueprint for urban development in the modernizing nation. It reflects hallmark characteristics of mega-events, such as the haste of its execution that eschewed careful planning to integrate the space into the existing built environment; the white elephants it left behind in the form of unused structures and spaces; and as with the events in Brazil of the last few years, the removal of racialized groups from the area that the authorities sought to reclaim. The ways in which the organizers represented and exhibited Brazil's society and culture closely yoked urban progress to racial progress. This notion was summed up in the prevailing concept of the *raça brasileira*, a homogenous "national" classification that in theory could include the diversity of the country's racial heritage, but in fact always reinforced whiteness as the default standard of civilizing achievement. Chapter 4 uses speeches, newspaper reports, commemorative publications, and visual records to explore the ways in which the fair materialized the desires of nation builders for the raça brasileira. It examines the space that the state and municipality created to project the social and cultural values it wished to inculcate. It also teases out conflicting reports on the participation of racialized subjects in events surrounding the commemorations. Some sources suggest a lack of interest in the formal events and a preference for celebrations in popular spaces, while others reveal an interest in accessing the spaces of the official celebrations, or in self-inscription into a centennial national narrative.

In order to facilitate discussion each of the four chapters focuses primarily on a different key aspect of how race makes space: discourse; visuality; spatial practices; and built or material form. However, all of these elements are intertwined, overlap, and produce each other, and they are all present to varying degrees in the analyses of all of the chapters. The impulse of this work has been to shed light on how these elements work to naturalize race and space, and the myriad ways in which racialized subjects defy this process. The effects of this naturalization are profound. In the 1920s the government decided that this neighborhood had value only if it were destroyed to create a stage for an international spectacle of modernization, and to open up land for real estate speculation. This is also a twenty-first-century story of mega-event development in Brazil. The state's violent removal of poor people from their homes for the sake of international events is part of a national project tying urbanization to whitening that is nearly a century old. To join some of these dots, as I begin to do in the epilogue, is to make historical links that might otherwise remain invisible. As Ann Stoler comments in the context of race and imperial ruination, such a critical move highlights the connections that make some people and places repeatedly susceptible to ruin (2013, 18). This book maintains that it is important to understand such undertakings as part of a racial project. A whole extra set of tools for combating these initiatives may then present themselves to those who organize and mobilize in Brazil in the contemporary struggle of people of color for the right to call some place home.

1

RACE, ETHNICITY, AND URBANIZATION

ON JUNE 25, 1921, A GRUESOME DISCOVERY halted demolition work on Castelo Hill. Two workers on the site were wielding their pickaxes on the flank of the hillside behind the School of Fine Arts when they came across a human head. After notifying their supervisor of the discovery, further investigation revealed a body buried in shallow dirt and the police were summoned. The body was that of a young, white man whose pockets contained only a few coins, handkerchiefs, a ticket from the People's Laundry for a pair of trousers, and a copy of the score to a samba song.[1] In the lengthy time that it took police medical and pathology experts to arrive at the scene, a large crowd gathered to witness the find. It grew as the officials carried out their business, with bystanders pushing and shoving in their attempts to breach the police cordon around the body, and sprinting up the hillside to get a better view. Sensational talk of murder dissipated later that day after the autopsy revealed that the body bore no signs of violence or a struggle. The medical examiners concluded instead that the young man had been the victim of an accident. Attempts to learn his identity failed until late that night when two men identified him at the police morgue. The dead man was one Manuel Jesus Gomes, a twenty-two-year-old Spanish immigrant. Gomes was a former employee at the Club Central, a stone's throw away on the Avenida Rio Branco (formerly the Avenida Central), the city's European-style boulevard created by the Passos reforms of 1903–1906. Gomes had formerly resided in a rooming house in the center of the city. Having lost his job, he had disappeared from his room without paying the rent he owed and was homeless at the time of his death. This version of events matched the manner in which Gomes's body was discovered—in a crouching position, covered with a newspaper that served as a blanket. It also provided the missing piece in the puzzle of his death. Gomes had been sleeping on the demolition site when earth from the hillside collapsed and suffocated him.[2]

Manuel Jesus Gomes and the two construction workers who found him, José Vieira and Cícero Pereira, would have remained entirely anonymous and invisible actors in the centennial reform project, one of the most extraordinary episodes in the capital's urban history, were it not for Gomes's newsworthy death. On the surface the incident appears to be nothing more than a sad footnote in a grand narrative of progress. However, these three individuals map out key coordinates of the racialized landscape of the city on the eve of its centenary. Gomes, the Spanish immigrant, described as "white" in press coverage, may have been a *gallego* from northwestern Spain, given the spelling of his surname; José Vieira was Afro-descendant; and Cícero Pereira was a northeasterner from the interior whose phenotype evinced the mixture of Portuguese with indigenous, and perhaps some black heritage. These men represent "types" that dominated social thinking on race at a moment when the country's elites were wringing their hands over how to reconcile its racial makeup with their aspirations to European-style modernity. The incident points to intersections of race, ethnicity, and urbanization in the city, and hints at the vast breach between the vision for the city held by ruling social groups and the lived experience of the city of those who serviced the modernizing project but were not its beneficiaries.

This chapter follows currents of optimism and pessimism in social thinking regarding race and Brazil's potential for achieving modernity in the early twentieth century. It then considers specifically how the racialized groups represented by the immigrant and the two construction workers fit into those discussions and debates. Finally, it explores how an intertwined discourse of race and progress understood urban space and shaped urbanization. Overall, the chapter teases out the anxieties but also the aspirations about race that lay behind the reorganizing of space for the centenary. Racialized discourse in the runup to 1922 was not frequently overt in urbanization language and policy, but by sketching out a panorama of race thinking at the time it is possible to glimpse the refracted or coded nature of racial discourse in the process of reimagining the city for the next century. In an important book on the rescripting of white supremacy through practices and policies of education in this period, Jerry Dávila (2003) unpacks how race thinking provided the conceptual framework for an ambitious reform of Rio de Janeiro's schools. Like the educators whom Dávila discusses, urban reformers were profoundly influenced by racial ideology in their vision and their actions. Consistent with the near consensus among the elites on the future path of the country, the modernization of the capital meant the whitening of the capital. The coexistence of different racial and ethnic groups in the poorest neighborhoods of the city has tended to obscure the centrality of whitening to urbanization in a great deal of the existing scholarship. However, as George Reid Andrews (2004) has observed, urban reform was a fundamental strategy of the whitening project, or what he calls "the war on blackness." Across Latin America the material and aesthetic transformation of cities sought not just to modernize their infrastructure but also to reconfigure their class and racial composition (118–20).[3] Urbanization and whitening were conjoined and fundamental to the pursuit of modernity. With the intention of creating a showcase for Brazil's modernizing ambitions, spaces of the city first functioned as a huge laboratory for experimentation with whether material changes to the built environment could result in at least a socially and culturally whiter population. The centennial reform was a project of monumental proportions, undertaken by the mayor's office and with the support of the president and the federal government.[4] It is, therefore, a stage on which shifting ideas about race in the 1920s were writ large and spectacularly enacted. Profound changes occurred in the occupation and distribution of space in the city at this time as a result of attempts to address Brazil's racial "problem."[5] This chapter seeks to make connections between urban and racial progress. Its sources are primarily chronicles, articles, and political cartoons from the press, as well as accounts by city officials. These narratives of urbanization are therefore told from the perspective of the governing classes and the emerging middle classes, though they can be ambivalent or critical with regard to the national project of modernity. Some press publications challenge aspects of that project on behalf of the city's poor racialized population, whose voices occasionally break through in the third person, or whose views are construed in cartoons.

BETWEEN OPTIMISM AND PESSIMISM

> Our latest sanitation project, modeled after the most progressive examples, visibly facilitates the strengthening of the race and increases its productive capacity.
>
> —Epitácio Pessoa, inaugural speech for the Centennial World Fair, 1922 (*Livro de ouro* 1923, 363).

President Pessoa's upbeat prediction that the hastily (and partially) concluded urban reform project to host the Rio World Fair would improve "the race" and, therefore, national productivity is not refracted or coded. In fact, he could not be more explicit in making the link between race, progress, and urbanization. But to what race was he referring? Not long before his pronouncement a gloomy sense that Brazil had no race pervaded and preoccupied its intellectual community.[6] Miscegenation, they believed, had doomed the country and produced a backward, unhealthy, and lazy majority population that was more "bestial" than it was civil society.[7] As Dain Borges (1993) has discussed, from the 1880s through the 1920s medicalized social thinking understood this problem as degeneration, and the notion persisted in following decades as a means of social analysis for Brazilian intellectuals.[8] Degeneration was a quasi-official ideology of the Republican government in its first two decades. It borrowed from European scientific racism and lamented that the tropical environment reduced individuals to unproductive laziness and society to a parasitic organism. The threat of degeneration hung over various modernization projects designed to cure a sick nation, including European immigration, urban renewal, and public health campaigns. The unequivocal goal of these projects, therefore, was achieving racial advancement (235, 256, 249). The voices of progress frequently wrestled with pessimism, their own and that of others, given the scope of this racial degeneracy. This is very much in evidence in the pro-reform press. The *Revista da Semana* frequently bemoaned, for example, that the space of "barbarity" that was Morro do Castelo persisted adjacent to the island of civilization that the Passos reforms had created downtown.[9]

Accompanying the gloomy outlook of degeneracy, however, was always a more optimistic current of thinking that was necessary to the effort of imagining a nation blighted by its climate and inferior peoples (Oliveira 2006, 25). This more positive vision of the country's future relied in part on a belief that white immigration could counter and gradually eliminate the weaker black race in the process of race mixing. One of the most buoyant predictions in this regard undoubtedly came from João Batista de Lacerda, the director of the National Museum. In the paper he delivered at the First Universal Races Congress in London in 1911, he projected that in one century the black race would be extinguished in Brazil (Skidmore 1993, 65–66); Schwarcz 1999, 3). In the meantime, however, impatient ideologues of nation, or those who doubted (privately or publicly) that there was an infusion of white blood sufficient to purge blackness from the population, were obliged to think more creatively about the country's racial dilemma. According to Lilia Moritz Schwarcz (1999, 42), Brazilian social thinkers demonstrated original approaches to evolutionist doctrine that made race theory borrowed from Europe very much their own. The First World War further encouraged a questioning of European ideas and provoked a feeling that Brazil could challenge the future that determinist racist thought predicted for it. At this time the competing theory from Europe and North America of race as cultural rather than biological was also circulating in Brazil, particularly in the work of the anthropologist Edgar Roquette-Pinto (Skidmore 1993, 146, 185–89). These factors coincided to produce a more "elastic" view of degeneracy, as an acquired, rather than innate condition (Dávila 2003, 6).

This expanded notion provided a logic for apprehending Brazil's racial realities to its nation builders (see Lima and Hochman 1996, 28). To return to Manuel Jesus Gomes, it explains why a European migrant who bore the hopes of the elite for the improvement of the Brazilian nation could be reduced to homelessness—a condition that the postabolition Penal Code of 1890 had criminalized as vagabondage and that affected Afro-descendants disproportionately.[10] From the perspective of degeneracy, a poor white obliged to coexist alongside the black population in difficult and insalubrious conditions could end up dissolute and dying like a *malandro,* with only a few pennies and a samba score in his pocket. A more fluid view of degeneracy also offered some hope for the social and racialized group to which the construction worker Cícero Pereira belonged. Improvements in education and living conditions presented the possibility of rehabilitating "backward" rural, miscegenated types from the interior. As far as the other worker, José Vieira, was concerned, theoretically this elastic degeneracy meant that in the right conditions it was possible for Afro-descendants to achieve some social ascension. However, given the hope held out by many officials and elites that the country was following a trajectory of racial progress from blackness to whiteness (Dávila 2003, 6), the section of the population to which he belonged would eventually be eliminated in any case.

Degeneracy is therefore the notion that provides the key link between urban reform and racial thinking. As Dávila has observed, although overt discussions of race may often be elusive in analyzing public discourse or policy at this time, racial meanings were diffused into the discourse of degeneracy (2003, 13). Ruling groups considered degeneracy a condition particular to people of color, and later, a condition that affected whites compelled to live in close proximity to them and who adopted their behavior. Race, therefore, was the motor driving the determined and concerted campaigns to extirpate degeneracy that preoccupied urbanizers in the First Republic, and beyond. This is why talk of "laziness," "filth," and "ugliness" by city administrators, engineers, and in the press is talk about race. Dávila is entirely right when he says in the context of his analysis of education that racial ideology is actually a *metanarrative*, a whole complex of values and concepts that guided policy and practice. Though frequently no one may be ostensibly speaking of race, race was embedded in assumptions about different social groups that shaped the intentions and outcomes of public policies (14). For example, when the head of the Settlement Service of the Ministry of Agriculture, Industry and Commerce calls repeatedly for the "homogenization of the national type" in his *History of the Colonization of Brazil* (1918), he never uses the word *whitening*, yet it is clear that he was calling for immigration by white Europeans with assimiliationist tendencies (Seyferth 1996, 55). This chapter, therefore, examines one strand of the metanarrative of race in Brazil at an important moment in the reorganization of space in the capital.

So, what concept of race is President Epitácio Pessoa openly invoking in his speech? According to Pessoa it is a "Brazilian race" in formation that the capital's latest urbanization project aimed to nurture. The national type or race that Pessoa envisages is ideally white, or more precisely, whitened. Although European immigration was to make a key contribution to this process, in his speech Pessoa clearly attributes a major role to urban reform in creating the appropriate environment.[11] It is significant, too, that he understands the entire engineering and architectural project of removing and destroying a neighborhood, flattening a hill downtown, and constructing a new mini-city of monumental buildings on the site primarily as a sanitation initiative. Sanitation was a central concern of those who fretted about the country's degeneracy, and one of the most important goals of the key urban reform initiatives of the Republic. Sanitation would prepare the stage for productivity, and the displays at the World Fair made it clear that progress would result from work regimes and norms that the state established (Neves 1986, 68–69). This vision of modernization effectively excluded the black population, given the preference for hiring European immigrants after abolition. Ruling social groups considered Afro-descendants bad workers, as opposed to European immigrants, who would facilitate the country's transition to a capitalist order (Chalhoub 1986, 75). The newly improved built environment would also help Brazilians to Europeanize culturally. According to Dávila, new policies of cultural or behavioral whitening emerged with the public health and hygiene movement of the second decade of the twentieth century and became central to the notion of the *raça brasileira*. The *raça* would eventually facilitate the idea of a racial democracy because it occluded the perpetuation of racial hierarchy within notions of a "common ethnicity" shared by Brazilian society (2003, 26, 27).

The idea of a Brazilian race was a catchall notion that favored diverse interpretations in the public sphere. In the official publications accompanying the fair, the organizing committee presented the raça as "Lusitanian," based on "one shared race, moral values, and language." The pro-urban-reform *Revista da Semana* took a more wide-ranging approach when it organized a competition in 1921 to find "the most beautiful girls in Brazil." It aimed to "gather together varying representations of Brazil's beauty, from the dusky miss from the North to the blonde types of the deep South." According to the *Revista*, the contest would "document the superior qualities of our Race, showing off Brazil in its most aesthetically pleasing human aspect." It assured its readers that this was no frivolous enterprise. In fact, this would constitute an archive of beauty that was both "artistic and patriotic," and would represent "a hymn of praise to our Race." The assurance was necessary in part to emphasize that this was not a prurient initiative that might wound delicate moral sensibilities; indeed, the photographs would compose "a gallery of both Virtue and Beauty."[12] Its emphasis on the imbricated values of aesthetics and nationalist fervor speaks directly to one of the main concerns of degeneracy thought—the nation's ugliness. Degeneracy thinking held laziness, dirtiness, ill health, and ugliness as some of the main characteristics and most troubling aspects of Brazil's population of color. The link between non-European physiognomies, unattractiveness, and racial inferiority is exemplified in Gilberto Freyre's infamous confession to his diary in the same year of the *Revista*'s beauty contest. On observing a group of mixed-race Brazilian sailors on shore leave in New York he recalled the verdict of an American traveler that Brazil's population had a "fearfully mongrel aspect" (Borges 1993, 243–44). Beautification was therefore an important buzzword and exhortation in discourse surrounding the centennial urban reform. At the time he assumed his post the mayor himself identified the two most pressing problems of the city as hygiene and aesthetics (Sampaio 1924, 5). Not surprisingly, the first seven women to be declared paragons of national beauty by the *Revista da Semana* from the states of Espírito Santo, Minas Gerais (two of their regional beauties made the cut), Paraná, Rio Grande do Sul, Maranhão, and Ceará, were all white.[13] The magazine duly paid lip service to the "diverse types of beauty" of the "race," while reinforcing whiteness as the unerring standard of female beauty. Gender and race ideology coincide here to produce the ideal attractive and virtuous female. The magazine also emphasizes heavily the curatorial aspect of its enterprise: it aims to "document," "archive," and "disseminate" this "gallery" of Brazilian beauty. It therefore charges itself with producing and transmitting knowledge about the ideal racial type. The discourse of the magazine is one of color blindness, but practically and visually it sutures whiteness to national pride.

More than two decades later, the polemic over the minister of education's commissioning of a statue to represent the raça demonstrated unequivocally that whiteness persisted as the desired model of Brazilian identity. When the sculptor planned to give the figure an appearance that was distinctly *caboclo*—that of the part-indigenous, part-Portuguese Brazilian from the country's rural hinterlands—Minister Capanema protested that to his mind the archetypal Brazilian was more of a "Southern Mediterranean" type, and canceled the commission (Resende 2000, 214). Lissovsky and Moraes reproduce an article from the September 23 *Correio da Manhã* in 1938 that represents the dispute in even starker terms:

> According to the account by [the sculptor] Celso Antônio, Mr Capanema suggested an Aryan type. . . . The sculptor did not agree. He claimed that there were no pure Aryans in Brazil. He was subject only to the principles of the plastic arts and would model the "Brazilian man" as he saw him from the Amazon to Rio Grande do Sul. He would not subject his art to the judgment of the doctors and anthropologists consulted by the Ministry. This typical Brazilian, Celso Antônio emphasized, is not the immigrant. He's from right here. Mr Capanema responded that there was no work of art without beauty and truth, and that the *mestiço* with the harsh features and thick lips that was taking shape in the studio repulsed him. (1996, 236)

Eugenics provided the social scientific language through which to articulate the idea of the raça. A science of "race improvement" that grew in popularity in Europe in the first decade of the twentieth century, it developed a "hard" strain based on the sterilization or genocide of inferior peoples, and a "soft" strain that posited that it was possible to improve hereditary traits. Nancy Stepan comments that many social reformers in Brazil preferred the "soft" strain that held out the promise that progress could occur from one generation to the next through education and changes to the environment (1991, 15, 11, 74).[14] In the 1920s the latter belief alleviated some of the elites' racial pessimism and appealed greatly to medical doctors and social reformers. Eugenics was most concerned with the social ills of the local population of color, but developed new anxieties about foreign-born factory workers, especially after the first national strike of 1917 (156, 50, 38–39). While urbanization projects sought to facilitate the possibility offered by "soft" eugenics of generational change through environmental improvement, there is also a harder strain in evidence in terms of the ruthless elimination of undesirable racialized groups from the downtown area. Creating urban spaces that deprive people of color of shelter and access to decent health care and employment opportunities while exercising violent, at times lethal control over them as they attempt to move through these spaces can be understood as a slow form of genocide (Nascimento 1989; Vargas 2010).

This chapter opened with the death of an individual blackened by his cohabitation with the city's Afro-descendant population. It is a death directly related to ideologies and practices concerning race and urbanization in the city. The Spanish immigrant falls victim to the very whitening project he was meant to serve. In addition to homelessness and unemployment, he suffers the violence of urbanization in a most literal way, buried by debris from the monumental construction site. He becomes collateral damage in an exercise whose main target was the population of color, because ultimately, while poor European immigrants were able to use the badge of white privilege for social advancement in subsequent generations, Afro-descendants remain(ed) at the bottom of all indicators of social improvement.

The census of 1920 also collaborated to produce a vision of a society that was successfully eliminating its black population. Despite the fact that there was no "color" question in the census, the official introduction to its publication measured Brazil's progress unequivocally in racial terms (Loveman 2009, 468). Its author, social theorist and historian Francisco José de Oliveira Viana, optimistically misrepresented the official numbers to provide evidence for Brazil's white future. Although the racial determinism that informed his analysis already sounded outdated in view of the possibilities for curing the country's ills offered by notions of "soft" eugenics, the essay's overall conclusion was one welcome to the elite: Brazil was becoming white, and this was a sign of national progress and what Viana called "Aryanization" (Loveman 2009, 464, 466; Skidmore 1993, 201). In any case, despite his praise for European racist thinking, Viana did not consider differences between inferior and superior races as absolute, evidencing the fluid approach of Brazil's nation builders to understanding racist theory in the context of a multiracial reality (Skidmore 1993, 201).

AFRO-DESCENDANT TERRITORIES IN THE FIRST DECADES OF THE TWENTIETH CENTURY

> Vade retro! (an American contemplates sending the black population of the United States to Brazil) (from the newspapers)
>
> You didn't manage to dispatch to Siberia,
> Uncle Sam, the dark segment of your population
> And so now you're going to try again
> To resolve your serious race problem.
> I sincerely applaud your enthusiasm,
> Because this is no joking matter
> It really is a most difficult thing
> I can't think of anything harder.
> For your sake let's hope the menace
> Disappears in the not too distant future
> But don't come here and fool around with our populace. . . .
>
> —João Rialto, *Careta*, August 6, 1921[15]

Rialto's poem appeared in the illustrated weekly *Careta* the year before the centenary in response to reports in the press that African American emigrationists had their eye on Brazil as a possible site for black colonization. In 1921 the Brazilian American Colonization Syndicate (BACS—one of several groups interested in Brazilian colonization) acted on the Brazilian government's promised subsidies for immigration and positive reports about the lack of racial prejudice in Brazil (see Hellwig 1992, 35–54), and advertised its project for Brazilian colonization in prominent black publications in the United States. Among those whose rosy view of race relations in Brazil fueled enthusiasm for these resettlement projects was one E. R. James, a black businessman and real estate developer who traveled throughout Brazil in late 1920 and in 1921 (Meade and Pirio 1988, 92, 90). In a series of articles in one of the leading African American newspapers, the *Chicago Defender*, James, struck by the lack of legal segregation in Brazil, also mistook the coexistence of the poor of all races and ethnicities for racial democracy: "Here in these districts we find all classes and all colors indiscriminately mixing and associating, large families of eight, ten or a dozen people living in little one- or two-roomed houses with dirt floors, children by the hundreds, yes by the thousands, playing in the streets only half dressed, dirty and ragged" (June 11, 1921, quoted in Meade and Pirio 1988, 91). Another traveler to Brazil in 1920 wrote in the December 11 *Tulsa Star* that both recent European immigrants and the descendants of slaves lived harmoniously with former Portuguese masters:

> We saw foreign people from the Mediterranean countries of Europe, who have been there only a year, joining with the native born in celebration of the numerous holidays. And why shouldn't they? I know of no place in the world where the conditions are more favorable to peace and comfort to the ordinary person than in this country.
>
> . . .
>
> Even slavery was never cruel and harsh in Brazil. The relation of slave to master was much in the nature of a hired servant. They belonged to the same church, observed the same feast days, and often married into the family of the master. Today the same fraternal relationship exists. (Cited in Hellwig 1992, 41)[16]

According to an announcement in the *Chicago Defender* in May 1921, several families had already left for Brazil and founded a colony in Pará (entering Brazil from British Guiana) (Meade and Pirio, 95–96). In Brazil alarmed politicians across the country warned against this "black peril" that would introduce black nationalism and disseminate racial hatred in their country's harmonious racial landscape. The Brazilian press began to publish accusations of a supposed plan by the US government to send their entire black population to Brazil (Mota 2003, 74, 73). Skidmore quotes the concern of the prominent man of letters and medical professor Afrânio Peixoto that "it will take us perhaps three hundred years to change spiritually and to bleach our skin so that we become, if not white, as least disguised and thus lose our *mestiço* character. . . . It is at this moment that America [the United States] intends to rid itself of her body of fifteen million Negroes and send them to Brazil. How many centuries will it take to cleanse this human impurity? Will we ever have enough albumin to refine all this dross?" (1993, 196). It was this kind of moral panic that provoked the poem in *Careta* cited above, whose Latin title recalls the prayer of exorcism "Vade retro Satana," or "Get thee behind me, Satan."

The government of the state of Mato Grosso canceled the land concession it had made to the BACS and informed the country's foreign minister (Mota 2003, 74–75; Skidmore 1993, 192–93). As a result, two deputies introduced a bill that produced animated debate in the lower house of the National Congress calling for a ban on entry into Brazil of "human beings of the black race" (Skidmore 1993, 192). Although their initiative was short-lived, immigration officials stepped in to impose the ban in practice by directing consuls in the United States to refuse visas to any person of color (Meade and Pirio 1988, 96; Ramos 1996, 66). The prohibition even extended to potential tourists—in 1923 the founder of the *Chicago Defender* himself, Robert S. Abbott, and his wife were refused visas "solely on the ground of being Negroes," as he put it, and only succeeded in obtaining them after pressure by a US senator (Hellwig 1992, 58).[17] In 1922 Brazilian consuls in Barbados and Panama twice refused a visa to a US citizen by the name of Edwin Kirk who intended to visit the Centennial Exposition. As justification, the Brazilian Ministry for Foreign Affairs cited Decree No. 4,247 of January 6, 1921, that foreigners could be refused entry "for reasons of public order or of national interest. This restriction is applied according to circumstances to all nonresident foreigners, no matter what their color." Clearly, although they claimed not to be operating under racial bias, there was grave concern that even prospective tourists might spread radical notions of Pan-Africanist identity and a black homeland (Meade and Pirio 1988, 100, 102). Two years later Viana would expound on this theme in the Chamber of Deputies, claiming that African Americans were uppity and aggressive, and if they proved to be "unfusionable" Brazil would have a serious political problem on its hands. He contrasted this with Brazilian blacks who were conscious of their own inferiority—in other words, who knew their place. (Ramos 1996, 67).

It is not surprising that immigration officials denied a visa to an African American seeking to visit the Centennial World Fair, when the fair was fundamentally an exercise in imagining a white Brazil. As Stepan (1991, 156) has observed, the intelligentsia's faith in whitening was reinforced by the use of informal mechanisms of social control over black mobility, as well as more institutionalized forms of repression, such as the use of the police to maintain the social and racial order. The major urbanization projects of the early twentieth century buttressed both these informal and institutionalized mechanisms to disappear black bodies from the modernizing space of the capital's downtown area. In 1890, two years after abolition, the largest group of migrants to the capital from outside the state of Rio de Janeiro was made up of 10,633 former slaves and descendants of slaves from Bahia (Tinhorão 1998, 264). The Bahians agglomerated in an area known as Little Africa, comprising the port area and the very center of the city. They concentrated in this area in the hope of finding work and in order to access the networks of solidarity established by earlier arrivals. Theirs was a highly conspicuous presence, and as mentioned previously, newspaper and magazine articles often disparagingly referred to the city as looking like an African street market (Moura 1983). In the postabolition period, carnival associations, street vendors, and capoeira fighters (all criminalized to varying degrees by the Penal Code of 1890) produced alternative geographies for collective identification that transformed public spaces (if temporarily) into battlegrounds for asserting their different regional origins in Africa and their neighborhood solidarities. In doing so, they challenged the feasibility and validity of the "civilized Rio" enterprise and imaginary (Leu 2014, 181–82). "Rio is becoming civilized" was the rallying cry of the city's first wide-reaching urban reforms between 1903 and 1906, led by Mayor Passos (Meade 1999). These infamous reforms aimed to sanitize and modernize the city, with Haussmann's Parisian urbanization project as a model. The reforms concentrated on precisely the areas where Afro-descendants lived to facilitate access to work: the port and the most densely populated parts of the city center (Needell 1984, 408). The demolition frenzy constituted a violent attack on the city and its humblest inhabitants, making way for the construction of elegant avenues, monuments, and high cultural institutions like the School of Fine Arts behind which the body of the Spanish immigrant José Manuel Gomes was discovered (Abreu 1997, 59–67; Meade 1999 84–94; Needell 1984, 400–403; Sevcenko 1993, 48–68). The Republic was clearly intent on implementing *topocide*: the deliberate annihilation of place (Porteous 1989, xi). Whole communities were reduced to rubble in an attempt to put an end to the street as a public space for the black population. The demolition, which became popularly known as the Bota-Abaixo, or "tearing down," threatened black networks of sociability in informal spaces such as the port, public squares, and gatherings around the street vendor's stall or tray (Velloso 1988, 200).

The creation of black territories was key to the myriad ways in which Afro-descendants in Rio responded to the violence of removal and disputed the meanings of space in the city. Among the best-known examples is the port neighborhood of Saúde, home to many Bahian blacks and the site of fierce resistance to the Republican government when it attempted to forcibly vaccinate the population against smallpox as part of its urbanizing drive (Leu 2014, 188). During the so-called Vaccine Revolt of 1904 rebels used guerrilla tactics that relied on their intimate knowledge of their neighborhood and the debris from demolished buildings in the old, narrow streets of Saúde, where they constructed barricades to keep out Republican troops (Sevcenko 1993). Others responded to the criminalization of black spaces in the city center by negotiating substitute spaces for collective identification. The annual Festa da Penha served as such a space of solidarity, shared values, and social and cultural practices in which Bahian women sold food, *capoeiristas* gathered to engage in combat, and musicians and singers performed carnival sambas (Moura 1983, 71–75). For a time, the space of the festival was a cultural and, on occasion, an actual battleground as the Portuguese community that originally organized it was gradually pushed out (Moura 1983, 71–75; Velloso 1988, 20; see fig. 1.1).

In spite of police presence and occasional police harassment, the festival was allowed to continue—partly because of the Bahian community leaders' contacts in the police—and endured in that form until the late 1920s as the largest street festival in the city after carnival (Velloso 1988, 20). By this time, it had been attracting people of all colors and classes and had become a space of encounter between Afro-descendants and other urban groups (25). This black space of tolerated transgression became a site for the production of an urban popular culture that began to attract wider interest and participation, and that would eventually end up dominating the production of a "national" culture. In these black geographies cultural expression both defied national myth making and later became adapted and appropriated to fit a national narrative of felicitous *mestiçagem* (Leu 2014, 188–89).

Both more enduring and contingent spatial practices represent small conquests that extend the notion and the extent of black territorializing at a time when key urban reforms of the Bota-Abaixo and, later, the centennial sought to violently eradicate a black presence from the city center. Geographer Andrelino Campos (2005, 31) has observed that twentieth-century Afro-descendant organizing, mobilizing, and resistance are significantly based on permanence in space—on the struggle to remain in appropriated spaces.[18] When Afro-descendants moved through the capital city, they negotiated spaces of violence, surveillance, and control. However, as Raquel Rolnik (1989, 2) has observed, black geographies are not confined to the experience of exclusion and the exercise of white dominion. Black bodies managed to transmit collective memory in spaces where they elaborated social and cultural repertoires and celebrated their belonging to a community. The organization of carnival groups in the late nineteenth and early twentieth centuries points to the diverse ways in which

Figure 1.1. Brawling at the Penha Festival. *O Malho,* October 28, 1922. The caption reads: "Oh my, we've had Women's Day, then Children's Day, there's even a Dogs' Day. Now these guys are inventing Thrashing Day . . . "

Afro-descendants negotiated and disputed space in the city. Carnival groups like the *ranchos* requested police permits to enable them to parade in the city center at carnival time through members who worked in the local magistrate's court (Moura 1983, 59). These ranchos consisted of groups of Bahians who had gained some status in wider society through jobs in the lower levels of the civil service (Tinhorão 1998, 274). Although they sought to confer respectability on their carnival processions, these attempts were undermined by the *cordões*. These smaller groups of rowdy revelers infiltrated the permitted space of the ranchos with unsanctioned occupations of the street, turning them into a disputed space. According to the contemporary chronicles of the journalist and flaneur João do Rio, the cordões engaged in violent conflicts with rival groups, often clashing "in the middle of Ouvidor Street", the most sought-after street downtown for carnival parades ([1906] 1997, 225). They framed these encounters with songs that named their suburban *cordão* and their group identity, and declared their takeover and control of the streets of the city center. He describes the roar of percussion and song in a meeting of four cordões:

> In spite of the heat, I was cold sweating; the confetti battles ceased; the shouts, the laughter, the jokes stopped, and alone, convulsing the street, as if shaking the houses, as if rising to the sky, the crazy, epileptic sound of the percussion, of the atabaque and tambor drums, the shakers, tambourines, the thumping on the big bombo drums, the bellow of songs belted out to dominate rivals, among the vibrating whistles, like mysterious signals that cut through the frenzied roar of the big drums as if bringing each and every person back to the reality of the job at hand. It was White Rose, sequined blacks from Cajueiros Street, the Flaming Terrors, the Night Dew Lovers and the Hummingbird Lovers! The blacks from White Rose, with their mouths wide open, sang:
>
> In São Francisco Square
> When the cornet sounded
> White Rose was victorious
> On Ouvido' Street. (239)

Using sound and their bodies the cordões took advantage of carnival to make a claim on the same streets from which the Bota-Abaixo reforms sought to eliminate them. Although the cordões' occupation of the Rua do Ouvidor is also temporary, it defiantly reimages and resignifies the street as a black space. David Crouch points out that the bodies of self and others can transform a space through a common identification, purpose, and action. Together these bodies can overwhelm the official imaginaries of that space, "as these become culturally deafened by the ritual of occupation" (1998, 167). João do Rio describes this phenomenon (as well as a literal deafening) in his chronicle. Using their collective occupation of the Rua do Ouvidor the cordões momentarily legitimize practices that the reforms had outlawed. The cordão even provides a space for performances of the much-persecuted serenade. The series of prohibitions that the mayor's office decreed to accompany the reforms—such as Decree No. 403, of March 14, 1903, ordering the removal of beggars from public places—led to police repression of street serenaders (Benchimol 1985, 608). The latter were usually mixed-race singers performing *modinhas,* a sensualized Brazilian version of the Portuguese courtly aria the *moda.*[19] However, João do Rio observes the performance of a serenade, defying police persecution, taking place in the middle of a cordão and ingeniously taking advantage of the protective chaos it afforded ([1906] 1997, 235).[20]

THE CABOCLO AND MODERNIZING BRAZIL

> It was the first time that the two of them had ever gone to Morro do Castelo. They began the ascent on the side leading up from the Rua do Carmo. There are many people in Rio de Janeiro who have never been there, many will have died, many more will be born and will die without ever setting foot there. . . . The steep, uneven, badly paved slope martyrized the feet of the poor ladies. Nevertheless, they continued up, as though doing penance, slowly, heads down, veils drawn. Morning brought some activity on the hillside: women, men, children going down and up, washerwomen and soldiers, the odd clerk, shopkeeper, priest, who all regarded them with some astonishment, even though they were very simply dressed; but they possessed a certain air of refinement that was not common in those parts. The very slowness of their pace, compared to the hurried step of others, suggested that it was their first time there. A black woman asked a sergeant: "What do you want to bet that they're here to see the *cabocla*?" They both stopped some distance off, overcome by that invincible desire to pry into other people's lives that often affects us all.
>
> In fact, the two ladies were surreptitiously looking for the number of the house where the *cabocla* lived, until they happened upon it. The house was like all the others, clinging to the hillside. One approached it by means of a little stairway, narrow, dark, and entirely appropriate to the adventure.

> . . .
> They had not wanted the carriage to take them all the way to the bottom of the slope, so the driver and the footman would not suspect their mission. At that time everyone was gossiping about the *cabocla* from Castelo, she was the talk of the town, people attributed infinite power to her, a series of miracles, strokes of good fortune, godsends, marriages. If they were discovered all would be lost, although many respectable people went there (Machado de Assis [1904] 1988, 1–2).

Joaquim Maria Machado de Assis's 1904 novel *Esaú e Jacó* opens with the sisters Natividade and Perpétua laboriously making their way up Morro do Castelo. Natividade has married well, and lives in the suburb of Botafogo just to the south of downtown that was still popular with well-off families in the period when the novel is set, around the proclamation of the Republic. She overcomes the potential shame of being discovered in the humble neighborhood of Castelo in order to consult a soothsayer on the future of her young sons. The soothsayer is a *cabocla*—as mentioned previously, a rural person from the interior of the country, usually of mixed Portuguese and indigenous heritage. The cabocla in the novel is from the *sertão*—the hinterland of the northeast of the country, and her father strums a *toada* in the background. The toada was a rural musical form that began to gain visibility in the city especially from the 1910s, whose lyrics frequently lamented the loss of an idealized country life ("Toada" 2015). In this brief sketch, as the old caboclo sings a northeastern folk song and his daughter divines the future of her client's sons by examining their portraits and locks of their hair, Machado conveys how caboclo subjectivities were articulated in the city. The opening of the novel constructs Castelo as a racially signified space and as a place of absolute centrality in the urban imaginary. He mentions twice that the mixed-race, migrant cabocla was the talk of all of Rio in 1871, irrespective of social class. Her celebrity imposes a mystical presence on the landscape of the capital, and the widespread interest and faith in her powers point to the limits of the rationalisms of modernity that the Republic would attempt to impose. Her visibility and the presence of the toadas in the country's capital suggest the persistence of caboclo rural values and sensibilities that would preoccupy social thinkers and nation builders in the first two decades of the twentieth century.

These concerns coalesce around the fictional character of Jeca Tatu, a caboclo from the interior of the state of São Paulo invented by the writer and publisher José Bento Monteiro Lobato. In Lobato's essay "Urupês" he describes the caboclo as a vegetating, squatting race "incapable of evolution, impervious to progress" ([1919] 1946, 164). Having already dubbed the caboclo a "nefarious parasite" ([1919] 1946, 179; "Velha Praga"), Lobato warms to the theme by comparing him to an *urupê*, a kind of fungus, on rotten wood. A mute, passive witness to history, when faced with any opportunity to improve his lot Jeca scratches his head, spits, and drawls: "Não paga a pena"—not much point ([1919] 1946, 164–65, 168). Jeca's dictum echoes satirically in that of the multiracial antihero of Mário de Andrade's novel *Macunaíma* (1928) who greets any action requiring effort with the phrase "Ai, que preguiça!" (Can't be bothered!).[21] Lobato did not think much of the regionalist vogue in *paulista* literature between 1910 and the early 1920s dedicated to rural life. A parallel impulse in historiography since the end of the nineteenth century had sought to recover indigenous customs in regional culture and reread the characteristics of the rustic paulista as the building block for the formation of a strong race (Oliveira 2006, 84, 87). The same vogue brought rural folk songs like the one crooned by the caboclo in Machado's novel to theaters and composers in the city who reworked them in their new context. These songs often homogenized the cultures and ways of life of different regions in the countryside into a national rural type who fused in the urban geographic imaginary simply into "the *caboclo*" (Oliveira 2006, 105).[22]

Euclides da Cunha's afflicted, ambivalent account of the Republican army's brutal campaign against a community of mixed-race peasants in the interior of Bahia (*Os Sertões* 1902), had provoked fierce debate about the huge breach between the modernizing coast of the country and what its elites saw as its atavistic hinterland. Lobato published his not at all ambivalent broadside just as "soft eugenics" was throwing a lifeline to nation builders that the worst characteristics of Brazil's mixed-race population might be improvable. In 1916, the same year in which medical professor Miguel Pereira had described the country as "one enormous hospital,"[23] doctors Belisário Penna and Artur Neiva published a report commissioned by renowned sanitation health expert Oswaldo Cruz on health conditions in the interior of Bahia, Pernambuco, Piauí, and Goiás. They concluded that epidemic and endemic disease as well as government neglect were the causes of the rural population's proverbial indolence, not race or climate (Skidmore 1993, 183; Lima and Hochman 2000, 317). The Brazilian Pro-sanitation League (Liga Pró-Saneamento do Brasil), founded in 1918, was led by Penna, and sought to obtain support among politicians and intellectuals for improving health in the countryside. The prosanitation movement became important in imagining a national identity that identified disease as a key characteristic of the country, and played a significant role in debates over the national character and national salvation (Lima and Hochman 2000, 314, 315). Penna and Neiva's article, reprinted in 1918 and widely debated in the newspapers and in academic and government circles, gained a great deal of traction and mobilized support for large-scale public health institutions and interventions (Skidmore 1993, 183). A storm of debate and disapproval, therefore, greeted Lobato's pessimistic outlook on the raça and forced a quite radical change in his perspective. In the same year that he first published his damning indictment of the caboclo in book form, he began publishing articles and booklets in the cause of redeeming him through public health. The book version of some of these articles, *Problema Vital* (1918), was actually published by the Eugenics Society of São Paulo and the Pro-sanitation League, and in it Lobato reconsiders Jeca's behavior and the fate of Brazil, declaring, "There can be only one patriotic mission: make Brazil healthy" (Mota 2003, 30; Skidmore 1993, 184). Included in this collection is the story of the "resurrected" Jeca, now cured of the hookworm that sapped his energy, and an advocate of hygiene and progress. In this morality tale Jeca manages to become a prosperous landowner—more successful than his Italian neighbor, he modernizes his property, and learns to speak English (Oliveira 2006, 85–86; Lima and Hochman 2000, 322)![24]

As Nísia Lima and Gilberto Hochman observe, there is something of a change at this time to the way in which race is understood with regard to social thought and public health discourse. Instead of accepting its fate as a country "condemned by race," nation builders entertained thoughts of using sanitation to attain modernity and construct a Brazilian identity (2000, 320). It is important to remember, however, that this approach to the racial question did not include the black population (Skidmore 1993, 184–85). They were not redeemable, as the caboclo might be, by any sanitation effort, however great, and were indeed condemned to disappear through miscegenation. The caboclo, therefore, played a key role in helping Brazilian intellectuals and governing elites develop a more optimistic racial outlook for the country.

JECA IN THE CITY

The rural mixed-race type started as a concern in the context of the Brazilian countryside. However, the presence of migrants from the hinterlands and their culture and ways of life in the cities made the caboclo the focus of the debate on the country's potential for progress in the runup to the centenary. According to Afrânio Peixoto, an influential thinker in the fields of health and education,

Brazil's interior (sertão) began where the Avenida Central ended (speech in honor of Miguel Pereira, May 19, 1918, quoted in Lima and Hochman 2000, 317, 330). Lobato himself insisted that the outskirts of cities should be a priority of sanitation campaigns (Lima and Hochman 2000, 317). As a result, Jeca Tatu became a critical icon of the dreams and doubts concerning the modernization of Brazil and its capital city, alongside the more recognized, official figures of the Republican imaginary. José Murilo de Carvalho has discussed the appropriation of the female figure from French Republican iconography to image the Brazilian Republic. Artists and sculptors never represented this symbol of the ideal Brazilian citizen as Indian, black, or mixed race (Carvalho [1990] 2003, 79, 84). Versions of this figure appear in the press in the year of the centenary, such as in figure 1.2.

Here the Brazilian allegorical figure with her Phrygian cap embraces a masculine counterpart in a shout of liberty to commemorate the first "cry of independence" by Emperor Pedro II that had marked the beginning of Brazil's separation from Portugal. The male figure appears frequently in commemorative representations of the centenary in magazine publications. He has European features and is dressed like a gaucho from the south of the country, a region in which German immigrants were concentrated and which received one of its largest intakes of Germans in the 1920s during the economic crisis of the Weimar Republic (Seyferth 2003, 230).

A month after the Centenary Exposition opened this idealized Brazilian male converses with a figure identified as a caboclo on the cover of the same magazine (fig. 1.3). The male allegory of Brazil stands astride and atop the Pão de Açúcar mountain, one of the city's reference points and internationally recognized icons, looking down at the caboclo. The latter is not represented according to prevailing perceptions of the time, as a person of Portuguese descent with some indigenous blood. Rather, he is a full-blown native, with feathers, bows, and arrows. The European type, simply dubbed "Brazil" in the cartoon, calls down to him: "So *caboclo,* what do you make of the success of this Exposition?" The native replies: "It's all fine. But if it weren't for Mexico, there wouldn't have been the slightest mention of me as a historical factor in your nationality!" Mexico's gift to Brazil on the occasion of the centenary was a replica of the Cuauhtémoc monument on Mexico City's Paseo de la Reforma (Tenorio-Trillo 1996, 205). The remark also alludes to the discourse of the "raza cósmica" produced by the mixture of Hispanic and indigenous blood that was embedding itself in Mexican national consciousness in the 1920s (Vasconcelos [1925] 1979). The exchange is remarkable

Figure 1.2. “Independence or death!” *Careta*, September 2, 1922. Biblioteca Nacional Digital Brasil.

Figure 1.3. “Viva Brazil!” *Careta,* October 7, 1922, Biblioteca Nacional Digital Brasil.

for the directness with which it broaches the subject of race and its representation in the fair. It represents a direct critique of the erasure of the indigenous presence from the showcasing of the country's history. In the context of the whitening project, however, it does not see fit to question the elimination of the black population from the national narrative.

Carvalho has discussed how caricaturists also focused criticism through the feminine figure of the Republic in order to ridicule the government, transforming the virginal or heroic symbol into a corrupted, fallen woman ([1990] 2003, 87). On the front cover of *Careta* shortly before the opening of the Centennial World Fair, the Republic becomes transformed into a feminine figure representing the exposition (fig. 1.4). She is a coquettish blonde, dressed only in her lingerie and performing her toilette in an improvised boudoir set up within the grounds of the fair. Helping her get ready for the inauguration is Jeca Tatu, looking somewhat out of his element in a smart blue suit decorated with stars from the Brazilian flag. At the door of her makeshift dressing room an old man representing the centenary peeks in, and Jeca warns: "Madame, the Centenary is already here." The Republic replies flirtatiously, "Send him in, I'll receive him just like this, in my underclothes." In an issue of *Careta* published three months later, it is the toothless rustic Jeca who has triumphantly obtained the keys to the city, while the Republic, sorrowful and defeated after only thirty-three years, prepares to depart (fig. 1.5). Her humble bundle of belongings highlights her fall from grace, as well as her playing of the guitar. As Lima Barreto reminds us, a guitar was a sign of dubious morality and playing it was not considered an appropriate activity for those who enjoyed high social standing.[25]

This is one of a number of appearances by Jeca in caricatures satirizing preparations for the fair. He becomes a critical voice in the context of urban reforms leading up to the centennial. In these appearances Jeca embodies alternative experiences of and relationships to city space, and the conflict between the rural, uncivilized other and the modernizing nation. The front cover of *O Malho* magazine in April 1921 features Jeca in response to the news that Morro do Castelo would be demolished to make way for the exposition (fig. 1.6). In this *charge*, or political cartoon, President Epitácio Pessoa is represented as "The Destroyer," operating the machinery that will obliterate the oldest neighborhood in the city. In the cartoon Castelo is labeled "Brazil," thereby standing in for historic spaces and traditional ways of life all over the country that would be assaulted by the juggernaut of the modernizing impulse. As Jeca observes the machinery he remarks to the president: "So, it's really happening then?" Pessoa

Figure 1.4. “The Centenary at the Door,” *Careta*, August 26, 1922, Biblioteca Nacional Digital Brasil.

Figure 1.5. "Celebrating the Anniversary," *Careta*, November 11, 1922, Biblioteca Nacional Digital Brasil.

Figure 1.6. "The Demolisher," *O Malho*, April 23, 1921, Biblioteca Nacional Digital Brasil.

replies, "It is. Until the Centenary everything's [going] down." The cartoon plays with the phrase *estar em baixo,* whose meanings include "down" in the sense of not functioning, and being down in the dumps, hinting at both government ineptitude and the impact of the demolition for residents. The phrase *em baixo* also recalls the Bota-Abaixo reforms of 1903–1906. The rather curious, hybrid steam contraption that Pessoa is operating indexes modern technologies of destruction. However, that modernity is made rather ambivalent by the noticeable patch on the machine, suggesting that Brazil's ambitions to the modern are hindered by aged, worn-out equipment.

In *Careta* in November 1922, in the context of the ongoing exposition and what the organizers considered a successful showcasing of Brazil's strengths, Jeca becomes the Destroyer, further illuminating the ambiguities and anxieties of Brazilian modernity (fig. 1.7). He drives a military tank decorated with the Brazilian flag over a heap of rubble from Castelo, underscoring the destructiveness and authoritarianism of urbanization and progress. Once again, he has sidelined the female Republican figure, who, displaced from the symbolic driving seat of modernity, smiles benevolently at him as though wishing him well. However, a doleful passerby, labeled "Pessimism," gazes incredulously at Jeca, who reproaches him: "What are you looking at, Mr. Parasite Face; this is the real Brazil! It's a fearsome tank that always wins the day and overcomes all obstacles, always moving forward!" Jeca remains toothless in this representation, and with the exaggerated facial features that always make him appear simple and prematurely old, but his dress recalls something of the idealized Brazilian male from the south of the country, as seen in figures 1.2 and 1.3. Evidently, he has also been sufficiently cured of the parasites that weakened him to cast aspersions on the health of others. However, the figure representing Pessimism does not appear convinced by Jeca's tank and new vestments, trappings like those on display in the Centennial World Fair.

A year later in *O Malho* the prolific cartoonist J. Carlos has Jeca questioning the actions and intentions of the city's mayor, Carlos Sampaio (fig. 1.8). The mayor energetically assists with creating the landfill for the exposition (and for real estate speculation to follow), but instead of using earth from the destruction of Castelo, he shovels money into Guanabara Bay. A concerned Jeca inquires in vernacular Portuguese: "And when will my money run out, Mister Mayor?"

"It already has," says Sampaio. "This here is borrowed." In these caricatures Jeca is Brazil's everyman, humorously undermining and making transparent the modernizing aspirations of the city and federal governments. He is the

Figure 1.7. "Lucky Star," *Careta*, November 4, 1922, Biblioteca Nacional Digital Brasil.

Figure 1.8. “Afterward, the Flood . . . ” *O Malho*, April 29, 1922, Biblioteca Nacional Digital Brasil.

uncivilized, racially impure counterpart to the symbol of the Republic, representing major obstacles to the nation's progress. Jeca is ultimately a bystander and victim of modernity. He is also frequently invoked as a figure that waits in the wings ready to be dressed up in the guise of a modern citizen, reflecting and critiquing the public discourse of the moment.

EUROPEAN IMMIGRANTS AND BLACKENING IN THE CITY

> They're knocking down Castelo
> Soon I'll have no place to be . . .
> I'll sleep on the Avenida
> For King Alberto to see . . .
>
> —"O povo é contra o attentado, e basta!" *A Noite*, August 26, 1920

In August of 1920, as government and city officials were gearing up for the visit of King Albert and Queen Elisabeth of Belgium the following month, the people of Castelo were criticizing both the visit and the plans to demolish their neighborhood with a subversively adapted popular song. Using the melody of the carnival "march" "Pé de Anjo," one of the year's biggest hits by the *sambista* Sinhô, a Castelo boy came up with the ingenious verse cited above. The lyrics register protest against a state that did little to make alternative housing provisions for those threatened with displacement. Moreover, they threaten an invasion of the elegant space of the Avenida created for Rio's elites and bourgeoisie—and for the purpose of impressing foreign dignitaries. The phrase "for King Alberto to see" had become regularly employed in the press as well, adapting the Brazilian idiom "for the English to see" meaning "to do something merely for show" (Caulfield 2000, 64).[26] Sinhô, a regular at carnival clubs and the Penha festivals, was a light-skinned *mulato* performer who preferred to describe himself as a caboclo, no doubt in the hope of avoiding prejudice ("Sinhô" 2017).[27] He became known, however, as one of the most important voices in the musical tradition of Afro-descendant social commentary and critique. João Cardoso, the young lyricist who appropriated and mobilized this critical voice, was of Portuguese origin, an example of how cultural expression was crossing over among the city's diverse population. This kind of crossover was facilitated by the extent of the coexistence between the black and immigrant populations, obliged to share overcrowded collective dwellings in the city. Such intense coexistence explains why a samba score could be found among the sparse belongings of the homeless Spanish immigrant Manuel Jesus Gomes.

Yet although European immigrants sang sambas and participated in carnival groups, they were wary of being lumped together with the black population in their new home. In fact, they often formed their own groups, and rivalry between black and Italian carnival clubs became so violent as to oblige the Italians to seek protection from their consul on occasion (Andrews 2004, 146). Italian immigrants identified as "white" in order to distinguish themselves from Afro-descendants and avoid discrimination, and quickly developed a sense of superiority over Brazilians of color (Bletz 2010, 134; Marques 1994, 93; Lesser 2013, 99). However, like the Portuguese they were willing to occupy the lowest rungs of the urban labor market in professions such as street vendor, shoe shiner, street sweeper, and construction worker (Menezes 1996, 77).[28] In the workplace rivalries of race and nationality played a key role when conflicts arose, and immigrants from the same country tended to stick together in disagreements and acts of violence involving Afro-descendants (Chalhoub 1986, 58–88). Working conditions were difficult, with low salaries, long working days, and frequent accidents, especially in construction, transport, and on the docks. Some of those on such low-paid jobs joined the ranks of the unemployed who wandered the streets, sometimes sleeping outdoors, in doorways, buildings in ruins, or taking to the hillsides, as Gomes did (Menezes 1996, 38, 49–50; Chalhoub 1986, 74). Brazil's nation builders began to express concerns that some of these immigrant groups might contribute further to the degeneracy of the country, rather than elevate and civilize it. Already in 1896 a report to the president of the state of São Paulo asserted that Italians committed the majority of crimes and infractions in the state (Mota 2003, 77–78).

Because the conditions in which many of these immigrants lived in the country's capital were shared with those of the black population, slippage between the groups occurred frequently in public discourse. Poor white immigrants became "blackened" by their occupation of spaces linked to racial anxieties in an official language of public health. This kind of slippage is evident in a 1906 report on popular housing by the engineer Everardo Backheuser to the minister of justice:

> Italian vagabonds snore away their days in these nauseating surroundings; black women with their wooly hair dripping oil croon ballads, washing clothes right there and laying them out on the roof, or even hanging them in their own rooms, a regular practice that fills them with hot, humid air, making it impossible to breathe; naked, dirty children drag along the filthy floor, making it even dirtier; and in the midst of all this, women of low extraction, usually blacks, outrageously dressed, mix together

> in the same beehive as poor, but decent girls, who do a great deal of sewing for the military, and who clean their little rooms almost excessively, decorating the walls with much loved portraits—these are islands of cleanliness in those oceans of squalor (1906, 108).

One of the most remarkable things about this glimpse into the living conditions of the poor toward the end of the Bota-Abaixo reforms is the equating of Italians with blacks. The report pathologizes both Italian male immigrants and black women as being unable to adopt the required behavioral, moral, and cultural norms of the modernizing city. The spaces they share and their spatial practices are defined as undesirable in relation to the building of a whitened social order.

George Reid Andrews provides examples of the blackening of the immigrant population in his discussion of black and white workers in São Paulo from 1888 to 1928. The shiftlessness and moral decay that the better-off ascribed to Afro-descendants were also qualities that moralizing, middle-class editors assigned to European immigrants in labor or neighborhood newspapers. Andrews (1991, 79) quotes a Spanish-language paper in 1899: "Owing to their sufferings in Europe, they are content with little salary, and settle into tenement slums and huts, housed like beasts, eating black bread and bananas. They live worse than pigs . . . these unhappy people differ little from the ex-slaves of Brazil." In Brazil's centennial year the main newspaper for the Italian community in São Paulo declared itself to be against immigration because recently arrived Italians were treated no better than former black slaves (Bletz 2010, 134). In 1906 the general commissioner of Italian immigration mentioned frequent marriages between Italians and blacks as proof of the former's decline in their host country (cited in Marques 1994, 93. The modest seamstresses mentioned by Backheuser, very probably European themselves given the importance of sewing as a source of income for female immigrants,[29] escape indictment and are described instead in terms of their industry and hygiene—both necessary qualities for the country's salvation from the perspective of government officials and social thinkers. Backheuser's description thus succinctly expresses the conflicting feelings that those in government and dominant social groups held about immigrants. Like other discourses concerning race in the first Republic, the pendulum swings back and forth between pessimism and optimism that it was possible to redeem Brazil's degeneracy and improve its population.

David Roediger has discussed the ambiguity of immigrant racial status in the

United States in the period 1890 to 1945, highlighting the "in-between" position of new immigrants from southern and eastern Europe.[30] Being in-between referred to the situation in which these immigrants were compelled to live, but that they might one day transcend. In other words, although migrants from Greece or Italy, say, were considered "less-than-white" in the late nineteenth and early twentieth centuries, they then followed a trajectory toward inclusion in the white race, processes of inclusion shaped by the continuing exclusion of people of color (2006, 13, 20–21, 45, 134). As in Brazil, US society quickly gave new immigrants lessons in antiblackness and white supremacy, and rapidly made them aware of the advantages of being white (119). In the United States the racialization of Italian Americans was particularly likely to conflate them with African Americans, but unlike the latter Italians could begin to "acquire" full whiteness at an intermediary moment when race was both biological and cultural (46, 35). In Brazil the connection between Italians and Afro-descendants tended not to question the supposed "biological" whiteness of the former but to ascribe to them cultural stereotypes assigned to the black population. As Roediger puts it, while frequent references to "filth" confused ideas of racial inheritance with cultures of poverty, a dirty immigrant could wash and be transformed (54). The sanitation drive that might redeem Jeca in Brazil therefore ultimately also offered the possibility of transformation to blackened southern European immigrants.

The coexistence of the poor white and the black populations has sometimes obscured the thoroughly raced impulse of urban reform. In the service of this project governments and the elites pursued policies of whitening at the same time that they blackened poor white immigrants who threatened to contaminate or endanger the initiative. Some immigrants were scripted in language very similar to that used to denigrate the black population and the caboclo before his redemption through hygiene. Spanish immigrants from Galicia, for example, were stigmatized as lazy, dirty, and ignorant. They both suffered prejudice and held prejudice against the black population (Oliveira 2006, 31, 32–33). Lená Medeiros de Menezes (1996) has discussed the profound ambiguity of the relationship between immigrants and modernity. By 1920 immigrants constituted 20.65 percent of the population of the capital, and city officials saw them alternately as agents of and impediments to the modern. The press branded those acting against the political, economic, moral, and social order—ultimately those contesting the vision of the city elaborated from above—as "undesirables" (63, 91).[31] Poor migrants were central figures in the anarchist and Marxist protests of the first decades of the twentieth century, and hundreds of "dangerous foreigners" were expelled from Brazil between 1907 to 1930 (24, 185). The government's fear in this case was not that the migrants would be contaminated by Brazil's degeneracy but that they would contaminate the country with their disorderly conduct, and in the case of working-class leaders, with their militancy and discourses of social revolution.

One of the best-known literary representations of the contamination of the European immigrant by the dissoluteness of Brazilian society is that of the Portuguese immigrant in Aluísio Azevedo's naturalist novel *O Cortiço* ([1890] 1980). The protagonist, João Romão, works excessively hard and is obsessively miserly in attaining his single-minded goal of economic success in Brazil. After becoming a wealthy (but no less miserly) landlord, owning several tenement dwellings in the center of Rio, he throws it all away when confronted with the irresistible sensuality of the *mulata* Rita Baiana. However, by the beginning of the nineteenth century the Portuguese immigrant was already less inclined to interracial relationships than is commonly imagined. Immigrant men showed a preference first for Portuguese women, or white Brazilian women descended from recent Portuguese migrants, or else white Brazilians with Portuguese heritage (Florentino and Machado 2002, 99). The Portuguese were a significant presence in the capital city. The majority who entered the country during the period of greatest influx between 1890 and 1930 did so through the port in Rio de Janeiro, and by 1920 they made up 15 percent of the population of the city (Ribeiro 1994, 633; Florentino and Machado 2002, 101). Portuguese immigrants became key figures in the city's housing market, owning the vast majority of properties available for rent, especially collective dwellings (Ribeiro 1994, 638; Oliveira 2006, 27). The housing crisis fed by the Bota-Abaixo reforms and subsequent reforms and removals, together with the ongoing arrival of immigrants and internal migrants, allowed landlords arbitrary power to charge and raise rents, and evict renters by force (Ribeiro 1994, 638; Chalhoub 1986, 95).

The Portuguese landlord features in caricatures around the time of the Castelo reforms as callous and all-powerful. One *O Malho* cover from 1920 comments on the August 17 decree sealing the fate of Castelo and on the municipal government's promise to build homes for the poor (fig. 1.9). The stereotypical Portuguese landlord—well fed, red-faced, with a luxuriant moustache, and in this case wearing ostentatious jewelry, looms over the scene. Jeca also features in this *charge*, hopefully asking President Epitácio Pessoa whether the planned housing will finally put an end to his residence on Hard Luck Alley. Playing on

Figure 1.9. "So Many Houses," *O Malho*, August 7, 1920, Biblioteca Nacional Digital Brasil.

the Portuguese *por um*, "to put a," the cartoon has the president erroneously hear *porão*, "basement," suggesting the hollowness of the government's promises and that the poor will end up in even worse living conditions.[32] Indeed, on November 11, 1922, the mayor's office was obliged to issue a lengthy statement on the subject to the *Gazeta de Notícias* newspaper to deny claims by Federal District senator Irineu Machado. Senator Machado denounced the treatment of former residents of Castelo who had been "cast aside or else housed in infected sheds in the Praça da Bandeira." The city argued that the accusation was "unfair and untruthful" and that the demolition was conducted without hardship to the residents and without any complaints from them.[33] It countered Machado's claims with a statement signed by sixty-six former residents then housed in shacks in the square. According to their statement they were very courteously treated by officials from the mayor's office, were more comfortable in the shacks than they had been on the hillside, and were paying not a penny for the privilege. Of the names included, 16 percent are of Italian origin and all but one of the remainder are Portuguese, though it is impossible to tell which of those are immigrants, Brazilians of Portuguese descent, or Afro-descendants with Portuguese names. In any case, visual representations of the Portuguese immigrant at this time repeatedly return to the avaricious landlord or the bar and corner store owner. In figure 1.9 the landlord comments, "Me, I'm inclined [playing on the Portuguese word for renter, *inquilino*] to think that nothing will change. Let them build houses, no one can stop me from bleeding the tenants dry at the end of the month." Among Brazil's intellectuals, opinion on the Portuguese presence and the country's Portuguese heritage also swung back and forth like it did with the caboclo. Lúcia Lippi Oliveira (2006, 27) observes that Portuguese immigrants faced waves of acceptance and rejection since independence in 1822. Their domination of aspects of economic life in the capital generated considerable anti-Portuguese discourse (Motta 1992, 19; Ribeiro 1994). They also competed with Afro-descendants for low-paying jobs. In 1908 the election of two Portuguese members in leadership roles in Rio's historically black port workers' union provoked disturbances that resulted in one death and the decimation of the union's membership (Fausto 1976, 36–37). In the early twentieth century it was important for many Brazilian intellectuals to affirm the European origins of the country in Portugal, while for others by the beginning of the 1920s the origin of Brazil's problems lay in its roots in backward Portuguese society, and it was national identity that should be affirmed (Oliveira 2006, 131).

URBAN DREAM AND REALITY

Nation builders' intertwined conceptions of race and progress had a profound impact on urbanization. At this time they were laying the groundwork for a pattern of spatial occupation that would keep the majority of Afro-descendants in the city impoverished, unable to advance socially, and vulnerable to police terror and other forms of violence. In the first decades of the twentieth century poor European immigrants shared the condemned spaces of the city with Afro-descendants, but with the exception of the "undesirables" who threatened the political and social status quo, they were redeemable by modernization projects by virtue of their race. As Giralda Seyferth (1996, 53) points out, ultimately, there is a fundamental division between whites, whether they were assimilable into Brazilian society or not, and nonwhites such as Japanese, *mestiços*, and blacks whose inferiority was understood as based on their varying degrees of distance from white civilization. European immigrants' relationship to space was structured differently in that they had the possibility of working their way out or up, whereas Afro-descendants remained the majority in the city's poorest neighborhoods. Northeastern migrants and their descendants would join them as a significant presence in the informal housing market that flourished partly as a result of urban reforms of the first decades of the twentieth century. Urbanization, therefore, also served the political project of reinforcing raced hierarchies of power and governance. As part of the Republic's economic project, it helped to prepare the city for emerging capitalist markets and industrial development by modernizing the port, improving transport systems, and creating a sociospatial order that would facilitate the control of workers.

Consistent with the country's highly ambivalent relationship with modernity, those who held power in the city and sought to reform it often belonged to traditional oligarchies. Others, like Carlos Sampaio, the mayor of the capital from 1920 to 1922, were part of a rising urban middle class. Sampaio graduated in engineering from Rio de Janeiro's polytechnic school and later taught there. As a professor, his courses and intellectual interventions reflected the school's positivist leanings toward the importance of scientific reason in promoting social progress.[34] Sampaio was a direct appointee of the president and a part of his inner circle. In turn, the mayor appointed his friends to high posts or gave them preferential treatment in city contracts (Conniff 1981, 61). He enjoyed wide-ranging power over the urban reform project to remove Castelo Hill, as well as the construction of the centennial exhibition site, and headed the centenary's Organizing Commission at the behest of the president.[35]

Carlos Kessel understands Sampaio's vision for the city, underlined by a twin concern with sanitization and beautification, as an expression of a civilizing project shared by bourgeois and elite society since the late nineteenth century (2001, 128). He characterizes Sampaio's relationship with the city using the metaphors of the mirror and the showcase. The mayor, Kessel observes, saw in every project to transform the city a reflection of his own civilizing ideals, and by extension those of dominant society. The city would also function as a showcase—a space to be exhibited to foreigners—in which its elites could see themselves reflected and take pride (6). That Sampaio did not intend such spaces to showcase Afro-descendant Brazilians became clear with the 1920 visit of the king and queen of Belgium to Rio de Janeiro. The mayor supposedly issued an order that all children of color be pulled out of a performance planned for the royals at the Quinta da Boa Vista, the former residence of Brazil's emperors (Kessel 2001, 65).[36]

In his justification of the demolition of Castelo, Mayor Sampaio (1924, 11–12) referenced a report by medical experts that was by then 126 years old and that identified the hillsides as a culprit in the city's epidemics. His economic motivation to open a new area downtown for real estate speculation, however, responded to more recent concerns with the generation of capital.[37] Like the Passos reforms that preceded them, Sampaio's urbanization projects aimed to make the city function more effectively in the service of modern commerce. In fact, his overall vision for public administration was to govern with the rationality and efficiency of private enterprise (Silva 2003, 44). The demolition proposal provoked fierce debates in political circles and the press between those to whom the presence of Castelo in the city center was an affront to civilization, and those who did not feel it necessary to raze the historic neighborhood in order to urbanize.[38] Sampaio enjoyed support from elite society who longed for the city's modernization to European standards, even as they continued to be linked to traditional forms of wealth accumulation (Silva 2003, 47). By and large, Sampaio's detractors in the press did not question the values of modernization and progress that the mayor cited as goals of the reforms, though they may have criticized the financial burden they placed on the city (Kessel 2001, 111.).[39] Some critics also suspected Sampaio's motives; although he claimed that the reforms would improve the city's finances (Sampaio 1924, 114), he had after all established a firm (the Company for the Demolition of Morro do Castelo) with the express purpose of destroying the hill for his personal enrichment. He obtained the concession to do so in 1890, but was unable to proceed with demolition due to the financial crisis of the late nineteenth century known as the "encilhamento" (Sampaio 1924, 43). One of his first actions as mayor was to decree the destruction of the hill and the urbanization of the resulting area, which he now sought to legitimize by invoking the urgency of the centennial celebrations (Silva 2003, 46).

Whether or not to destroy Castelo became the focus of intense discussion concerning the nature of modernity and nation in Brazil (Motta 1992, 6–7; Silva 2003, 48). As Marly Motta has discussed (1992, 18–35), the opposing views on the demolition among state builders reflected at least two very different visions at the beginning of the 1920s. A strong current of traditionalism conflicted with a desire to demolish all traditions, although members of both schools of thought proclaimed themselves the agents of modernity. While the first group believed that a truly modern Brazil should be rooted in the solid values of its rural tradition, the second enthusiastically sought to embrace the fast-paced urban and industrial world. While the traditionalists believed that Brazil's impressive landscape and geography could redeem it, some in the other group felt a need to dominate nature in order to attain progress.[40] Among the traditionalist thinkers were members of an agrarian elite in crisis, including Viana, the proponent of "Aryanization", and Jeca's creator, Lobato. In response to the decision to destroy Castelo, Lobato ([1920] 1965, 413) wrote an impassioned plea calling the area "the sacred hill that should be our Acropolis," and "the greatest in the wonderful string of pearls that Rio possesses." Lobato may have considered Castelo the city's most valuable jewel, but Mayor Sampaio dubbed it a "rotten tooth" that needed to be extracted. As Motta observes, the destruction of Castelo revealed such divergent visions and versions of modernity (1992, 54, 62). Competing descriptions of Castelo in the press and public discourse also reflected these impasses about what held value in the modern nation.

The prodemolition press denounced the neighborhood as a "garbage dump" and an "aesthetic monstrosity," and evoked racist slurs in marking it out as a place in which the "stain" of colonialism persisted.[41] For them it was an "African village" or a "Botocudo Indian settlement" (Motta 1992, 58). The existence of a downtown neighborhood in which the perceived fanaticism, superstition, and backwardness of indigenous and African customs persisted presented a great obstacle to the modernizers aiming at European standards of civilization (57–58).

Castelo was the site of premodern rationalities and mystical beliefs associated with race, such as the fortune telling cabocla or the *macumba* priest João Gambá, described in Luiz Edmundo's chronicles (1957, 221–22). Despite conflicting views about whether or not to demolish Castelo, both sides united around the need for sanitation and whitening as fundamental to progress. As discussed at the outset of this chapter, among the anxieties that plagued intellectuals in the early 1920s engaged in the task of imagining the nation was a profound anxiety about race. Urban reform provided a stage on which to imagine a modern nation, as well as materialize who belonged and did not belong to this community by means of the reorganization and redistribution of space in the capital. As Lúcia Silva has pointed out, while public health provided legitimation for the demolition in the arguments of the engineers working for the mayor's office, the rationalization of urban space was equally important. Castelo was a hindrance to the functional organization of space because it consistently attracted people from different social classes to its cultural and social events (Silva 2003, 49; Motta 1992, 58).[42] Although Silva does not mention race, the rationalization to which she refers sought to reclaim this central area for the benefit of the city's white elites.

Silva (2003) has explored how the First Republic signaled a new form of governance driven by concerns over hygiene. Just as educators had an important role to play in this regard in terms of changing the culture and customs of the population, so did engineers and architects by means of urbanization. In fact, the two areas of intervention were linked in the minds of some intellectuals in the 1920s who began to see the city as a civilizing agent that would provide an appropriate environment for educating the population. The capital city became the privileged locale for the implantation of modernizing values of work, education, and hygiene (55, 32, 56). The 1920s therefore marked the beginning of a process of constituting a group of urbanization professionals within the municipal administration. Architects began to develop new ideas about the social utility of their art, and to recognize the state, rather than just the elites as a major client. Engineers were already seen as agents of progress at the beginning of the century, and in the 1920s they confirmed their vocation as a governing elite. During the same period the Clube de Engenharia was consolidated as an influential forum in which to address the capital's problems (25, 88, 89, 90, 50). While some engineers were in favor of regeneration rather than demolition, two engineers who worked on the project, Carlos Soares Pereira and José de Oliveira Reis, consistently rearticulated the views of the mayor's office that the destruction of Castelo was an act of progress. In interviews for the Museum of Image and Sound in Rio they tend to view the residents of Castelo as obstructions rather than as occupiers of lived space.[43] A more complex view emerges from the 1906 report by Backheuser cited previously, in which the gap between vision and reality in the city is laid bare, and demolition is questioned as the best solution to the housing crisis.

As Gladys Sabino Ribeiro (1994, 639) has pointed out, the real-life "drama" of the old Republic was that thousands of people lived badly or distantly after the demolitions of the beginning of the century and of Castelo, or had no homes to go to at the end of the day's work. Those who lived badly tended to occupy rooming houses. An 1890 census estimated that a quarter of the city's total population lived in tenement buildings in its central areas. The majority of Afro-descendants who lived in the city center resided in some type of collective dwelling. The term *cortiço* came to be used generically for collective housing, but Backheuser (1906, 105–6) explains that it referred specifically to housing that was often added on or adapted for partitioning into rooms or cubicles.

The Bota-Abaixo made these collective dwellings the target of its ruthless sanitizing, fueled by a discourse of social medicine that linked urban disorder directly to a physically and morally degenerate population (Benchimol 1990, 114–17). Moving out of the center to escape the urbanization drive was only possible for those with some resources and was not a viable option for many who lived on unstable incomes, who were forced to move around the city to escape persecution from the police for vagrancy (288). This itinerant population rented rooms on an ad hoc basis from remaining, already overcrowded tenements, making for insufferable living conditions. In the middle of the Bota-Abaixo reforms João do Rio (2005, 277) described such conditions in his chronicle "O sono da miséria" (Misery's slumber), after a visit to a *cortiço* at the foot of Castelo Hill. There he observed the unwashed, naked bodies of sailors, soldiers, and humble workers piled together in the darkness and suffocating heat.[44] Those without employment of any kind paid what little they were able to beg off the streets for a space outside, in the building's backyard, which they used to avoid nightly roundups by the police.

Initially, displaced city dwellers fanned out from the downtown hub to nearby areas such as the port neighborhoods of Gamboa and Saúde, and the Cidade Nova area just north of the center. In his 1915 novel *Numa e ninfa* Lima Barreto describes how the latter neighborhood sprang up out of necessity: "Cidade Nova didn't even have time to develop beyond the swamp it was; . . . but it ended up as the dumping ground of the growing city, of the races that populate us and were brought to these shores by the slave ships and the immigrant ships, by force and free will" (Barreto [1915] 1961, 83). Roberto Moura's research on Praça Onze in the Cidade Nova area has shown that the square was a point of convergence for Bahians seeking to reconstitute their communities, and a meeting point for malandros, capoeiras, and musicians from the carnival associations. It was also a focus of resistance to modernization, as it maintained some precapitalist socioeconomic relations after the Bota-Abaixo, offering food and accommodation for any recently arrived Bahian until work could be found (Moura 1983, 28, 36, 68–69; Rocha and Carvalho 1986, 81). Praça Onze is, therefore, an example of the kind of black territory that Rolnik describes as a form of highly structured, Afro-descendant community constituted within a particular space. It was a site in which collective memory helped Afro-descendants claim a place within the city's modernizing landscape. However, Rolnik (1989, 2) makes the crucial point that signaling certain spaces as black territories does not mean that they were exclusively black. As evident in Lima Barreto's observations, the area also attracted European immigrants affected by the city's housing crisis. During the 1920s it became a central site of Jewish social and cultural life (Malamud 1988). Bruno Carvalho's (2013) fine-grained analysis of the cultural history and the meanings of this space has unpacked the dynamic interracial and interethnic character of Praça Onze and the Cidade Nova.

During the 1910s and 1920s new suburbs sprouted along the four main rail lines out of Rio with the introduction of commuter trains running to the northwest where land was cheap. Speculation meant uneven development and provision of services, and the *subúrbios* were already beset by problems in 1920, isolated from the city by poor, patchy transport and with decreased quality of life and land values (Conniff 1981, 27). Still, they often represented the best prospect for the city's poor. By 1940 the majority of the city's residents lived here, as did the bulk of its Afro-descendant population (Dávila 2003, 84). In 1920 the prospect loomed of improved rail services for these residents when the city borrowed funds with the intention of converting the commuter lines to electric power. However, the money was diverted to the Castelo demolition project, to the dismay of residents compelled to endure the frequent accidents and breakdowns of the aged system (Conniff 1981, 25, 28). The decision to destroy Castelo with diverted funds from the train services therefore also resulted in the increased segregation of a large segment of the black population of the city. Ironically, the explosion of growth in the new suburbs was one reason city officials were unable to sell the lots of land created by the Castelo demolition and landfill, which ended up as government buildings and parking lots by the mid-1930s (Conniff 1981, 25).[45]

The reforms also spurred the growth of the favela as a significant mode of collective housing in the city. Reputedly the first systematically occupied illegal settlement in the city, the Morro da Favela, or Morro da Providência, was conveniently located just behind the Central do Brasil rail station, thereby avoiding the commuting nightmares of those who settled in the subúrbios later. According to Ney dos Santos Oliveira (1996, 74–75), Afro-descendants "played an active if unrecognized role" in the creation of favelas, which were initially overwhelmingly black, until they came to be inhabited by poor whites as well, including European immigrants arriving in the late nineteenth century. The presence of poor whites should not blind us, however, to the antiblackness contained in the metanarrative of degeneracy that imagined the favela in public discourse. The *morros* had long been imagined as obstacles to public health, because they were thought to prevent the circulation of purifying breezes. Doctors looking for ways to combat periodic epidemics had advocated their demolition since imperial times (Benchimol 1990, 117). Once the hillsides began to be informally occupied by the black population they became fixed in the urban imaginary as sites of physical and moral degeneracy. In the 1920s, from the perspective of the city's authorities and well-off they were a "leprous scourge" infecting the landscape that in an ideal world should be extirpated.[46] During his term in office Mayor Sampaio also initiated favela "beautification" projects that removed a large number of people from Morro da Favela, Santo Antônio, and Gávea-Leblon (Gonçalves 2013). With the centennial celebrations only two years away from when he assumed his post, beautification focused on favelas in the city center or in emerging bourgeois South Zone neighborhoods. In light of his attempts to make these spaces more socially and culturally European, the magazine *Careta* parodies two stock urban figures with exaggerated Afro-descendant phenotypes discussing plans for the beautification of Morro da Favela (fig. 1.10). In racialized, vernacular Portuguese the malandro with his knife tucked into his waistband informs the washerwoman that they, too, will soon be able to enjoy the leisure activities of the well-off, like promenading and taking morphine.

Much of the reaction to such projects by the racialized population comes to us mediated and imagined by the press, which also provided glimpses into the living conditions of the poor. The reports written by Backheuser also constitute one of the best sources on the latter from the perspective of the urbanizers. As evident in the previously cited extract of his report, the racial metanarrative that links filth and laziness to blackness heavily influences his technocrat's view on sanitation problems. However, his vivid, detailed snapshots of everyday life in

Figure 1.10. "The Slum," *Careta*, August 28, 1920, Biblioteca Nacional Digital Brasil.

collective housing make his report seem more like a chronicle at times. From these documents we have a clear picture of the myriad types of collective dwellings in the city. For him, among those presenting the worst affronts to sanitation and morality were cortiços, "some of which you enter with a handkerchief over your nose and exit overcome with nausea," and *albergues,* which rented rooms or space on the floor for a night where "adults and children of both sexes were piled together in promiscuity" (1906, 110, 106). Many types of housing had shared toilets, but no bathrooms; some had cooking facilities like the *avenidas* that were permitted by mayor's office and the informal *estalagens* (small houses grouped around a central patio); others, like the cortiços, sometimes did not.

Backheuser's sanitizing discourse is frequently as severe as any government official's of the day. On one occasion he expresses support for the idea of disinfecting the cubicles in rooming houses where occupants kept their clothes. He describes the *casas de commodos* as "the most anti-hygienic, the most detestable kind of collective dwelling." They were "big old houses divided and sub divided many times over by wooden boards and even burlap bags, even including the space between the insect-infested ceiling and the roof, making for a kind of communal living and appalling promiscuity" (1906 109, 108). Yet he does not call for their demolition, advocating instead that they be transformed into habitable spaces without having to turn families out into the street. As a member of a commission investigating the city's housing crisis he criticizes proposals to destroy Castelo, expressing both public health concerns that an "epidemic focus" would then be spread out across the city and a more humanitarian concern that those displaced from Castelo would be treated as vagabonds by the police (115). Backheuser also calls for more purpose-built *villas operárias* like the Villa Ruy Barbosa on the Rua do Senado downtown, challenging the impulse to displace popular housing to the suburbs (109). His description of the multiracial work and social spaces of the *estalagens* betrays a subtle admiration for the brio of their inhabitants: "In the main patio black, Portuguese, Italian, and a few Spanish women, mostly washerwomen, gather around the tubs and their daily chores, among broods of impish, high-spirited little ones, they spend their days in a bewildering noisy tumult." According to Backheuser their dwellings lend the city "a picturesque quality with the touch of originality that their customs possess, molding nocturnal troubadour types who play the viola and accordion, losing themselves late into the night in insipid tunes or in fandangos, at gatherings that often end in a brawl or knife fight" (110).

REAL AND FICTITIOUS GEOGRAPHIES

Backheuser paints a portrait of interracial spaces that the governing elites hoped to eliminate by means of their urban reforms. In their dream of a sanitized city—a city appealing to assimilable white immigrants and external capital—there was no place for people of color. Their dreams and also their anxieties about race produced lasting, material changes to the distribution and occupation of space in the capital. The new dynamic of expansion that was initiated in the 1920s would thereafter leave Rio's poor, and especially its nonwhite and northeastern migrant population, fending for themselves or vulnerable to predatory, often lawless housing markets. Between 1906 and 1924, the period marking the end of the Bota-Abaixo reforms up to the end of the Sampaio administration, the city's poor began to spread out to distant suburbs or increasingly to the hillsides (Menezes 1996, 39). Although such reforms reinforced the classed and raced status quo and reclaimed downtown for the state and private enterprise, in many ways the centennial reforms were a failure. Sampaio failed to get engineers to come up with a well-considered plan for the city because of personal and political differences within the group (Silva 2003, 41). The lack of interest by investors in the lots put up for sale after the exposition that were supposed to bring in revenue for the city, the ad hoc layout of the site, and the housing crisis created by the reforms provoked severe criticism of Sampaio's motives and competence, leading him to defend himself vigorously in the pages of the press.[47] As a result, the rest of the 1920s signaled a shift away from an approach to urban problems that responded piecemeal to the exigencies of the moment (Conniff 1981, 19–20). Yet in the evictions and annihilation of communities of color all over the city for the 2014 World Cup and 2016 Olympic events the problems of the poor were thrust aside in the urgency to stage Brazil's long-awaited "achievement" of an elusive modernity. People of color still make up the majority in Rio's poorest settlements. These neighborhoods contested the fictitious whitened geographies imagined for the city in the first decades of the twentieth century, as they do today.

Figure 2.1. *Fundação da Cidade do Rio de Janeiro* (*Founding of the City of Rio de Janeiro*), Antônio Firmino Monteiro, 1881. Photograph of work in the Palácio Pedro Ernesto, Rio de Janeiro, by Halley Pacheco de Oliveira, CC BY-SA 3.0.

Figure 2.2. *Primeira Missa no Brasil* (*Brazil's First Mass*), Vítor Meirelles, 1860.

2

RACE, ETHNICITY, AND VISUALITY

IN THE LATE NINETEENTH CENTURY the Afro-descendant artist Antônio Firmino Monteiro broke through the empire's tight circle of artistic recognition and patronage with his oil painting *Fundação da Cidade do Rio de Janeiro* (*Founding of the City of Rio de Janeiro*) (fig. 2.1). His expansive study depicts the refounding of the city of Rio de Janeiro on Morro do Castelo in 1567 after the expulsion of the French from the area around Guanabara Bay. The painting recalls the famous foundational work *Primeira Missa no Brasil* (Brazil's First Mass; 1860), by Vítor Meirelles (fig. 2.2), but advances the history of Portuguese colonial expansion beyond the first mass celebrated in 1500 to settlement and construction. The work reimagines the event along four horizontal planes. Occupying the foreground is a group of Portuguese soldiers alongside indigenous men. The soldiers wear armor and the sunlight glints off their weapons and helmets, highlighting the tools of conquest in an area of the canvas in which darkness predominates, in spite of the daylight scene. They are grouped on the left of the canvas, subordinating, not only with the violence threatened by their poleaxes but also by their higher position in the scene, the group of "Indians" sitting or crouching below them. However, this latter group occupies the center of the foreground. While the presence of native peoples echoes the Indianist paintings of the period in imagining the nation, Monteiro's representation is somewhat more complicated.

Unlike Indianist literature, Indianist art and sculpture in Brazil in the second half of the nineteenth century tended toward tragic representations of dead or dying natives, as opposed to strong or powerful warriors (Jorge 2010, 39). While the soldiers' poleaxes may well portend a violent end for these native men, they appear to be a somewhat rowdy group, not content to mutely and passively watch the spectacle of creation of the colonial city but waving their own weapons around, and with one turning his back on the event. In this shadowy area of the canvas, and in counterpoint to the soldiers' weapons, the light glances off the animal skins worn by two of the native men. This spotlighting imbues the skins with symbolic meanings that index savagery, but also convey the prowess and courage of the native hunter. However, the skin worn by the last member of the group, who is set off a little to one side of the rest, acquires a more ambivalent meaning once we become aware of the identity of its wearer. In addition to the substantial animal skin slung across one shoulder, this native wears a jerkin, doublet, and hose. He is Martim Afonso de Tibiriçá, reputedly the first convert of the Jesuit missionary Padre José de Anchieta in the settlement of São Paulo (Moreira 2016, 86). On his conversion Tibiriçá received the name Martim Afonso, after the colonizer who founded settlements in the areas of present-day Santos and São Paulo (Godoy 2014, 194). As a cacique, Tibiriçá may indicate rank within his community through his animal skin, and in Monteiro's painting he wears it juxtaposed on European garb to indicate both his traditional power and that acquired through new alliances.

What, then, to make of the apparent exchange of glances between Tibiriçá and the man seated on the stone below him? This nameless native is minimally dressed and almost certainly does not possess the status enjoyed by the cacique. Indeed, he is positioned at Tibiriçá's feet. Yet his extremely relaxed body language and the quizzical tilt of his head suggest both a lack of respect and an inability to understand the hybrid being before him. There is a challenging and questioning air that Giovana Moreira has read as impudent, as if the "savage Indian" were staking out a place in the scene in defiance of the acculturated one (2016, 86). Though both men's bodies are in shadow, the space between them is well lit, drawing attention to the breach between these two very different natives at a key "civilizing" moment of colonization. Their mutual drama of looking is located in the very center of the foreground of the painting, complicating the dichotomous spectacle of power and the gaze that the painting enacts between colonizer and colonized.

This prominently situated exchange of gazes seems to stage the internecine conflict provoked by colonialism in this founding moment. In a letter from 1563 written by José de Anchieta relating the death of Tibiriçá, he mentions that the cacique had made enemies of his own family members for his adherence to and defense of God and his church (Anchieta 1988, 197, cited in Godoy 2014, 192). Tibiriçá is the noble savage who enters history via a national narrative that eulogizes his sacrifice of community for the Europeans' civilizing project. The unknown native seated before him challenges this myth of colonialism with his gaze. In his insolence we glimpse a counter to another myth—that of passive native acceptance of Portuguese culture, and the "naturalness of conversion" evident in Meirelles's *Primeira Missa* (Moreira 2016, 87, 89–90).

The second horizontal plane of Monteiro's painting is bathed in light and portrays the dignitaries of colonial governance. Squarely in the middle, in a direct visual trajectory out from the breach between Tibiriçá and the nameless native, the scene symbolically enacts territorial conquest. The governor-general of Brazil, Mem de Sá, presents the keys to the city to the *alcaide-mor* (a kind of military administrator and nobleman). In an echo of the figure of Tibiriçá a featureless but dark-skinned boy in formal European dress, probably a convert, is positioned between the two men and plays an important supporting role in the pageantry by offering the key on a tasseled cushion. Our gaze is drawn to him more than it otherwise might be because of his lightly colored clothing, which contrasts markedly with the somber dress of the new city's governors, as if to spotlight the civilizing possibilities of colonization. To the right of them stand the ceremonially attired members of the municipal council, with one of their number holding a white flag which may bear a cross of São Jorge, like those toward the left of the painting decorating the walled city. These and the flags fluttering from the galleons in the bay symbolize Portuguese dominion over land and sea, and connect in a horizontal axis across the painting.

Occupying more or less the entire right side of the scene are the religious figures who have just celebrated mass and consecrated the new city. An altar has been constructed that appears to rise out of the tropical vegetation and is framed by bushes and a large tree. Moreira observes that the integration of altar and vegetation suggests a communion between nature and the Catholic faith (2016, 88). Despite the exuberance of nature in this corner of the painting, however, it is a large wooden cross that dominates the landscape because of its positioning with the pale blue waters of the bay behind it. Distance and perspective make the cross appear to loom larger than the Pão de Açúcar mountain across the bay. The cross appears three times in this portion of the painting—there is a smaller one with the crucified Christ at the foot of the large wooden one, and Padre Manuel da Nóbrega brandishes a cross that is perhaps made of silver.[1] The bishop of Salvador, D. Pedro Leitão (standing behind Padre José de Anchieta), also bears aloft a gold crosier, and the silver cross and gold crosier can be connected to the wooden cross in straight lines that form a triangle of sacred space over the altar. This altar is in reality a flimsy "set" (Brand 2006) with its improvised red carpet that puts on a theater of ecclesiastical power for the benefit of the natives.[2]

The administrators and priests are positioned on a pathway that leads to the city gate, to which Mem de Sá gestures. The adjoining city walls compose part of a third plane, outside of which a crowd of Portuguese men gather—among them presumably the first settlers—to witness the event. None of the figures are discernibly women, and in contrast to Meirelles's *Primeira Missa,* in which naked and near-naked native women populate the canvas, Monteiro entirely denies us women as the object of coloniality's prurient gaze. The crowd appears to be waiting to gain access to the city after the dignitaries, and they are positioned obliquely opposite the group of indigenous men in the foreground, for whom the city walls appear as a symbolic form of segregation. This incipient but solid and rectilinear built environment is an index of conquest and represents an organization of space that orders, separates, and fixes meanings based on race. Indeed, a contemporary commentator reads the painting in terms of the establishment not only of a new city but of racialized difference: "The ceremony takes place on Castelo Hill, in the open air; there are Indians and Portuguese. With many variations in physiognomy the artist managed to imprint on both races their norms, their true types" (*Revista Illustrada,* December 1881, cited in Moreira 2016, 73).

The painting's fourth plane is composed almost entirely of blue sea and sky. Although it forms the backdrop to the historic events depicted, the sky in particular constitutes a full half of the entire canvas. The painting's spatial dissection into heaven and earth makes the deeds of men seem small in comparison to the vastness of the sky and the majesty of the distant mountains, which also dwarf the galleons and the commemorative smoke issuing from their artillery fire. Might this be a contemplation of colonial hubris? Might the portal with its door firmly shut be a commentary on urbanization's fundamental dynamic of exclusion and inclusion? Are the racial hierarchies and differences that foundational paintings tend to naturalize decoded and unveiled for us here, despite a superficial adherence to the themes and forms of the genre? It seems that Monteiro, an Afro-descendant of limited socioeconomic means in a slave society, may have created a more nuanced view of the implantation of Portuguese civilization in

Brazil than the painting's warm reception by the imperial establishment might suggest.[3] This rendition of Castelo is a picture of a beginning that presages an end—the beginning of the implantation of white supremacy in new urban space and the consequent ruination of nonwhite subjects.

In this chapter I want to use images of Castelo—a foundational site of colonial civilization that became an obstacle to modernity—as a way of thinking about civilizing violence, modernity, and race. The story of Castelo is a story of loss, displacement, and destruction of what had become a vibrant, interracial and interethnic community by the 1920s. It is also the story of the enactment of a national project of modernization, and of various forms of refusal of this process. Visual materials document this drama and shed light on the role of urbanization in dealing with race difference during this process. The rest of this chapter uses images as a way of thinking about how race makes the neocolonial space of the nation. Unpacking the discursive and ideological constitution of space in the iconography of this historically important neighborhood demonstrates that urbanization and whitening are intimately intertwined. The chapter examines the workings of an imbricated visual language and spatial configuration of race. It explores ideas of race and ethnicity as "part of a parallel and enabling history of visual and spatial technologies" (Poole 1997, 216) that shape the city. Methodologically, this chapter is animated by the conviction that although the voices of the indigenous peoples, slaves, descendants of slaves, northeasterners, and European immigrants who appear in these images have been silenced by the brush, pen, and camera, the images speak volumes about modernity and its discontents. Deborah Poole's work has been of fundamental importance in understanding the role of images in structuring the scientific knowledge, cultural understandings, and aesthetic norms of Latin American modernity in general, and modern racial discourse in particular. Such images do more than simply reflect contemporary understandings of racial difference and the civilizing missions of empire and nation. By inscribing on other bodies a specific sort of difference they play a key part in forming the racial culture of modernity (1997, 5, 12, 37). To trace some of the visual history of this neighborhood where the city was born and whose demise was deemed necessary for the city and the nation to progress is to consider the origins of modern racial thinking and highlight its continuities with the present.

My analysis is attentive to various aspects of the visual economies of the images: their content, production, archiving, and circulation (Poole 1997, 9–10). I am guided by Gillian Rose's basic precept that visual culture refers to the ways in which the visual is part of social life (2016, 4). In other words, vision is constructed through various practices, technologies, and knowledges, drawn from a range of economic, social, and political relations. Therefore, the ways of seeing that an image mobilizes are crucial in the production and reproduction of visions of social difference (23, 25, 22). In the section that follows I use an 1835 engraving to think about cultural constructions of blackness in terms of the social context of viewing, the production of the image, its intended circulation, and the visualities that its intended public might have brought to its viewing. I will also consider how the embodied subject might refuse such representations.

BLACKNESS AND VISUALITY IN NEWLY INDEPENDENT BRAZIL

The city gate of Monteiro's painting is clearly visible in a landscape from 1835 titled *Morro do Castelo e da Praya d'Ajuda* (Castelo Hill and Ajuda Beach).[4] The version of the image included here as figure 2.3 was produced by lithograph, an important printing technology in postindependence Brazil.[5] Lithographs arrived in Brazil only three years after Portugal's king Dom Pedro I, still in residence in Brazil after fleeing the Napoleonic Wars in 1808, declared Brazil independent and installed himself as the country's new emperor. Anxious to secure recognition by European powers, he invested in lithographs as a way of disseminating positive representations of the country abroad, including images of the emperor himself. In 1825 the Swiss lithographer Johann Jacob Steinmann arrived in Brazil under a five-year contract with the state. At the time lithography was still a novelty in Europe and the arrival of the technique spoke to the new country's desire to participate in the production of a global circuit of images. Steinmann was charged with engraving and printing the maps produced by the Royal Engineer Corps, so that lithography also had a key role to play in the modernizing of map production in Brazil. The latter was important to defense, the occupation and administration of territory, and the building of infrastructure, as the emperor sought to stabilize and centralize the new state.

Although in Brazil lithographs were intended as an official way of imagining the new nation and constructing the state, they often acquired a life of their own. Steinmann was a wily businessman and persuaded state officials to allow him to set up the lithographic studio in his home. This afforded him much less oversight than working in the military archive, the originally intended location for his studio (Ferreira 1994, 329). Lithographic technique also permitted faster reproduction and in greater quantities than etching designs into wood or copper. As Walter Benjamin observed, this opened a wider market for graphic arts for

Figure 2.3. *Morro do Castelo e da Praya d'Ajuda (Castelo Hill and Ajuda Beach)*, Friedrich Salathé/Johann Steinmann, 1835, Biblioteca Nacional Digital Brasil.

the first time (1982, 117). Steinmann cannily took advantage of this emerging market, which extended to the emperor's court as well as the illustrated press, given lithographs' ability to register contemporary events quickly and cheaply (Santos 2008, 59). Steinmann's artistic production reveals this change in the themes portrayed by the engraved image. He strayed from representing official events to recording well-known figures from the streets of Rio, and transformed paintings of the city into lithographs for sale in the court and subsequently in Europe (Santos 2008, 54, 63).

The production and circulation of one such image reveals much about the process and role of lithography in the creation of an image-world of newly independent Brazil.[6] In 1824 the emperor's representative in Paris, charged with negotiating French recognition of Brazil's independence, reported on the awestruck

Figure 2.4. *Panorama do Rio de Janeiro* (*Panorama of Rio de Janeiro*), Friedrich Salathé/Johann Steinmann, n.d. (probably 1820/1830), Biblioteca Nacional Digital Brasil.

reception of a panorama of the city of Rio viewed from Morro do Castelo (fig. 2.4). A public space along the Boulevard Montmartre served as the exhibition site for the lithograph, thus displaying Brazil's landscape to any and all passersby in the French capital. While the state's representative deemed this image to be a great propaganda success for Brazil, beyond its official function the lithograph had quite an extraordinary trajectory of artistic production and commercialization. The Frenchman Guilherme Ronmy painted the original image, based on 1821 drawings by Félix Émile Taunay. Taunay came to Rio from France in 1816 as a young man accompanying his father, Nicolas Antoine Taunay. The elder Taunay was part of the French Artistic Mission, the Portuguese Crown's initiative to institutionalize the teaching of art in the colony turned metropolis by the exile of the court. Steinmann edited the panorama after his return to Europe, and his compatriot and collaborator Friedrich Salathé applied watercolor. The final product, therefore, reflects a multilayered form of artistic production that defies the auratic in favor of a kind of early production line of technical reproducibility in which there is no auteur, but several artist and artisan contributors.

In the right-hand corner of the lithograph reproduced here as figure 2.5 the emperor makes an appearance on Castelo Hill. He is accompanied by the empress Leopoldina and their entourage, with both white subjects and slaves surrounding them. Like the lithograph that opened this section, *Morro do Castelo e da Praya d'Ajuda*, to which I will return shortly, the overall picture is one of

perfect balance between a landscape of stunning natural beauty and its taming through the ordered civilization of the built environment. Slaves are represented as part of this harmony of nature's and man's order. They are naturalized as part of the exotic quality of the landscape—indeed, Steinmann described some of the cityscapes he offered for sale as containing "negroes in the background."[7] Slaves also appear as a key element in the maintenance of the social order. In this strategic portrayal of the emperor strolling in the place where European civilization in the capital began in earnest, it is as if his power and sovereignty are constituted in significant part by his dominion over slaves, who predominate in the scene.

The landscape that opens this section, *Morro do Castelo e da Praya d'Ajuda*, also traveled with Steinmann to Europe. Steinmann lithographed the landscapes in Switzerland, with some printed in Paris and London, before their return to Brazil to be sold by Casa Laemmert publishers in the 1840s (Santos 2008, 85). The trajectory of these images is all the more noteworthy when we consider that there was significant demand for these images back in Brazil by travelers from Europe and North America.[8] In some cases, therefore, the pictures would have originated in Brazil, been finished in different cities of Europe, returned to Brazil for sale, and then ended up being purchased and brought back to Europe by travelers! In this circular network in which the iconography of the capital of the empire transited, there was a certain convergence of ideas in renditions of city scenes and landscapes, with the presence of slaves being one of the most prominent themes (Sela 2008, 153, 162; Zenha 2004, 31; Vaz 2000, 8). There are

Figure 2.5. Detail, *Panorama do Rio de Janeiro* (*Panorama of Rio de Janeiro*), Biblioteca Nacional Digital Brasil.

repetitions and resonances in the image world of the Brazilian empire that these pictures create as they travel across places and cultures. In this visual world slaves become image-objects through which Europeans imagined, desired, and othered the tropics (Poole 1997, 7). Yet the representation of slaves in these landscapes would surely have resonated very differently within Brazil and abroad. These lithographs were being offered for sale after the passing of the Abolition Bill in England (1833). The presence of slaves in iconography intended to display the newly independent nation as progressive would have surely confounded many viewing the pictures in Europe. For Europeans viewing and buying the images as souvenirs, or for those unable to travel to such places but desirous of accessing the fantasies they promised, in these images that were part landscape and part natural history they could indulge in the "emerging idea of race as a material . . . and biological fact" (Poole 1997, 15).

The landscape *Morro do Castelo e da Praya d'Ajuda* differs from the panorama mentioned above in fig. 2.4, *Panorama do Rio de Janeiro*, in placing slave figures not "in the background" but in the foreground of the image. The slave woman is positioned at the very center, with two slave men to her left. Steinmann portrays the figures taking a break from work; they are probably *escravos de ganho na rua*—urban slaves who offered services on the streets. The man in the middle is carrying the large basket of the itinerant peddler that many European artists reproduced in their street scenes. As slaves working in the streets, these figures would have enjoyed more mobility than plantation slaves, and some even lived separately from their masters (see Klein and Luna 2009, 137–38). Castelo appears in the top right-hand corner of the lithograph, distant, but very visible, as a looming symbol of a very recent and present colonial memory. The lithograph was one of twelve or sometimes thirteen reproduced in editions of Steinmann's album of landscapes *Souvenirs du Rio de Janeiro* ([1835] 1944). The print shows the balance of stunning landscape with ordered civilization characteristic of the genre, but the slaves appear prominently, as opposed to as tiny figures set against the land or cityscape. They also appear without any whites in the scene, and this absence diminishes somewhat the visual rhetoric of other landscapes in which the presence of masters and mistresses with slaves confirms the social order. Although mute, their circle of conversation among themselves creates a blurring of their knowability as image-objects with the nonknowability of their subjectivities, which escapes the gaze that the consumer of the image directs at it.

The elaborate visual frame decorated with arabesques and exotic vegetation that Steinmann uses for this print and all the others in the album invokes and recycles various elements of the image-world of Brazilian colonialism. This frame adjoins the bucolic landscape, but presents a whole other set of visual and discursive narratives of indigenous and slave life, which sometimes contradict the representation of the main scene and suggest a rural location. At the top center of the frame slave ships arrive in Brazil, but the rest of the images evince no evolutionary, civilizing tempo and place—a naked native hunting a tiger and another clinging to a vine share the space of the left margin with a clothed slave with an agricultural tool. The curious juxtaposition is the result of Steinmann's plundering of figures from three different works by Johann Moritz Rugendas that the latter eventually published in his *Voyage pittoresque dans le Brésil* (1835): *Chasse au tigre,* which takes place in a forest setting, as does *Ponte de cipó,* showing the hanging native, and *Nègre e nègresse dans une plantation* (Sela 2008, 167).

Interestingly, the native physiognomies that Rugendas depicts so clearly in his prints are blurred in Steinmann's appropriation so that it is virtually impossible to tell that the hunter, the figure on the vine, and the ones crossing the bridge on the right margin, which are also adapted from *Ponte de cipó* are, in fact, indigenous. The frame thus collapses black and indigenous peoples into one subjugated category on which colonialism is founded. The indigenous figures are distinguished from the slaves only by their nakedness, although the figures being punished by overseers in the bottom left of the frame are also naked. These figures, however indistinct, communicate the abuses of slavery with a visual language that would have no doubt been easily recognizable to the European consumer of these albums. Shackled, humiliated, hunched over in pain, and in one case possibly buried to the waist, they profoundly disturb the tranquil scene of the central landscape image.[9] They are placed in the frame next to the catechizing violence of Jesuit priests, a small but eloquent scene in which dark-skinned figures surrounded by the symbols of religious power reach toward the missionaries positioned above them. Hanging over this mini-scene is the symbol of the Divine Eye, or all-seeing eye of God. In this micro-representation in the margins of the lithograph, therefore, Steinmann enacts the constitution of the authority of visuality in the New World.

According to Nicholas Mirzoeff, visuality's first domains were the slave plantations, and modern ways of seeing emerged from the oversight of black bodies (2011, 2, 48). The hypervisibility of black bodies that Saidiya Hartman identifies in the plantation's surveillance system articulates clearly this nexus of vision, race, and modernity (1997, 36), where modernity is "constituted in a dialectical relation with a non-European alterity" (Enrique Dussel quoted in Mignolo 2007, 453). The micro-scene of conversion gets at the heart of the violence and exploitation of racialized bodies that underlie modernity through multiple acts of looking as power—by the priests and their God, by the colonizers and overseers, and by the consumers of the iconography and ideology of racial difference. It stages Mirzoeff's idea of a "complex of visuality"—a set of social organizations and processes that trains minds and deploys bodies in the establishment of its authority. However, one of the constitutive forms of visuality is the knowledge that it is always already opposed and in struggle (2011, 5, 6). The rest of this chapter will explore this drama of visuality and countervisuality.

RACE, SPACE, AND THE POLITICAL CARTOON

The reproduction of images by lithograph led to a surge of representations in caricatures in the press in the second half of the nineteenth century. By the beginning of the twentieth century new printing technology ushered in transformations for periodical publishing, as more efficient techniques of photozincography and photoengraving replaced lithography (Süssekind 1997, 48). During this time a number of illustrated weeklies appeared whose content was frequently satirical in tone and in which the *charge* featured prominently. The *Revista da Semana*, founded in 1900, was the first weekly to make use of the new printing technologies in-house. It illustrated current events and crime reports copiously and used photoengraving to produce sharply defined caricatures on high-quality paper (Lima 1963, 138, 143). Over the fifty years of its existence the *Revista da Semana* declared itself to be focused on "striving above all to provide interesting illustrations and articles to all" (Lima 1963, 143). The equal emphasis on illustration responded to the realities of contemporary readership, as only 33.1 percent of the country's population was literate at the time of the 1900 census (Needell 1987, 299).

While periodicals were of central importance to the capital's intellectual milieu due to the paucity of published books, their readership was limited to those with the means, leisure time, and ability to consume print culture (Needell 1987, 197). However, the growth of the bourgeoisie early in the century helped to stimulate the consolidation of periodical publishing into an industry (Sodré 1977, 315). Improvements in graphic design also helped boost interest and audiences for the satirical weeklies whose production and distribution outpaced those of even the largest daily newspapers (Corrêa 2012, 73). According to Herman Lima the *Revista da Semana*, which published the first cartoon discussed in this section (fig. 2.6), was a popular choice for middle-class families (1963, 143). The second *charge* analyzed below (fig. 2.7) comes from *O Malho*, which appeared in 1902 and lasted for fifty-two years. In contrast to the *Revista da Semana* it oriented itself very much toward the working classes, at least until 1918, when its content became more literary (Lima 1963, 146, 149). Proclaiming, "Ever the defender of the popular classes, our good old weekly exists because of the people and for the people!" it sought to appeal to this readership with cartoons lampooning contemporary politicians and the use of popular language in its captions (Corrêa 2012, 78). Caricaturists of these and other weeklies chronicled varied aspects of early twentieth-century urban life, creating images that conveyed the vertiginous experience of living in a city undergoing profound transformation (Dealtry 2009, 119).

Caricatures, alongside photography, would image the city in the period of urban expansion of the first decades of the twentieth century (Santos 2008, 86–97; Vaz 2000, 2). During this time, in the decades following the abolition of slavery, caricatures clearly continued to understand the production of space

Figure 2.6. Detail from "In the Capital," *Revista da Semana*, No. 446, 1911, Biblioteca Nacional Digital Brasil.

in the city as racialized. The 1911 cartoon from the *Revista da Semana* (fig. 2.6) satirizes recent events in the capital. The left half of the cartoon (reproduced here) lampoons fashion trends among the black population. The caricature discusses the popularity among women of the *bombacha*, a baggy style of trousers that was "making waves in the suburbs" and "would undoubtedly soon make its appearance in Morro do Castelo."[10] The artist imagines the jealous punch-ups that will ensue among the "pessoal da lyra," troublemaking revelers, when the first *mulata* dons a pair.[11] According to journalist Jota Efegê, wearing the bombacha was synonymous with capoeira fighters and *capadócios* (1978, 223). The press often used the latter word synonymously with capoeiras, vagabonds, and hooligans (Oliveira 2009, 53), and the *Pequeno dicionário brasileiro da língua portuguesa* defines *capadócio* as a "roguish individual; ostentatious; swaggering; a crook; a trickster" (Ferreira 1971). An account by João do Rio recalls the intense street life downtown of prostitutes, naval fusiliers, people strumming guitars, and "young lads in jerseys and white *bombachas* with the supple bodies of the scoundrel" ([1905] 2005, 96).

The jersey and white bombacha were part of a signature style of the *malan-*

dro, or black street tough, who constructed himself as a public figure partially through his distinctive clothing. A white linen suit, two-toned shoes, and Panama hat was another staple look of the malandro's wardrobe that Matos describes as aspirational to bourgeois respectability but also ultimately parodying it (1982, 56). The two black men punching each other in the cartoon do not sport the trademark clothes of the malandro, except for the straw hat. On the surface their clothes do, in fact, suggest modest bourgeois dress. Yet the cartoon mocks that aspiration by the way they quickly fall back into their uncivilized ways at the merest provocation, and the rendering of their faces that make them appear simian—like apes dressed in men's clothing. Their representation neatly brings together ideas of medical criminology in circulation at the time regarding race, physiology, phrenology, and moral degeneracy. The fact that the woman wears clothing favored by capoeiras masculinizes her.[12] Likewise, her facial features are not only exaggeratedly racialized but masculinized. This is patently not the *mulata* of post-1930s Brazil—the sexualized icon of Brazilian racial mixing. Her large breasts and behind are a nod to the pathologizing of black women's bodies as excessive and hypersexed, but the muscular forearm clutching the alcohol suggests that she is as tough (and immoral and debauched) as any man. In fact, this may be a pictorial rendering of the *malandra*, the female rogue who abandons the home frequently to spend nights carousing, and the subject of a subgenre of samba compositions of the 1920s and 1930s (Matos 1982, 146–59).

Significantly, the little scene played out here is motivated by the act of looking. One or the other of the men eyeballs the woman and this provokes the fight. Indeed, they attack each other so violently that the man on the right punches the eye of his rival clean out of its socket, literally depriving him of sight. Mirzoeff (2011) has discussed how under slavery in the United States, the enslaved were forbidden to look at the white population, a prohibition that was continued throughout the period of segregation and is still in evidence in today's prison system. Black men received especially terrible punishments for transgressing this injunction if they dared to make white women the object of their gaze (2011, 167). In this cartoon black-on-black looking also results in violence, denying black males any right to the gaze whatsoever, for that gaze is always understood as animalistic. For her part, the black woman throws a dismissive look over her shoulder at the men brawling over her sexuality.

An earlier political cartoon published in 1907 in *O Malho* (fig. 2.7) demonstrates more sympathy for the subjects it portrays. Titled "Descendo do Castello" (Descending Castelo Hill) it shows a family of northeastern migrants being

Figure 2.7. "Descending Castello Hill." *O Malho*, September 2, 1905, Biblioteca Nacional Digital Brasil.

evicted from their home on Castelo as part of the Passos reforms. Holding an infant and bundles of their belongings, the wife berates her husband bitterly: "You said this was a civilized place . . . Well, some civilization! Give me my backlands village any day! . . . They want to tear down the hill? Fine, but put up some shacks for the poor who have nowhere to go! These people just abuse us with no shame. . . . I tell you if I were a man I would raise hell!" Hunched over by the weight of the family's furniture that he is carrying on his back, the husband retorts, "Shut up woman! Shut up and get on with it! Here is just like everywhere else: they treat the rich like kings and the poor like dirt. But one day we will have our revenge. Oh yes, we will!" The dialogue that the illustrator imagines between this husband and wife reflects remarkably closely the *sertanejo*, or backlands, worldview that Euclides da Cunha describes in his magnum opus *Os Sertões* (*Rebellion in the Backlands*), published five years earlier. As is well known, da

Cunha was a civil engineer and journalist who went to Bahia for the newspaper *Estado de São Paulo* to cover the brutal and total war waged on the messianic community of Canudos by the Republican army (1896–1897). The community's Catholic lay leader, known as Antônio Conselheiro, resisted the authority of local church and Republican leaders, and as Canudos kept growing it presented an increasing threat in the eyes of coastal leaders and elites.[13] Although the eviction emasculates the husband in the cartoon, as his wife's imprecation suggests ("I tell you if I were a man I would raise hell!"), he threatens that the poor will one day rise up against their oppression by the wealthy. Levine described the country's coastal elites, when they thought about the north of the country at all, as nursing an anxiety about the mixed-race population of the interior, who they understood as ignorant and superstitious, and a real obstacle to the government's modernizing goals (1995, 18).

This concern was borne out in news reports from Canudos, that for the first time reporters in the field transmitted swiftly back to the cities by telegraph, fueling fears of a monarchist plot by racially degenerate religious zealots (Levine 1995, 22, 24). Da Cunha's narrative contains both this horror at the atavistic *mestiço* he encountered in the *sertão* and gradually and increasingly, a sneaking admiration for their survival skills and toughness. This, he rationalized, was a different kind of mestiço, not the degenerate mix that made Republican elites despair for the future of the country, but a "pure" "subrace" that centuries of isolation in the sertão had melded from Brazil's three primary racial groups: indigenous, Portuguese, and black (Zilly 1999, 45). Da Cunha's account revealed that the sertanejo imaginary divided space between sertão and civilization, with no concept of country or nation (Zilly 1999, 19), as the wife in the cartoon does. He recounts how sertanejos referred to the unknown urban coastline as "terras grandes," just as the wife speaks of a "terra civilizada": "It is all the rest of the world, the whole of civilization, which they fear and avoid" (Cunha [1902] 2002, 184). In the cartoon civilization is, indeed, something to fear; it dispossesses and inflicts violence on the vulnerable, who are kicked out of their homes (*aos ponta-pés*). The cartoon reinforces this with the presence of the infant and small child—the latter clutching the mother. Uprisings in the rural northeast threatened the legitimacy of the Republic and the very concept of civilization the Republicans were promoting, and the Canudos rebellion represented the most direct assault on the Republic and its civilized image (Meade 1997, 24, 25). The illustration's critique appears to echo da Cunha's questioning of the country's leaders who eliminate whole communities in the name of civilization.

PHOTOGRAPHY AS A TOOL OF MODERNITY

Figure 2.8 shows demolition work on a colonial-era house in a street that disappeared as a result of the project to tear down Castelo Hill. The city's official photographer, Augusto Malta, is the author of this image and many others that record the communities that the urban reforms eliminated from the landscape. These disappeared geographies also tell of the removal of racialized bodies from the city center. As Lilian Vaz (2000) observes, there is a wealth of iconography from the beginning of the nineteenth century featuring the extensive black presence in city spaces that so fascinated European artists and travelers. However, the reforms of the early twentieth century sought to turn a slave city into a modern bourgeois capital, and the modernization of collective transport, waste management, street lighting, communication, and the sale of goods meant a dwindling black presence in public space. By the end of the nineteenth century and the beginning of the twentieth images of public squares highlight buildings and rarely show the presence of black people. Many squares seem almost deserted, recalling little of the image of the slave city (Vaz 2000, 1, 8, 9). This photograph of the demolition is unusual in Malta's work in that it features a single black subject so prominently. This dearth in the archive of Malta's prodigious production seems to reflect the vanishing presence of which Vaz speaks. She reminds us that the era of the reforms marked the invention of Rio de Janeiro as the "Marvelous City" (2000, 1). As we contemplate the marvelous city's image and imaginary then and now, therefore, we must never forget that they emerge from a process of racialized cleansing.

The photographer's lens captured the narrative of transformation of urbanization at every stage—before, during, and after. We have a significant collection of images of Castelo as a part of that process that record lifestyles, buildings, and public spaces—and their demolition with pickaxes and water jets to yield an idealized city space. The richness of the archive reveals the importance that city and federal officials placed on documenting this progress with a view to imagining and reimagining the city's history. According to Maria Inez Turazzi the Republican government's awareness of the potential of photography for state propaganda and the creation of an official memory is clear in the excessively expensive photo album of new buildings on the Avenida Central that it commissioned after the Passos reforms, and the appointment of Malta as photographer to the Directorate of Works and Transport by the mayor's office in 1903. While the photographs recorded for posterity the role of the state in advancing the nation's progress,

Figure 2.8. "Demolition on Train Street," Augusto Malta, n.d., G. Ermakoff Archive.

they also served to memorialize the engineering profession and valorize its contribution to society (Turazzi 2006, 71, 75, 69). The Republican government and its agents increasingly mobilized photographs of other large-scale engineering works, such as new roads, railways, and sanitary campaigns in the service of the notion of a new civilization in the tropics (Martins 2013, 5). This process is also evident in the legitimation of the architectural profession in Brazil in the context of the mini-city constructed for the fair on the site where Castelo once stood. In fact, Turazzi ties the history of the development of photography in Brazil to its history of national and world fairs. Both are concerned with legitimizing the present and making viable some future realization of a national identity (1995, 109). Inspired by the photograph above, I want to explore photography's dynamics of forgetting and invisibilizing. During a period in which Brazil's representative to the First Universal Races Congress in London declared that the government's whitening policy was working and that Brazil would become a white nation in one hundred years, photographs echoed scientific and official discourse of blacks as a disappearing race.

As Luciana Martins has observed, modern visual technologies supported the survey of territories as they became incorporated into the circuit of industrial capitalism (2013, 3). It was no secret that Rio's mayor had wanted to destroy Castelo for real estate speculation and development, with a company he had established for the purpose obtaining the concession to do so in 1890. Photography served as a tool in the elimination of racialized and ethnic communities with this end in mind. It was also a technique of governance, visualizing authority through images of urbanization. Beatriz Jaguaribe and Maurício Lissovsky call this visual rhetoric "pedagogies of the gaze," which train the public to imagine modernities and communities in line with official discourses of progress (2009, 176). In his work on the role of photography in processes of modern social regulation, John Tagg (1988) underscores that photography was a technique of power-knowledge that was central to urban planning and slum clearance, sanitary reform, and policing. In the context of his study of late nineteenth-century Britain, photography was a strategy of social engineering that became meaningful when inserted in certain official discourses on health and housing. Urban reformers in Britain used photographs to advocate for clean, open city streets, and photographs of streets scheduled for demolition were among the first occasions on which photographs were presented as evidence to a select parliamentary committee (64, 141–48). In Brazil photography also generated new kinds of knowledge of the city's poor and became a site for reimagining the social order. As part of the legitimization of the state's national project, it also rationalized violent interventions into daily life and the spaces of people of color through sanitary and engineering works. At the same time that photography documented these spaces, therefore, it was complicit in their eventual destruction.

PHOTOGRAPHY AND THE VIOLENCE OF RECORD

We owe many of the extant photographs of Castelo to Augusto Malta, whose work over thirty-three years in the mayor's office provides a register of dislocation and dispossession from 1903 to 1936. The city hired Malta to capture all stages of the reform projects and create a visual record of buildings marked for destruction for the purposes of indemnification (Ermakoff 2009, 18). History remembers Malta for the extensive but also detailed archive he created of the then capital city. He generally noted the street, house number, and date on the official photographs, a documentary precision that served as evidence in countering false claims from owners about the size or value of their properties. This meticulousness was necessary as the urban reforms' unseemly haste meant that the city frequently paid compensation only after buildings had already been demolished. Malta was attentive to both this practical function of his documentation and his contribution to the production of knowledge about city life, commenting at the end of his period of service that his material represented not only an archive of the city's history but a way of denouncing unsavory buildings to the mayor's office:

> I took more than a thousand photographs of the remodeling of the city, which I think represents a magnificent document of its history at a moment when it underwent its most radical and profound transformations. And I didn't stop there. In his concern to demolish ruins and blots on the landscape, old Passos always greeted any information about their whereabouts with alacrity. So I also sought to serve him in this way.
>
> . . .
>
> With my case slung around my shoulder, at a time when cameras were great big things, I spent hours wandering the city, snapping hovels that deserved the pickaxe. I acquired something of a reputation for this and many times I had to get out of there pretty quickly because the owners of the buildings to be condemned—of the stores, bars, and kiosks of the city—would come after me seeking revenge. At times it wasn't easy to save myself and the camera from attacks by those backward-looking types. (*O Globo*, August 1, 1936; cited in Ermakoff 2009, 23)

To avoid threats from owners or residents in the course of his duties, he would occasionally disguise his actions by arranging local children in front of targeted buildings and passing himself off as an amateur (Ermakoff 2009, 23). Malta, therefore, was an active agent of urbanization, not just due to the modern technology represented by his camera in the service of the city but as a willing collaborator in the individual and collective trauma that urban reforms of the period inflicted on poor racialized and ethnic groups.

As James Scorer contends, the photograph is both loss and displacement. It offers us only a trace of what is left over from the original moment, and it displays the objects it represents separately from their site of origin (2017). In Malta's work the photograph is doubly a site of loss because it is also a record of the material destruction of the site. It also doubly displaces the subjects and objects it captures to commemorative photo albums and city offices and literally portends the physical removal of its subjects. Press coverage at the time repeatedly refers to how the reforms (and their photographic record) uncovered shockingly crowded, insanitary, and immoral living conditions and lifestyles. Malta himself characterized his work as being in line with investigative journalism, in a retrospective interview on his career given to *O Globo* (cited in Ermakoff 2009, 23). The rhetoric of revealing or bringing to light also recalls archaeological discourses of excavation. It "others" cultures that the elites and bourgeoisie understood as belonging to the past. The documentary, quasi-scientific gaze of Malta's camera, therefore, revealed and recorded social groups condemned by modernity. Like the inverse of what Elizabeth Edwards calls "salvage ethnography"—an anxiety to photograph and somehow preserve dying cultures (2009, 67)[14]—Malta's photographs presaged and occasioned their ruination. There is a poignancy and affective charge in images of people posing in front of homes and businesses earmarked for destruction. The presence of so many children in Malta's images, in particular, is a potent symbol of the stymied future of a generation that official discursive and visual rhetoric produced as undesirable (see fig. 2.9).

It is worth considering briefly Malta's social position and the ideological formation that made him such a zealous supporter of urban reform. Malta was born in 1864, which meant that he lived twenty-four years of his life in a slave society. He was a sertanejo, born in the interior of the northeastern state of Alagoas. Echoing the language of criminal anthropology of the time, a weekly publication described him in 1945 as having a "typically northern appearance"—brachycephalic, with a protruding jawbone, and almond-shaped eyes (cited in Ermakoff 2009, 12).[15] During his time as an army cadet in Recife, Malta became an ardent supporter of the Republic and arrived in Rio a year before its declaration, the year of the abolition of slavery. Of the latter he opined: "As I see it, Abolition was ruinous for the plantation and for the slaves themselves" (cited in Ermakoff 2009, 17). Malta boasted some of the key ideologues and executors of the urban reforms as his friends or acquaintances, such as Paulo de Frontin, Carlos Sampaio, Francisco de Paula Rodrigues Alves, Joaquim Nabuco, Oswaldo Cruz, Ruy Barbosa, and Lauro Müller.[16] He was particularly proud of his relationship with Mayor Passos, the godfather to one of his daughters. As someone who was identifiably northeastern in appearance, who was one of the lowest-paid functionaries in the mayor's office, and who spent most of his career in debt, these acquaintances would have conferred considerable social prestige on Malta, and he repaid the

Figure 2.9. "Estácio de Sá Street," Augusto Malta, n.d., G. Ermakoff Archive.

attentiveness of Passos, in particular, with considerable diligence and zeal: "Even though I had a secondary, supporting role, I was proud to contribute to the glory of the great work. It required the faithful and incontrovertible documentation that only good photographs can provide. So the passable amateur grasped his responsibility and sought to be the best professional photographer possible" (quoted in Ermakoff 2009, 23).

Malta is clearly aware of the role that he has assumed as knowledge producer on behalf of the city. His enthusiasm for the urbanization projects, therefore, stemmed from his positivist formation in military school, as well as the sense of responsibility and importance that this inaugural role of city photographer conferred upon him given his somewhat precarious socioeconomic situation. The staging of urbanization in his photographs was more significant than his modest description of them as secondary or minor. They both reflect and produce Republican discourses on housing, health, and progress. His images also registered and recorded the elimination of colonial spaces to lay the ground for a visual economy reliant on invisibilizing race difference. The photographic archive, therefore, acts as a system of documentation that is complicit with the state's whitening project. His photographs accompany the process of identifying and naturalizing insalubrious obstacles to the modernizing project; the elimination of these communities; and the implantation of a built environment signifying order and progress in their place.

Malta gathered ninety-eight images of Castelo Hill before and during the demolition into an album, *Álbum de fotografias do morro do Castelo* (1922). The album tells a story about built and lived space, but also about time. On the surface it dramatizes positivism's idea of linear progress—displaying the premodern that gives way to the urbanizers' pickaxes and shovels. As Cláudia Quelhas Paixão has noted, however, Malta did not display the photographs in chronological order, preferring instead to create two sequences according to which he arranged the images. The first, at the beginning of the album, focuses on the Morro's poverty versus the material and symbolic wealth of its historic buildings. In the second part of the album the sequence highlights the contrast between the occupied space and the process of its demolition (2008, 56–57). Paixão has observed in the latter sequence a number of pairs of images juxtaposed on opposing pages in which one page shows locals in the streets and the other demolition in progress, such as images 76 and 77. In this pair of photographs the demolition image appears first on the left and the other photograph, of children outside decaying houses in Largo do Castelo, appears after it (2008, 62–63). This order inverts the "before" and "after" chronology of the urbanization narrative. In this instance Malta has, however, ordered these two photographs chronologically: according to his handwritten dating system he took the demolition photograph on July 30, 1921, and the picture of the children months later, in December of that year. This means that when we look at this pair of images what we are seeing is children living in the middle of a process of ruination of their communities. The banality of their presence in the square acquires significant poignancy in the light of this realization. Paixão highlights another example of this pairing of everyday life with demolition in images 78 and 79 (2008, 63). Photograph 78 shows the Ladeira do Castelo, or Castelo Slope, with adults and children, including one boy who occupies the center foreground of the frame with a ball under his arm (fig. 2.10), while photograph 79 records demolition work on the Capuchins' church. In this pairing the photograph of everyday life comes first, followed by the demolition photo, which has human figures and washerwomen's laundry dotting the landscape, so we are witnessing the disappearance of this community in process from

Figure 2.10. "Taken from Castelo Square," Augusto Malta, March 11, 1922, Biblioteca Nacional Digital Brasil.

one image to the next. Although the destruction appears as if in stages from one photograph to the next, Malta actually took them on the same day. Once we realize the simultaneity of these two images we understand that the drama of loss is being played out before our eyes: that ways of life, spaces, and people are literally disappearing as we watch. We cannot help but imagine how their lives continue even as the demolition has already begun.

The album documents the drama of transforming a colonial landscape into a space to serve the needs of twentieth-century capitalism—the international market represented in the spectacle of a world fair. The images are produced as archive, but presumably also for sale. The album therefore represents posterity and profit. Given the topocide of the neighborhood, the album endures as a ghostly trace of that material site that it is no longer possible to visit, occupy, or view. However, the people in these photographs haunt the present and the future with their own materiality in the images—their corporality, and their day-to-day activity and occupation of streets, squares, and courtyards. While

Figure 2.11. "Castelo Square," Augusto Malta, March 11, 1922, Biblioteca Nacional Digital Brasil.

many of Malta's photographs are posed, they are not studio portraits, and some are dynamic snapshots of street life.

In figure 2.11 a busy moment of daily life makes for a rather unusual image compared to the rest of Malta's oeuvre, with its good lighting, clarity, and careful framing. Here most of the bottom of the photograph is poorly lit, making it difficult to discern the faces of those in the center foreground and the two girls standing to the left, as if they have resisted capture by the camera. Although we see these figures only in silhouette, the female water carrier and the other two figures near the middle (one bent over by her load) convey strength and constitute the visual core of the photograph. The right of the image teems with children who seem to reflect Castelo's demographic by the time of its destruction, with European immigrants outnumbering Afro-descendants. Although some of the faces of the children are indistinct, a group of five clustered to the right is clear and well-lit and provides a visual focus to this side of the photograph. This little group is particularly racially diverse: the older girl who looks to be about ten years old, but who already appears to have the demeanor and responsibilities of an adult, holds a young child in her arms and both appear to be of mixed race; the boy scowling at the camera next to her and the entirely naked child are white; and the boy seated next to him with what appear to be crutches and gazing impassively back at the camera is black. The backdrop for the four is the crumbling wall of a colonial house that bears the sign CASTELO ALLEY, seemingly indexing the place name with decline and neglect. The rundown setting and the lack of light on the left of the photograph that accentuates the grime of the cobbled streets and buildings mark this space out as unhealthy and decaying. The gaze behind the camera measures these tenement buildings falling into ruin against an ideal space that was healthy, orderly, and European. It also legitimizes the large-scale ruin-making of the state by presenting this alley as uninhabitable space.[17] Yet there is something about those engaged in the daily business of survival and leisure, and the fact that the image seems unable to properly contain the people it portrays, several of whom are exiting the frame or spilling over its edges, that resists being fixed and typed by the photographer and those who would seek to condemn them.

As mentioned previously, one of the constitutive forms of visuality's authority is the fact that it is always already opposed and in struggle (Mirzoeff 2011, 6). I want to return to figure 2.8 to further explore the dynamics of the condemning gaze and the ways in which the camera's subjects may counter it. Poole (1997) proposes two ways to think about the racial scripting of photographic portraiture and the subjectivities that can nevertheless emerge from such images. Early twentieth-century portraits in Latin America molded and formed subjects in accordance with a vision of modernity borrowed from Europe, but subjects also subverted or resisted the enframing technologies of race and photography and suggested their own experiences of the modern (213). In analyzing this photograph I will introduce the issue of space into the intersection of race and the visual rhetoric of photography. The photograph shows a young black boy seated on top of a house that the demolition work in Castelo has reduced to ruins. It appears that all that is left of the house is its façade, which is cracked, pitted, and damp. Most of the space within the frame is occupied by the façade, whose outline organizes the bulk of the frame into a horizontal plane. This plane has a slightly oblique trajectory that urges us to follow it with our eyes to the boy sitting in the top right-hand corner. Despite the house's advanced state of disintegration there is still a kind of geometrical order present in its façade—with its horizontal form broken up by the three vertical apertures—that speaks to previous attempts to order space that the photograph now presents as obsolete and undesirable. Someone has placed salvaged bricks in the window, perhaps to prevent what is left of the house from falling and thereby recycling its debris in an attempt to slow down the process of its ruination. Yet the rubble at the side of the house—wooden planks that look like the protruding entrails of the gutted building—foretells the inevitable future of this modernization project. In fact, from our twenty-first-century vantage point there is a temporal tension between a colonial past that the demolition is violently effacing in the present time of the contemporary observer, and the reverberations of these projects into the future in the elusive search for modernity. The boy in the photograph brings our vision of the present time of the image into sharp focus by compelling us to think about the everyday of those who lived in and among these ruins. His position on top of the crumbling wall appears precarious and potentially dangerous and provokes speculation about his being there. Has he made this ravaged building into his playground? Was this once his home?

While we will never know the answers to these questions, to contemplate them is to speculate on this boy's active, affective, and embodied engagement with the ruins around him. This in turn undermines the ways in which the photograph scripts him and the neighborhood he called home. The portrait may construct him as a racialized presence that merits ruination and elimination like the space he inhabits. Yet as buildings disintegrate around him he stays, like many other *castelenses* did. Newspaper reports of locals killed or injured due to the demolition work emphasize residents' stubborn refusal to leave. Their persistent habitation tells a story about the geographical histories of coloniality in the Americas. As mentioned in chapter 1, twentieth-century Afro-descendant organizing and mobilizing are significantly based on the struggle to remain in appropriated spaces, which geographer Andrelino Campos traces to black forms of territoriality such as the *quilombo* (2005, 31). Even as the city makes this community uninhabitable its occupants' refusal to leave confers a different meaning on the place—as home. Home was not a concept that city officials attached to Brazil's black population in the period of the Old Republic. In contrast to the classed and raced idea of the homes of the white bourgeoisie as inviolable, poor black domestic spaces appeared (and still do) to be imminently violable and invadable (Campos 2005, 43).

Undoubtedly, by naturalizing this degraded landscape as home, in which the boy seems quite at ease and in which he communicates a sense of belonging through his position atop the house, this photograph racializes ruin and displacement as black. Indeed, these were and continue to be fundamental aspects of the Afro-descendant experience of urban space, and the afterlife of this image can also stand as testament and critique of a history of dispossession. Therefore, on the one hand this photograph constructs this place as eliminable and its occupants as disposable in order to imagine new material and symbolic landscapes of national community. In so doing it mobilizes and attempts to fix notions of racial and sociocultural difference in the service of a political project based on the exclusion of some social groups from modernization.

However, as James Ryan and Joan Schwartz remind us, although the camera is a form of technological power that prescribed and proscribed particular ways of picturing place, there is a range of relationships embedded in photographs—between representation and reality, intention and impact, and photographer and viewer, which means that their meanings, though bound up with myriad forms of power, are constantly negotiated (2003, 15, 11, 5). This photograph documents a geohistorical moment in which the city and the state made violent claims for ownership of public and domestic urban spaces that would define much of the Afro-descendant experience of city space thereafter. The boy's presence atop the ruin also communicates a right to inhabit the space and recalls other castelenses' refusal to leave. He also exercises his right to look by gazing directly at the camera, and does so from a superior position above it. His returned gaze is also a gesture of refusal in the drama of black visuality played out in the photograph.

The image is intended to produce historical and geographical knowledge about the neighborhood and document its incompatibility with modernity. In a parallel and related move it seeks to make blackness visually knowable or apprehensible within certain regimes of meanings that rationalize its "troubling presence" (Fleetwood 2011, 6, 3). The photograph understands the boy, his neighborhood, and his social group as doomed to disappear and visibilizes him in the historical and geographical record as part of what the country must and will overcome. In the photograph certain meanings associated with blackness mark out and occupy the distance between photographer and subject, but the boy's gaze also hints at subjectivities that are beyond knowability. As Fleetwood remarks on black visuality: "Blackness fills in space between matter, between object and subject, between bodies, between looking and being looked upon. It fills in the void and is the void. Through its circulation, blackness attaches to bodies and narratives coded as such but it always exceeds these attachments" (6).

What escapes these interpellations and the camera's gaze is also hinted at in the shadowy figures of a woman or women at an upstairs window behind the ruined house. Their domestic scene is a part of an unknowable black lived experience that remains hidden from our gaze.

"INAUGURATING RUINS"

Ruins and ruination closely accompany the ambitious urbanization projects of the capital city during the first decades of the twentieth century. A political cartoon called "The Government Inaugurating the Outline of the New Avenue" appeared in September 1904 in the current affairs magazine *O Malho* (fig. 2.12). It shows then president Rodrigues Alves together with Rio de Janeiro mayor Pereira Passos; José Luiz Bulhões de Carvalho, medical doctor and statistician for the Director General of Public Health; the engineers Lauro Müller and Francisco Bicalho; Minister of War Francisco de Paula Argolo; Minister of the Interior and of Justice J. J. Seabra; Navy Minister Júlio de Noronha; Minister of the Exterior the Baron of Rio Branco; and Minister of Transport and Public Works Paulo de Frontin. These high-ranking officials are attending the inauguration of the construction of the Avenida Central, a project that destroyed one of the slopes of Castelo Hill. The text of the cartoon subversively imagines the following dialogue between the country's pillars of government:

> R. Alves: Did you fall, Bulhões? Serves you right! You can't perform gymnastics like we São Paulo folk . . .
>
> Bulhões: My good man! Better get out of here before I fall again! What on earth was Lauro thinking to inaugurate ruins . . .
>
> Lauro: Ruins, he can talk! You're the one with the ruins, Bulhões; you know what I mean . . . [18]
>
> Seabra: Let's not argue, chaps. You just need a bit of skill, like me, so you don't take a tumble . . .
>
> Noronha: Ouch! I just took a grenade to the head! This is Barbosa Lima's doing!!
>
> Argollo: Careful, colleague! Positivism can be a tough brainteaser to crack! What do you say, Baron?
>
> Rio Branco: Hold on, I have no idea how I'm supposed to scale this mountain. It's like a pilgrimage up to Our Lady of Glória . . . *uff!* . . .

Figure 2.12. "The Government Inaugurating the Outline of the New Avenue," *O Malho*, September 3, 1904, Biblioteca Nacional Digital Brasil.

To "inaugurate a ruin" is to claim the power of deliberate ruin making for the state, as well as to create a spectacle of ruination that was fundamental to the visual rhetoric of the modernization project. Many photographs of the inauguration of the Avenida show half-demolished buildings dressed up for the occasion with palm fronds, leaf garlands, and bunting. These rather rudimentary "sets" on which a crude theater of modernization was performed is what the cartoon mocks mercilessly. It was also the butt of jokes in commentaries in other weeklies. On September 8, 1904, the magazine *Tagarela* jeered: "The inaugurations of the Avenue are going to stretch out into an endless commemoration. We just had the axis, soon it will be the first sidewalk, then the first urinal." The daily *Jornal do Brasil* described the scene, dominated by "an arch simulating a ruin," that paid homage to President Alves, the engineer Müller, and the construction workers. This heroic representation of the workers was rather different from the cartoon's portrait. On the faux ruined archway there was a painting of a "manly worker with his sleeves rolled up, hat in hand, looking serenely into the distance in the direction of the Presidential convoy."[19]

In the above cartoon the workers are bent over from the physical demands of their tasks and one in particular is far from a complicit participant in the modernization project. At the top left of the cartoon we see a black construction worker demolishing a building and dropping stones on the head of Noronha. There was significant black presence in the workforce of the city's ships and ports, and the overwhelming majority of Brazil's navy was black.[20] The potentially surreptitious gesture is carried out right under the nose of Mayor Passos, and suggests acute political resentment on the part of the black population against those who exercise oppressive control of their lives and govern the city. The minister's reaction references the ongoing debate in government and the press over the law requiring compulsory vaccination against smallpox. Federal deputy Alexandre José Barbosa Lima opposed the law and would cofound the League Against Compulsory Vaccination in November, stoking popular resentment of government interference and an "obscene law" that would enable public health officials to enter homes and expose intimate parts of the bodies of female family members to their immoral scrutiny. He and other leaders of the league made inflammatory speeches aimed at the city's working classes, particularly maritime workers, encouraging an all-out rebellion in the streets over the passing of the law (Sevcenko 1993, 15, 18). The rocks dropped on Minister Noronha's head therefore represent a small act of vengeance against an authoritarian initiative that

Figure 2.13. "The Inauguration of Central Avenue—On the Presidential Train," *O Malho*, September 10, 1904, Biblioteca Nacional Digital Brasil.

engaged in no public education or psychological preparation of the population and required their unconditional submission (Sevcenko 1993, 15).

Jon Beasley-Murray observes that "ruination and modernity go hand in hand: the modern displaces the ancient and marks it as irredeemably part of the past precisely by construing it as ruined" (2010, 212). This symbiosis is rendered visually and succinctly in another political cartoon from *O Malho* published a week after the previous one (fig. 2.13). Titled "The Inauguration of the Avenida Central—on the Presidential Train," it shows the president of the Republic touring a chaotic building site in a ceremonial train festooned with flags. The chief engineer of the project, Frontin, remarks to him, "You see, Mr President, there are ruins and debris everywhere, but without them we could only build imaginary Avenues." Ruination is necessary to modernization, and the materiality of the rubble inspires the utopian modern imagination. That rubble is also part of a visual language of ruination that works to exclude and to naturalize hierarchies of value in reordered space. This visual regime also has a temporal impulse by which the lifestyles, behaviors, and bodies of certain groups are identified with the debris and consigned to disappear in the past. In the previous cartoon, however, the black construction worker whose physical labor is building the modern city is engaging in his own act of restitution. He repurposes the debris to which black and popular neighborhoods are being reduced to cause physical harm to the navy minister. The cartoon therefore opens a space for the construction worker's experience of modernity that the pomp and ceremony of the inauguration ritual would seek to silence. His moment of political resentment disturbs the discourse and the iconography of progress.

Photographs also documented the demolition of Castelo at every stage in order to claim the ruination process for the state. The spectacle was important to affirming and collectively imagining the destruction of the colonial legacy of the "slave city." Rather than the ritual of inaugurating ruins, Sampaio's urbanization project emphasized a process of archiving ruins: of visually cataloguing places before erasing them, repeatedly uniting the power and violence of urbanization with the technology of photography. The violence of record was conjoined with novel "technologies of spatial obliteration" (Gordillo 2014, 77). Initially, pickaxes carried out the demolition work and horse carts carried the debris away. They proved too slow, however, and the engineers brought in excavating equipment from outside the city and abroad. The diggers removed the soil and loaded it onto open freight cars that took it out to the bay along three railway lines. Humble city

Figure 2.14. "Castelo Hill: demolition," photographer unknown, [1923–193?], Biblioteca Nacional Digital Brasil.

dwellers accompanied the spectacle of the demolition and the modernization of the machinery of destruction firsthand and at all hours of the day.[21]

Figure 2.14 constitutes a pictorial analogue of technology's mastery over the landscape.[22] The foreground of the photograph is occupied by a flat dirt surface, which is the fate that awaits the mound of earth in the background, in the top right-hand corner of which we can glimpse a building still standing even as the hill is being dug out from under it. Horizontally dividing this "before" and "after" of progress more or less down the middle are the open-bed freight cars and the tracks on which they run. The tracks and cars form linear, straight lines of perspective that propel the gaze to a point outside the frame, which we know is the destination of the dirt as it becomes a landfill and new urban space in the near future. The straight lines and rectangles of the tracks and cars impose themselves on the natural landscape and dominate it. This visual and geographical order sets the stage for the central character in this performance

Figure 2.15. "Castello Hill [demolition]," Augusto Malta, October 9, [1]922, Biblioteca Nacional Digital Brasil.

of destructive modernity: the backhoe captured in motion pouring soil into the cars. The motion materializes as blurs on the glass plate, making the viewer a witness to this act of geographical transformation almost as it occurs. The backhoe occupies the middle of the frame and its vertical position cuts across and looms over the horizontal planes created by the cars and tracks, dwarfing the worker operating it. The photograph's perspective makes its shaft rise higher than the remaining hillside and project into the empty sky. Next to it, paralleling its vertical trajectory, is the smoking stack of the freight car, whose black plume rises into the sky almost as high as the backhoe itself, indexing industrialization.

When the backhoes failed to deliver destruction at the necessary pace, however, the city imported British water jets to speed up the process. A news report describes "powerful hydraulic bombs" never before used in South America, and the president of the country and the city's mayor attended a solemn inauguration of their use (*Gazeta de Notícias*, June 8, 1922). Malta documents the water jets at work in a number of images that neatly connect their destructive force with modernity's advances. In figure 2.15 the jets are photographed as part of a panorama of the bay in a kind of perverse reference to the countless panoramas of the city's stunning coastline, now radically transformed by the machines. The photograph's scale emphasizes the huge task before the city's engineers, but the gaping entrails of what is left of the hillside testify to technology and man's ability to meet the challenge. Throughout this chapter many of the images I have examined contain subjects who "look back" at modernity's authoritarian gaze. These photographs of a landscape ruined by new technology, however, disappear residents from the scene. They are registers of topocide, Douglas Porteous's previously mentioned term for the annihilation of place (1989, 230). They reduce the landscape to earth and rubble. While other images analyzed here explore rubble as "affectively charged matter" (Gordillo 2014, 5) with which people living in ruins engage on a daily basis, here the sense of place, of home, of sociality is erased—washed into the bay with the dirt. These photographs of the ravaged landscape disappear those who lived, worked, and died here—some actually killed or injured because they stayed on during dangerous demolition work, literally sacrificed, therefore, to progress. One can only imagine the astonishment of city dwellers in the face of this alarmingly effective tool of modernization that could wash a whole community into the bay. According to the samba singer Noel Rosa, the spectacle of the rapid disintegration of the neighborhood shocked the city's population of color.[23]

VISUALITY, REPRESSION, AND REFUSAL

> Every day, between 9 and 10 o'clock in the morning, one could see blacks lined up and awaiting punishment. They move along with their arms restrained, two by two, escorted by the police to the place designated for castigation. These public displays, firmly reestablished in 1821, were suppressed in 1829 and conducted since then in a single place which is steep and out of the way: outside the prison gate on Castelo Hill.
>
> —**Jean-Baptiste Debret,** ***Viagem pitoresca e histórica ao Brasil,*** **cited in Nonato and Santos 2000, 69.**

Jean-Baptiste Debret, a member of the French Artistic Mission appointed by the Portuguese Crown and who painted memorable scenes of slave punishment himself, describes an everyday spectacle of violence against black bodies that traversed city space and culminated at Castelo Hill. A watercolor by the Australian painter and traveler Augustus Earle (fig. 2.16) portrays the destination of

Figure 2.16. *Punishing Negros at Cathabouco*, Augustus Earle, 1822.

this wretched convoy: the *pelourinho*, or whipping post, outside Castelo prison. This was a slave prison located at the bottom of the hill that operated as such at least since the time of the Royal Court, which arrived in Brazil in 1808.[24] Of the 198 prisoners held there in 1833, 192 were recaptured slaves, or slaves accused of some impropriety by their masters who sent them there to be whipped for a fee.[25] Only 6 were actually serving a sentence or involved in a criminal process (Holloway 2009, 256). In the 1820s the prison charged a minimum of 160 *réis* per hundred lashes, and a total of 1,786 slaves were sent there by their masters to be whipped, with the majority receiving two or three hundred lashes (Coaracy 1955, 470; Holloway 2009, 255). In 1783 those fees were used to fund the construction of the Passeio Público, Rio's first public park, built just below Castelo Hill (Coaracy 1955, 471). The Passeio Público was the first urbanized area of the city, designed to exhibit the power of the Portuguese Crown to the local populace. It was actually built using the forced labor of those imprisoned for vagrancy and convicts from the Ilha das Cobras prison. Imprisoned slave labor was used for various urbanization and building projects around the city, including the new prison complex whose construction began in 1833 (Holloway 2009, 259). The city was literally constructed, therefore, through the use and abuse of black bodies. As a site of one of the city's pelourinhos, Castelo was a key reference point in this geography of spectacular racialized violence.

In his history of Rio de Janeiro writer Gastão Cruls (1952) describes a sixteenth-century map of the new city drawn by the Frenchman Jacques de Vaudeclaye, who visited Rio in 1579 on a secret mission of behalf of the French government. The map shows clearly the presence of a pelourinho on Castelo at this early moment in the city's history (72). According to journalist and writer Vivaldo Coaracy, the pelourinho was both a symbol of the power of the Crown and an instrument of punishment on which the condemned would either be lashed or simply displayed for the public gaze. As such, it was an essential part of the built landscape of any settlement. In small hamlets it might just be a robust wood post with iron rings screwed into it. In more significant settlements it was made of carved stone and decorated at the top with the royal coat of arms (Coaracy 1955, 58). Once the colonial authorities abandoned Castelo they installed a pelourinho in the Terreiro do Carmo, the large public square that is today's Praça Quinze. For a time this square was also known as the Terreiro da Polé, using the popular term for pelourinho, although the *polé*, or pulley, was a different instrument of torture. The pelourinho moved again after the Portuguese court transferred to Rio de Janeiro in 1808 and took up residence in the Terreiro do Carmo, in order to avoid subjecting the courtly gaze to such a spectacle. There was also a "polé dos militares" near today's Campo de Santana, on which soldiers subject to military justice were punished (Coaracy 1955, 58, 60, 59).

As Christen Smith observes with regard to the presence of the pelourinho in Salvador, Bahia, it was both an icon of (neo)colonial authority and a material and symbolic representation of slavery's culture of terror (2016, 56). In Earle's painting the slave about to be punished has been stripped naked, pointing to both the racialized and sexualized spectacularity of the pelourinho (57). He is lashed to the pole and we become witnesses to his torture in medias res, as his body is already bloodied and the whip is held high, in sharp relief against the blue sky, and about to fall and tear into his flesh again. The executor of the punishment is a slave. According to Thomas Holloway those who dispensed the lashes were themselves prisoners serving out a sentence at the *calabouço*, or prison, such as one Antônio who was serving life, and Joaquim Benguela, sentenced to ten years (Holloway 2009, 256). In her discussion of antiblack violence in Brazil, Smith discusses how black subjects are obliged to act as enforcers of their own communities, abusing and disciplining fellow blacks in the maintenance of white supremacy (2016, 49). Another punisher waits, seated in the right foreground of the painting, perhaps ready to take over when the first tires, or when the next slave in line is brought forward. It is not clear who the two black figures standing in front of the pelourinho are. Perhaps they are also prisoners who wield the whip, but their expressions and body language as they stand not two feet away and facing the bleeding slave exhibit a relaxed indifference, suggesting the quotidian nature of the spectacle of torture. The man to the viewer's right actually appears to be smoking, while the man to his left wears an almost bemused expression. In the background it is business as usual, as a master leads his slave through the gates and a female slave speaks through a window, perhaps inquiring about a friend or family member imprisoned there.

The painting unites the entire group clustered around the pelourinho in the foreground in a simultaneous drama of looking. All eyes are on the body being flagellated, except for one slave master who apparently shields his gaze with his hands, as if the proximity and intensity of the flogging were too awful for his fine sensibilities. The next prisoner to be flogged has an expression of terror on his face, but cannot help but look even as his body shrinks away toward the edge of the frame from the horror before him, while the look of the slave master in riding boots and top hat is one of sneering satisfaction. Perhaps the most disturbing gaze, however, may be that which the punisher appears to exchange with the man he is whipping. The latter has his back to the viewer, so we are denied his gaze, but his head is angled toward his torturer and the latter's line of sight leads directly into his. On the punisher's face is an expression that is unmistakably one of pity, and his countenance contrasts strikingly with his arm holding the whip aloft and on the verge of inflicting further pain. This jarring note speaks eloquently of his own subjugation and the psychic suffering of his role as enforcer of slavery's brutality.

According to Holloway the conditions inside of the calabouço were infernal, and it functioned as a kind of human scrapheap where masters would simply abandon their slaves if the cost of their upkeep and punishment exceeded the amount that the master deemed his chattel to be worth (2009, 257). The prison was, therefore, also a site of slow, ruinous violence against black bodies through horrendous sanitary conditions and lack of adequate nutrition. Additionally, the authorities neglected the wattle-and-daub building itself, which fell into such a state of ruination that in 1631 members of the town council informed the superior crown magistrate that prisoners were frequently exploiting the precariousness of its structure to effect their escape (Coaracy 1955, 24). In so doing they demonstrated a proactive, physical engagement with ruins in order to secure their liberty. The landfill created by imported water jet technology buried this site of abuse, abandonment, and refusal (Holloway 2009, 279).

In the latter half of this chapter I have used pictures of the debris and rubble from this disappeared hillside "as a lens to examine the places that were negated to create the geographies of the present" (Gordillo 2014, 11). These images from the past have much to tell us about technologies of governance of racialized spaces today. In analyzing them we denaturalize certain contemporary geographies that construct some spaces as more susceptible to and deserving of violence than others, by tracing continuities in a history of racialized destruction.

Past and future frequently overlap or collide in ruins. In figure 2.17, an image of gleaming new pavilions in the mini-city constructed for the fair, the ruins of Castelo still loom in the background, for a time monumentalizing the relationship between progress and destruction. While they stood there the organizers no doubt viewed these remnants as a symbol of the mastery and daring of their civilizing mission to overcome the past and call into being the city of the future. Modernization projects elicit powerful imaginaries of the future, but their promises are constantly deferred while being simultaneously entangled with the colonial past (Rao 2013, 292). This entanglement assumes visual, material form here in the skeletal remains of the Jesuit convent whose presence seems to suggest the precariousness of previous utopian modernizing endeavors. From the perspective of today's viewer, aware that many of the new buildings that arose in the place where Castelo once stood were themselves later demolished (such as the colossal Pavilion of the Brazilian States that dominates this photograph), the ruins captured here trouble the visual rhetoric of the new that the image articulates. It is as if, as Jaguaribe says, modernity's future is always already in ruins, and this building on the verge of collapse above the new pavilions functions as a sign of how easily the future projection of our present can unravel (2014, 54). In writing about the ruined landscape of the nitrate industry in the Atacama Desert, Louise Purbrick also observes how such photographic archives can "reveal an unfulfilled future" (2017, 15). While they document early twentieth-century industrial plenty and indicate progress, she explains, they are records of the

Figure 2.17. "Exposition to Commemorate the Centenary of Brazilian Independence," G. Ermakoff Archive.

failure to come. The photographs themselves can become ruins that foreshadow devastation and violence, but also resistance.

The photograph of the young boy on the ruined house (fig. 2.8) foreshadows the image below (fig. 2.18). The photograph is from 2015 and shows Pedro Berto, a resident of Vila Autódromo, a favela community decimated to make way for the Olympic Village, in front of his family's ruined house. Viewed together, the early twentieth-century photograph becomes a powerful portent that seems to anticipate the future writ large for black people in a city that continues to use urbanization as a weapon against them. These subjects have experienced ruination as a slow drama of loss (Purbrick 2017, 18; Nixon 2013); for example, in the form of unequal access to social services and the job market. Additionally, the disappearance of their communities as Rio was being remade in the name of mega-events was swift and spectacular. The speed and scale of their ruination were in direct correlation to the intensity of the imbricated desire for modernity and disavowal of blackness. There are no ruins of Castelo to contemplate today; all that remains of the hillside is the start of the steep path that once led up to

Figure 2.18. Pedro Berto, resident of Vila Autódromo, June 8, 2015. Courtesy of Catalytic Communities, *Rio On Watch*.

it via the Misericórdia Slope—now "a path to nowhere," as the title of a recent novel on Castelo describes it (Carvalho 2014).[26] "Nowhere" is a conceptual and material space inhabited by "no-bodies"—black and blackened people who are casualties of urban violence and the violence of urbanization. It is the place where what should "happen to nobody" continues to happen every day (Silva 2009, 212).

Figure 3.1. Chácara da Floresta on Castelo Hill behind the School of Fine Arts. Augusto Malta, July 29, 1921, Biblioteca Nacional Digital Brasil.

Figure 3.2. Chácara da Floresta. Augusto Malta, July 29, 1921, Biblioteca Nacional Digital Brasil.

3

ALTERNATIVE GEOGRAPHIES AND SPATIAL PRACTICES

> Rio is the most paradoxical city in the world. Just 50 meters from the theater where the *Parcifal* is performed and ecstatically received, which provides ample proof of the elevated level of our culture and our aesthetic sensibilities; just 20 meters from the Palace of Fine Arts, in whose collection we hold the highest endeavors of the artistic talent of our race; just 15 meters from a grand national library and the Supreme Court of Justice—one can see goats grazing on Morro do Castelo.
>
> —*Revista da Semana*, July 31, 1920, 25 (quoted in Motta 1992, 58)

> Rio de Janeiro is the city of contrasts. On exiting Rio Branco Avenue you suddenly find yourself in alleyways from colonial times. You can see richly dressed ladies and the most fashionable men in the streets, and shamelessly mixing in with them filthy, ragged, and barefoot individuals in dingy undershirts. On one side you hear courteous phrases exchanged between well-educated people, and on the other random obscenities hurled by those who frequent carnival and samba groups. And to top it all off, when you enter Rio Branco Avenue and your gaze hovers to the left, up on the hill just a couple of steps from the beautiful boulevard, a piece of Africa suddenly appears before you. Take a look and you could imagine that it's Dakar or São Vicente right there in front of your eyes!
>
> —*Revista Fon-Fon*, October 10, 1914

ONE OF THE SUMPTUOUS NEW BUILDINGS that emerged in the city center as a result of the Passos reforms of 1903–1906 was the Palace (or National School) of Fine Arts. High cultural institutions such as this one were monuments to elite ambitions to Europeanize and modernize the city.[1] The fine arts school was obliged, however, to coexist in uncomfortably close proximity to Castelo Hill, about twenty meters away.[2] Indeed, as is evident in Augusto Malta's photograph, the terrace of the fine arts school afforded an unobstructed view of the tenement dwellings, yards, and alleys in which residents conducted their daily lives in Chácara da Floresta, a micro-neighborhood within Castelo (figs. 3.1 and 3.2). This juxtaposition of the old and new city affronted publications like the *Revista da Semana* that supported the civilizing project. They fumed that Castelo was akin to an "African village," or a settlement of "Indian tribes wearing lip plugs" (Motta (1992, 58).[3] The persistence of racialized geographies in the center of the urbanized downtown area repeatedly thwarted the dominant geographies that the Republican and municipal governments sought to impose. These defiant spaces were produced by people whose forms of living, working, and leisure were perceived by those in power as immoral, criminal, or simply incompatible with the ideal whitened city.

This chapter examines ways in which *castelenses* established territory and negotiated their way in the city. Following Katherine McKittrick, I explore Castelo as a site of interethnic geographies; in other words, with the understanding that densely occupied, urban racial and ethnic spaces are not generally enclosed or discrete (exclusively black, for example) but are configured by the spatialities of other subjects (2006, 108). I therefore understand racialized geographies not just in terms of segregation, though this would certainly become a fundamental experience of black spatialities in later generations, as the descendants of European immigrants ascended socially. Different racial and ethnic geographies even in a single neighborhood like Castelo met, connected, and came into conflict. They also had a complex relationship with dominant geographies; often challenging them, sometimes articulating with them, but always transforming them through these interventions. Those invested in a Rio redesigned according to Parisian Belle Époque ideals found their model cityscape continually interrupted by these defiant and deviant spaces. The material examined in this chapter highlights the alternative forms of geographical knowledge produced in such spaces, whose cultural and social practices frequently came to extend in some form across the city, affecting social relations more widely. The chapter also denaturalizes and deessentializes racialized and ethnic geographies by rethinking the notion of territoriality. I explore how a diverse population in a densely occupied site challenges notions of geography as "biocentrically partial," as McKittrick has put it. In her study of black diasporas in North America McKittrick raises the importance of thinking of black geographic experience as multiple interethnic encounters. She suggests mappings of the black diaspora produced through intersections that reveal racially diverse and interracial subject positions (2006, 108).

The chapter also engages with a discussion of black territories by Raquel Rolnik, in which she points to the tendency within studies of urban Brazil to contrast racialized ghettos in the United States with Brazilian city spaces in which poor people of all races and ethnicities coexist in a shared condition of deprivation. Urban sociology, Rolnik argues, has attempted to understand the insertion of popular classes in the Brazilian city without acknowledging the importance of race (1989, 1). There is much at stake in Rolnik's insistence on urban black territories, as their existence admits a segregating impulse and undisguised antiblackness into discussions from which they had previously been sidelined. This compels us to understand spaces in which Afro-descendants moved as spaces of violence, surveillance, and control. As mentioned previously, Rolnik's definition of black territories is not confined, however, to experiences of exclusion and the exercise of white dominion. She gives the example of the authoritarian layout of the plantation in whose yard slave bodies managed to articulate and transmit collective memory. That space was eventually transformed into the *terreiro*, or back yard, a space of fundamental importance in the production of urban black territories. In such spaces, Afro-descendants elaborated social and cultural repertoires, and celebrated their belonging to a community (1989, 2). Rolnik defines these black communities as groups that identified themselves by their cultural singularities and by shared sociocultural practices that they produced and transformed over time. She emphasizes, however, that the black communities created and affirmed in such spaces were not homogenous or unitary forms of social organization. Within such groups, tensions and conflicts of many different kinds also existed. Additionally, Rolnik makes the crucial point that signaling certain spaces as black territories does not mean that they were exclusively black. As I contend in the introduction, spaces populated by the racially heterogeneous poor came to be blackened, or imagined and dealt with as black spaces, and assigned a racialized script that gave certain meanings to the diverse spatial and cultural practices of their inhabitants. This chapter focuses on how such racial and ethnic meanings became attached to the Castelo neighborhood.

LOCATING CASTELO

> Favella and Providência Hills aren't much different from the one that concerns us here—except that Castelo is in the heart of the city, it has a history, the longest and grandest in Rio de Janeiro, and there are important public services on its peak. Therefore, it certainly deserves more attention.
>
> —*Jornal do Brasil,* March 1, 1920

In a commentary piece in 1920 the daily *Jornal do Brasil* exhorts the mayor to make some improvements to Castelo Hill. The paper describes it as a neighborhood that is as degraded as the city's growing informal hillside settlements. However, Castelo differed in that it was a historic site and the first officially planned area of the city (despite the presence of illegally built dwellings there). The article also mentions the neighborhood's central location as one of the key reasons for an urgent upgrade (*Jornal do Brasil*, March 1, 1920). Its location was precisely why the next mayor, Carlos Sampaio, would seek to demolish it, anxious for the profit that the creation of real estate in the city center would bring. That location, overlooking the redesigned streets and newly commissioned buildings of the Avenida Rio Branco (formerly the Avenida Central), shattered the illusion that Rio had, in fact, been "civilized."[4] In a stroll through some streets at the foot of Castelo where Chinese immigrants had their opium dens, João do Rio's observations make clear the incompatibility of the area with the new boulevard: "Dom Manuel Street looks like it belongs in some distant neighborhood. The city morgue with its grassy field and wire fence, behind which gypsies converse, has the look of the suburbs. It's like you've arrived . . . at the city limits. On street corners, where ne'er-do-wells with neckerchiefs and a bounce in their step while away their time with whores with sprigs of rue tucked into their kinky hair, you see dark, narrow little streets emerging from the terraces of Castelo" (Rio [1905] 2005, 172).

These streets are narrow, dark, and colonial in design. They look not like downtown but like the suburbs to which the poor were increasingly being displaced. Instead of a city center demarcated for capitalist production, an air of idleness prevails. The presence of people of color—gypsies, street toughs with the swagger associated with Afro-descendant *malandros*, and black women working as prostitutes—disturbs the façade of downtown's urban European chic. Those who traversed the hillside and the city center streets that led off it mapped defiant geographies that denaturalized the ideological landscape as established by official arbiters of space.

Descriptions of Castelo's physical landscape uniformly emphasize the steepness of the hill, which made a tortuous ascent the only way to enter the neighborhood. This contributed to notions of Castelo as a space characterized by inaccessibility, remoteness, and marginality. However, Castelo belied the "proper" place of ethnic geographies by also being absolutely central and visible. By the end of the nineteenth century it occupied a large triangular area in the downtown district of São José, from São José Street up to today's Cinelândia, with the Santa Luzia beach and the sea bordering the foot of one of its slopes (see fig. 3.3). In

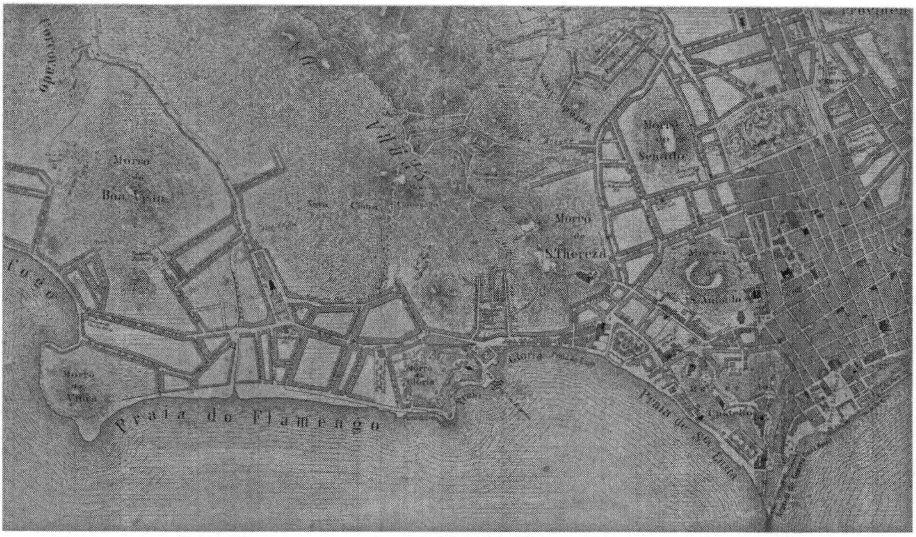

Figure 3.3. Detail from 1875 map of the city, Antônio José Fausto Garriga, Biblioteca Nacional Digital Brasil.

September 1921 Castelo was a large, thriving community with 408 buildings and 4,200 people (Kessel 2001, 74). It was reached via several slopes that led off from downtown streets, and lost one of its slopes to the construction of the Avenida Central during the Passos reforms. On this slope was a Jesuit seminary that members of the Capuchin order had occupied in its last years. After they vacated the historic building and in the five or so years before its destruction, it had been appropriated for use as an enormous tenement building (Fluminense 1905, 43).

In 1905 Américo Fluminense (a pseudonym of the writer and art critic Gonzaga Duque) made his way to the very top of the hill via a vertiginous path in front of the Convento d'Ajuda. Once there he declared, "You could say that we're now in the heart of the primitive city" (43). However, Castelo's residents belied the naturalization of its time-space as past and remote with their continuous mobility up and down between the hillside and the city. The difficulties of access, clearly aggravated by the Passos reforms, did not prevent their daily interventions, interactions, and negotiations into and with the downtown area. One contemporary observer was taken aback by the amount of foot traffic up and down the hillside: "The slopes leading up the hillside are neglected and dirty. However, they are full of life, serving that enormous human beehive, energetic and noisy, that settles and lives there. Those slopes are always crowded with people. People going up and people coming down" (Edmundo 1957, 203–4).[5] Despite the semirural aspect of Castelo's public spaces, as suggested in newspapers and captured in some of Malta's photographs, residents were deeply embedded in the life of the city below them for work and leisure, and attracted nonresidents to the hill for festivals and musical performances, as evident in newspaper reports on these events. Castelo also had its own football team, O Paulistano, whose grounds were located downtown, next to Praça Quinze, and whose games were attended by many of the residents (Paixão 2008, 177).

Despite perceptions of its remoteness, Castelo's central location made it both a site of and a witness to some of the major events in the history of the city. The hill found itself in the crosshairs during the Revolt of the Whip in 1910, when navy sailors organized a revolt against a brutal regime of corporal punishment that culminated in a state of siege in the city and a wave of barbarous repression against the rebels.[6] With cannons aimed at the shoreline, many *castelenses* evacuated the hill, but an exploding grenade killed two children at house number 16 in the Bastos tenements.[7] The rebel leader, João Cândido, visited Castelo after the fatalities to express his sorrow to the community. Castelo also became associated in the urban imaginary as a space of tragedy and disaster due to periodic landslides that affected the area and often the city below. These came about as a result of the *aguas do monte*, or hillside floods, a phenomenon reported since at least 1756 (Nonato and Santos 2000, 85). This recurring disaster was immortalized in the popular song "Vem cá Bitu" (Come here, Bitu), which recounts how the terrible floods of 1811 washed away Bitu, a black castelense and a well-known figure who put on a puppet show in the streets of the city (Engel 2001, 21–22; Cruls 1952, 395). Castelo's decline into a neighborhood of the racial and ethnic poor meant its neglect by municipal authorities in addressing the issue. One hundred years later, after a family living in penury in a flimsy shack in Chácara da Floresta was buried alive by a mudslide, the press berated the government for ignoring a problem that presented itself right behind the School of Fine Arts and a stone's throw from the Engineering Club.[8]

The naturalization of Castelo as remote also lent itself to its characterization as a space of criminality. According to one account in Augusto Maurício's *Templos históricos do Rio de Janeiro* (1946), as residents gradually began to abandon Castelo for the plain below by the end of the sixteenth century, "thieves and layabouts began to seek out the place as their hideout and territory" (cited in Nonato and Santos 2000, 62). Fluminense's profile of those who inhabited Castelo at the time of his visit in 1905 mentions penniless students, modest families of public functionaries without friends in high places, and old widows living on a state pension (43). The racial and ethnic profile of the population of Castelo and the streets leading off it was also eclectic. As mentioned in the introduction, municipal and national censuses from 1908 and 1920 did not record race, though they sometimes recorded the country of origin of immigrant residents, with Italy and Portugal predominating. According to Fluminense, by 1905 Italians were the overwhelming majority ethnic group in Castelo over Afro-descendant "nationals" and the Portuguese.[9] As he observes an old woman having her siesta in the street, he notes that the predominantly black population of the hill has dwindled. He nostalgically draws an analogy between the authorities' abandonment of Castelo and of a racialized group that appears superfluous to the requirements of the modern state: "At the end of the day, old Castelo, you are worth no more than that old black woman. You are the ruin of an existence that an inevitable degradation will carry away on the mists of memory. But something enlivens you still, just like the old black woman, something delicate that in her is the tragedy of her past, and in you is the poetry of legend that cloaks your ruined walls in indistinct longing" (1905, 45–46).

In his wanderings around the alleys of the Misericórdia area at the base of Castelo Hill, João do Rio describes a site of overlapping geographies and multiple interethnic connections:

> There are men on mats, sleeping in the street as if they were at home . . . Music Alley or Noblewoman's Alley duplicate the soul of the streets of Napoli, Florence, Portugal, Africa, and even . . . ancient Egypt. And why? Because they are streets near the sea, well traveled, with a view of other horizons. I peered into one of the pigsties that make up this organism. There were Chinese drugged up on opium, brutishly drunken sailors, sorceresses wailing sinister songs, all of that strange port life. And these alleys have all the treacherousness of the ocean, the misery of migration, and the great vice of the sea and the colonies." (Rio [1905] 2005, 62)

This tangle of space-times, of those displaced by slavery and migration who invoke other geographies and other historical moments, creates a site in which ethnicities are being configured in a diasporic situation, and are configuring each other through contact. João do Rio connects these geographic subjectivities in the process of becoming to Brazil's colonial past, which is not easily erased with the demolition of buildings. These streets evoke what Katherine McKittrick calls historically present geographies, in which past experiences of space shape the present (2006, 106). The colonial system created spaces of itineracy, and normalized and hierarchized racial difference within them. This process continued under sociospatial conditions particular to the Republic's national whitening project, in which the promotion of immigration results in multiple ethnicities, differential notions of whiteness, and the persistence of blacks at the bottom of sociospatial hierarchies.

The economic profile of castelenses was also somewhat heterogeneous. Some, as the Laemmert Almanac and Fluminense attest, were minor functionaries and professionals. Some were small business owners, like the Portuguese businessmen that Luiz Edmundo describes with an old piano in the living room and a portrait of Mouzinho de Albuquerque, "hero of the Africa campaigns, hanging on the wall of the room where visitors were received" (1957, 207). According to an article in the *Jornal do Brasil,* Castelo had eight taverns and four *botequins* (corner shops with a bar), as well as a haberdashery belonging to an Italian immigrant (Emygdio 1927). Contemporary accounts of castelenses' forms of employment, however, emphasize poor working immigrants: "According to what we found out, the majority of these people are Italian, maybe as much as 70%. . . . Most of the men work as fishermen or street vendors. The women wash clothes for their clientele in the city below."[10] Another press account remembering Castelo after its destruction mentions the porters in the streets—"Italians with a black band tied around their waists and a velvet cap, and the Portuguese with their satchels, caps, and wheelbarrows" (Secioso de Sá 1928). The washerwomen whom Luiz Edmundo describes in his chronicle were a constant presence at the tanks and in the patios and back yards of collective dwellings, and the landscape was permanently littered with the fruits of their labor. Women also worked as seamstresses and midwives. Former residents Florinda Alói and Francisco Moreno's mother was a midwife who attended to women on Castelo, as well as on Misericórdia Street below. They claimed that their mother even gave presentations on labor and delivery at the medical school at the invitation of one of the professors. They recalled that seamstresses worked at home, but collected their work from stores in Rua do Carmo and Rua da Quitanda in the city center. Luiz Edmundo mentions young Portuguese women who had their older brothers collect and deliver sewing in order to preserve their honor (1957, 207). Alói herself claimed to have visited the city below only once, to pose for a family portrait, until she was engaged to be married (Nonato and Santos 2000, 198–204). Within Castelo, however, photographs, paintings, and illustrations show young women and girls as more visible in the streets than their bourgeois counterparts, working, carrying out chores, socializing, or haggling with the vegetable vendor.

WALKING CASTELO

> What really impresses those who climb the pathways of those steep, rough slopes is a series of stone faces, strong, massive, supporting walls, old ramparts, some two or three centuries old, on which the neighborhood sits; mansions that the poverty of residents transformed into makeshift rooming houses, palaces split up into cubicles, many of them with compartments divided by burlap or partitions lined with paper, airless, dark, where countless families sleep promiscuously; people who leave home in the early hours to work in distant places, their lunch pails wrapped in newspaper; men with pale, drawn faces, with overgrown hair and beards who are evidently unwell or extremely poor; women who are the pillars of their homes, real work horses, looking unkempt and wretched, their skirts hitched up, rags tucked into their waists, damp from the wash basins where they work all day. . . .
>
> The interiors do not possess the slightest comfort. Cold, crumbling walls, lined here and there with paper from twenty years ago, covered in humid stains, smudged by filthy children's hands, rotting floors, tiled roofs, and the sparse furnishings associated with colonial times.
>
> —**Edmundo 1957, 202–6.**

We owe this detailed depiction of the neighborhood to chronicler Luiz Edmundo. His perspective in this passage is purely visual; there are no conversations or interactions with residents here that might afford us a glimpse into their experiential, imaginative relationship with the space. However, even as he reads the built space and its inhabitants in terms of poverty and degradation, these wan, overburdened residents are producing a lived space of survival and fortitude. The area is a ruin that evokes the colonial past, yet it is a place that is clearly shaped by the day-to-day activities of a large community.

Luiz Edmundo's survey of the architectural style of the houses reiterates the notion of ruin and decline, but also points to the alterations, reworkings, and redesigns of the buildings:

> On the whole the houses have one or two stories and are built in the "strong and ugly colonial style."
>
> They have a jumble of dismal grey roofs, constructed in a mismatched and shoddy way: disarticulated, dirty buildings, that are the remains, however of once noble dwellings, now in architectural tatters. Here as the path curves there is an old mansion, now a poor man's shack, with long verandahs, full of birdcages and laundry

> laid out to dry. . . . The row of houses is enormous, untidy, and confused. At times it leaps over the hill's steep slope, expanding into stories and rooftops, at others it squats into backyards and gardens. Shacks and mansions climb or roll down the escarpment, jumping over crevasses and gullies, hanging off cliffs, in the midst of clumps of vines and croton bushes, surrounded by flamboyant trees or palms, giving life and sound to the glorious landscape.
>
> Among all of these constructions, wooden shacks appear with regularity, too many to count, with rusty zinc roofs and christophene or passion fruit flowering alongside them, protecting them from the harshness of the sun.
>
> From a distance the scene is pleasing to the eye. Above all, there is a great deal of color in the varied foliage and much movement in the irregular line of the huge, extended roofs. (1957, 203–4)

In this passage Luiz Edmundo erases the residents from the scene he describes, ascribing the active voice in his narration to the buildings themselves. The shacks, for example, seem to spring unbidden from the earth, and hovels hang off escarpments as if forming an organic part of the landscape. The passage occludes the residents as social actors who had an impact on the built environment, by constructing their shacks in between existing buildings; by transforming the meager lodgings they rented into opportunities for participation in the informal economy; by bringing beauty and pleasure to these spaces with birdsong; or as Luiz Edmundo notes further on, by rearing pigs, chickens, and goats in the yard to augment the family diet (206).

Despite his overwhelmingly negative appraisal of the buildings' incoherent styles and irregular morphologies following the landscape, he betrays a certain attraction to the place in the final two lines of the passage. Significantly, however, he declares the scene pleasing to gaze upon "from a distance," like a "painting," rather than as experiential space. His final gaze is reminiscent of the panorama city that Michel de Certeau describes (1984, 95) in which totalizing images from a distance obscure those who inhabit the space, and whose identities and rationalities lack readability and transparency for dominant society. The repurposing of space in which mansions become hovels, in which architectural styles are jumbled together in a bricolage of practicality and need, and in which farm animals wander through urban public spaces, defy the pretensions of the rational city to which the Passos reforms had aspired. This description acknowledges an aesthetic and practice of informality that was becoming the norm for those displaced by the Republican government's neglect of housing for the poor and the acute crisis created by urban reforms. The heterogeneity of the dwellings on Castelo was a practical response to both the landscape and the existing built environment.

Luiz Edmundo observes innumerable *chalés* and *casebres* during his tour. The former were flimsy wooden houses, which proliferated in the city until the municipality prohibited their construction; the latter were shacks that could be easily self-built on the outskirts of the city or on hillsides, where they might escape detection by the authorities. Therefore, while some dwellings contained residents who had occupied the land without permission, many others were regulated by the city, like those in Chácara da Floresta discussed below. Lilian Vaz observes that it was not unusual for large areas of collective housing at the turn of the twentieth century to contain illegally constructed shacks (1994, 591). Castelo was therefore not a favela, which at this moment in the city's urban history meant an illegally occupied neighborhood of auto-constructed housing, though it did contain such dwellings.

TENEMENT LIFE

Various types of collective dwelling proliferated in response to the acute need for housing for the poor in the city center. City engineer Everardo Backheuser describes a number of them in his 1906 housing reports (105–6), and any definitions provided here are taken from his classifications. The mayor's office at the time of his report prohibited the construction of *cortiços*—small rooms made of wood, sometimes installed at the back of buildings, at times one on top of the other, which were difficult to access. The word *cortiço* also applied to an old building clandestinely divided using wooden partitions to form rooms or cubicles, and the term came to be used for all kinds of dwellings characterized by the collective use of toilets, cooking areas, tanks, patios, and corridors. Cortiços were big business due to the number of small spaces that could be rented out and the high rents charged. Owners would often turn their lands or houses over to a third party who invested a small sum in construction or subdivision of existing buildings (Vaz 1994, 583). At the top end of the housing spectrum were *avenidas, estalagens,* and *casas de pensão.* Avenidas were permitted by the mayor's office and were made up of small private houses with their own sanitary and cooking facilities, and with all houses facing a central street. The city prohibited the construction of estalagens, but these were still airier and more comfortable than most tenement buildings, consisting of small individual houses with the front door and window facing a patio, and with a front room separate from the bedroom. The *casas de pensão* were generally clean rooms for rent in private residences with food provided. At the other end of the scale were the *casas de cômodos* and other rooming houses, some of which, like *hospedarias* and *albergues*, could be rented by the hour, day, and night. Those who could not afford the humblest of these accommodations occupied ruins, empty buildings, and caves on the hillsides (Vaz 1994, 590).

Castelo's housing also reflected this diversity. The two former residents cited previously, a brother and sister who lived in Castelo until 1922, recalled that Chinese, "Arabs," and Italians without families lived in cheap pensions on the Rua da Misericórdia just below the hillside (Nonato and Santos 2000, 203). According to press reports lack of space for new roads on Castelo led to the emergence of out-of-the-way (and probably illegal) agglomerations of hundreds of poor families called Buraco da Formiga (Ant Hole) and Cova da Onça (Jaguar's Den) (Emygdio 1927).[11] The Estalagem do Bastos in which the two children met their deaths during the Revolt of the Whip spread over a large area that backed onto the Santa Casa da Misericórdia hospital.[12] According to a contemporary press report, Bastos was full of life and noise, and over six hundred people lived there (*Jornal do Brasil*, September 25, 1927). Former resident Florinda Alói remembers many communal parties in estalagens, to which everyone had to be invited in order not to cause offense: "It was like one big family" (Nonato and Santos 2000, 203). Analysis of crimes committed or allegedly committed in collective housing in Castelo, however, shows that acts of aggression and robberies were also common (Paixão 2008, 160, 159). However, evidently, so was persecution by the police. Cláudia Quelhas Paixão cites four incidents from 1916 in which the police chief ordered four Castelo residents to be detained in the Santa Casa as indigents. Paixão surmises that the reason for their internment, despite having a fixed residence and apparent employment, was that all four lived in casas de cômodos. Three of them lived in Chácara da Floresta: one white woman listed as a maid, one Portuguese man listed simply as "worker," and one domestic worker described as black ("de cor preta"). The fourth person picked up by police was a white male listed as a driver, who lived in Praça do Castelo, number 24 (2008, 158).

The extremely dense occupation of often poorly adapted and maintained living quarters created difficult living conditions in which privacy was hard to come by.[13] Rooms were sparsely furnished, as residents had limited means, and in order to make space for other members of the family, other families, or strangers sleeping in the same room at night. Many inhabitants who did not leave the neighborhood for work preferred to spend most of their day outside in the streets, or in the patios and yards of the collective dwellings. Luiz Edmundo expresses his disapproval for this life in the streets that flew in the face of the bourgeois ideal of separating domestic from public space. In Castelo, he protests, houses were always open to the streets, and people spent their time spying on and gossiping about their neighbors (1957, 208). He is particularly taken aback by the ways in which children occupied the neighborhood: "Yellowish, skinny children with a sickly appearance, their bodies covered with scars, but infernally noisy, swarm the houses, the yards, scrambling up the walls and the streetlights; dirty, rowdy, terrifying, arguing amongst themselves with slang, profanities, and stone-throwing, annoying passers-by with their vile bellowing, punching, and scuffling" (203). His zoomorphic description of a kind of "swarming" plague of children recalls the literal meaning of the word *cortiço*—a "beehive," which Vaz surmises was probably where the use of the term for collective housing originated (1994, 583). Descriptions of cortiços and the neighborhoods they occupied as beehives appear frequently in contemporary chronicles. Even given Luiz Edmundo's censorious account, we glimpse the confident dominion of communal and public spaces by these children, with a group identity underlined by a shared form of communication using slang.

Although Luiz Edmundo does not distinguish distinct areas within Castelo, the neighborhood contained micro-communities such as the Estalagem do Bastos, Estalagem do Marinho, and Chácara da Floresta. Floresta, as residents called it, was a large group of dwellings located on the rough terrain of the slope facing the Avenida Rio Branco. Its entrance was located where the Biblioteca Nacional stands today, and it contained 164 houses, and about 1,000 residents (Kessel 2008, 74). As mentioned earlier, passersby on the Avenida Rio Branco below could easily glimpse grazing animals and the ubiquitous washing spread out to dry that was a feature of the spaces of the city's poor. Castelo's police post was located in Chácara, facing its entrance, and of the crimes analyzed by Paixão in the period 1916–1922 the community had the highest incidence of robberies within residences (2008, 155). Former residents Florinda Alói and Francisco Moreno (Nonato and Santos 2000, 198–204) remember Floresta as an "avenida," which they describe as long and tree lined, which would make it an area with a better quality of dwelling overall.[14]

In 1906, when the Passos reforms had already claimed the slope leading to Floresta, the Directoria Geral de Saúde Pública (Public Health Directorate) inspected the buildings at the behest of the owner of the properties, who was interested in developing them. Its report, dated September 4, 1906, gives considerable insight into the types of dwellings that made up the micro-neighborhood. According to the report, Floresta comprised sixteen groups of individual houses. The groups varied significantly in size, style, and numbers, as well as the conditions of the structures. Group 4, for example, consisted of two parts, both two-story dwellings, the first part of which was deemed suitable for reform and dividing up for renting out rooms. Group 9 consisted of thirty-two two-story houses that were judged not of a suitable condition for renovating, as was the case with the three houses in Group 11, and the fourteen houses in Group 12. The ten houses in Group 8 and the six in Group 13, however, were new and well built, while Group 16 was "a simple little house" with "wooden partitions." The owner of these properties was the Condessa de Wilson, the member of a well-off family of Portuguese descent married to a British Brazilian businessman. In considering the request for a license to carry out the works, the directoria also required the owner to make a number of improvements that responded to authorities' concern with sanitation and morality. These included the installation of more sanitary facilities; isolating the latter from the kitchens; raising room divisions to the roof to increase privacy; installing new divisions to increase the size of rooms; building more tanks for washing clothes; and demolishing provisional constructions (Directoria Geral de Saúde Pública, 1906).

GEOGRAPHIES OF RESISTANCE

> The streets have such human qualities, they are lived and formed so much by their inhabitants, that there are even streets that clash with other streets. The rogues and toughs on one street look at their counterparts on another as enemies. . . . There are the Senate Street folk, the folk from the alley of the same name, the Catumbi folk . . . the well-known fighters today add their given names to the name of *their* street. There's Senate Joe, Harmony Juca, Castelo Lindinho . . .
>
> —João do Rio, *A alma encantadora das ruas* (2005, 69–71)

In a chronicle for the *Gazeta de Notícias*, João do Rio describes various subcultures and rivalries based on different streets of the city, and in particular the *malandro*'s identification of his courage and strength with his street or neighborhood. By exercising power in their street and local area, which then became known across the city, Afro-descendants conferred value on the most disparaged spaces of the city and made their own geographical knowledge. This construction of black geographies challenged official mappings and discourses of the city—the city as a landscape of power oriented around its brand-new monuments and avenues (Leu 2014). Retrospectives of the neighborhood in the press after its demolition emphasize that it was known for its "famous tough guys," such as João Vandeck, Pernambuco, and Bonitinho from Castelo (see Emygdio 1927; Secioso de Sá 1928). Denied any kind of meaningful citizenship, some Afro-descendant men looked to notoriety as a substitute. In a society bent on their literal and metaphorical erasure, their prowess in the art of capoeira, at least, defied their anonymity and elision from official narratives of the city.

Capoeiragem also afforded an opportunity for intervention into the political scene from which the black population was almost entirely excluded. Prevented from voting, for the most part, due to the literacy requirement, capoeiras, known as *capangas* in this context, were nevertheless a visible presence at election time, used by competing politicians to attempt to influence the vote (see Carvalho 1999, 87, 23). One press account recalls the role of Castelo's famous hoodlums during elections: "Some of their names became famous in the history of capoeiragem and of the election battles of the time that involved stealing urns and scaring off voters—strong-arm victories!" These enforcers traditionally took on noms de guerre such as the street-affiliated ones mentioned by Rio. The names of two renowned Castelo toughs were clearly intended to inspire fear and respect for their strength: Couraça (Steel-Clad), and Treme-Terra (Earth-Shaker) (Secioso de Sá 1928). "Treme-Terra" was a rather subversive appropriation of the nickname for the precursor to the state's military police. Another legendary Castelo malandro is named in the press article as "Pernambuco (the original)," who clearly self-identified, or was identified by his regional origins, and who inspired imitators throughout the city. The exploits of such figures would have inscribed themselves in the collective memory of the city. The article recalls the time that these "famous capoeiras" defeated a whole mounted police force, which tried to eject them from their hiding place on the top of the hill in Cova da Onça. No less memorable and newsworthy was the incident involving the capoeira described as the "agile Cisy," whose dexterity appears to have deserted him during a bout of drunkenness in which he fell off the hillside to his death (Secioso de Sá 1928).

João do Rio observed that malandros articulated their loyalty to their streets by identifying themselves as part of a "povo," literally "people" or "folk," or alternatively a "crew." Their self-desgination as "povos" recalls José Murilo de Carvalho's discussion of the building of "little republics" based on ethnicity and place, at a time when there was no sense of belonging to a larger collective entity of the city or country. People identified with their "colônias," or settlements of European immigrants and immigrants from outside the state of Rio; with Little Africa, the community of Bahians in the Cidade Nova; with Saúde, the Afro-descendant area near the port; or even with their cortiço, such as the "cortiço republic" on Senate Street in Botafogo described in Aluísio Azevedo's novel (Carvalho 1999, 38–39). The 1928 retrospective on Castelo in the *Correio da Manhã* reveals that within the neighborhood young men also engaged in ritualized conflict based on ethnic and interethnic identifications and affinities. These groups were known as *partidos,* and their nomenclature also emphasized micro-communities belonging to streets or squares in Castelo such as the Povo do Moura, Povo do Castelo, and Povo de Santa Luzia.[15] According to this account, these were highly planned and well-executed battles. A partido or partidos comprising mainly Italians, with "shirts open to the waist and black caps on their heads," would take up a position of defense on the Morro. The attacking partido would consist primarily of "nationals," or Afro-descendants, and the Portuguese, who would advance from below in an attempt to wrest control of the hill from their foes: "They were made up of unemployed youths, strong and fearless, that battled it out with stones. They fought some epic wars, following military techniques: they posted guards on the parapets of the old walls at the beginning of Ajuda Street, and more on the Santa Luzia side, where attackers could converge; the rest of the forces lay await in ambush around the old Seminary slope that began in Mão do Bispo Square" (*Correio da Manhã,* September 9, 1928).

This was a skirmish that involved the use of the entire hillside and its points of entry. The enemy would approach cautiously, using guerrilla strategies to hide as best as they could. Combatants used a system of whistling to communicate with each other. Once the lookouts on the Italian side gave the sign that the enemy was approaching, they would run at full speed to join their defense forces, while the attacking group would hurl themselves at the defenders in the trenches, roaring and striking them with pieces of stone, or occasionally pieces of iron—munitions that they had been hoarding in preparation for the battle. The confrontation occurred in daytime, and the fighters frequently caused damage to surrounding property, amid protests by residents, which went unheeded in the heat of combat. The attacking group of Afro-descendants and Portuguese would advance resolutely, gradually taking control from the morro's defenders. The latter would withdraw and take up other positions, as they continued to throw missiles at the invaders. It was not unusual for the battle to end only with the intervention of the police and local residents. Once the combatants had fled, they left behind shattered windows, broken roof tiles, and occasionally an injured fighter, bleeding copiously, who had to be stretchered off to the Santa Casa da Misericórdia.[16]

The account of this conflict is invaluable as a glimpse into the kinds of ethnic and interethnic alliances that were made in Castelo, and the profound investment of individuals in the groups with which they identified. The alliance in this instance between black Brazilians and Portuguese immigrants is also significant, given the fierce rivalry between the two groups. The two are united in this instance, one may speculate, through language. These unlikely allies forge new geographic subjectivities in their coalition against the Italians.[17] The enactment of this battle for Castelo elicited passionate involvement by the "armies," with both relying on an intimate familiarity with the landscape, and engaging in a remapping of their neighborhood along ethnic lines. On some level, their actions can be read as subaltern geographies that echo dominant spatial practices—seeking territorial conquests and making ownership claims. However, through their combat they also seize opportunities to express themselves as geographical subjects, capable of imagining, and temporarily producing, different distributions and occupations of space. This form of territoriality—though ephemeral—is a repeated and ritualized spatial practice that constitutes a small conquest and extends the notion and the extent of racialized and ethnic territorializing at a time when the Republican government sought to violently eradicate that presence from the city center. In a letter to the *Jornal do Brasil* in 1930 a former resident of Castelo maintains that these partidos were common all over the city, and that in Castelo they had names that divided the neighborhood geographically into "Upper Castelo" and "Lower Castelo." For their members the partidos were an important distraction, comparable, he says, to the passion and loyalty inspired by football. While the partidos' clashes may have occasioned some deaths, Castelo was not unique in this regard in the city, he maintains, and partidos had a role to play in settling scores and calling people to account for questionable behavior (*Jornal do Brasil*, January 23, 1930). Additionally, the conflict belies elite perceptions of subaltern violence at this time as spontaneous irruptions of irrational mobs (Carvalho 1999). The battle for Castelo that these groups enacted was a meticulously planned and executed spatial practice that marked out an area of control and power.

All too often, however, poor and especially black city dwellers found themselves subject to the arbitrary power of the authorities in public places. On April

11, 1920, the *Jornal do Brasil* reported that in the early hours of the previous day the police had shot a man in the back in Castelo. They named the injured man as Acacio Gomes da Silva, who was "Brazilian," and a resident of Saúde Street. Other press reports describe Silva as black (*preto*) and a working man—variously a cart driver or coalman by profession.[18]

According to the victim he was asleep on a street in Castelo when he was violently awakened by a military policeman who ordered him to get off the street.[19] He obeyed the order and began to descend the Ladeira da Misericórdia, when the soldier shot him in the back.[20] The reports condemn the shooting as a pointless, cowardly act of aggression, and the police authorities declared that they had opened a "rigorous inquiry" based on the victim's account, but this and other incidents make clear that police persecution appears to have been a fact of life in Castelo. This shooting, however, was extreme in terms of police abuse, and no doubt the victim's race made him a particularly devalued subject in the eyes of the soldier, who, whatever his own race or ethnicity, may not have felt accountable for potentially taking a black life.[21] It is not clear why Silva was sleeping in a Castelo street. According to the *Gazeta de Notícias* report he was seeking to "rest there awhile" (April 11, 1920), perhaps tired out from work, or sleeping off a night of excess. Given his race and his age (twenty-seven), he could also have been profiled as a criminal by the police officer. In her analysis of crimes in Castelo or involving castelenses between 1916 and 1922, Paixão mentions the use of the hill as a refuge for those involved in criminal incidents fleeing the police. On February 7, 1917, medical assistance was given to Manoel José da Silva and Eustáquio Alves Brito, both found wounded in Chácara da Floresta and taken to the Santa Casa, but who were residents of Saúde and Ilha dos Ferreiros, respectively (2008, 163).

It is clear from the location of a police post outside of Chácara da Floresta that authorities viewed Castelo as a site that required special attention from the forces of law and order. A story in the *Jornal do Brasil* from 1920 affords a glimpse into the repressive control that the police force sought to impose on residents. The paper reports that it had recently received many complaints against "authoritarian acts" practiced by the officer in charge of the police post installed on Castelo. The report portrays residents sympathetically as honest workers: "There are no millionaires there, just workers, laborers, men with the responsibilities of large families on their shoulders who work by day, so they can eat at night." According to the report castelenses were being persecuted by a tyrannical police officer who seized residents' livestock, arbitrarily carried out searches on businesses and demanded licenses, and indiscriminately arrested people during the night, especially on Misericórdia and São José Streets and surrounding areas leading up to the hillside. Those arrested would be held until three o'clock in the morning, before being released. Residents complained that the police were not doing the job they were supposed to do—there was no officer on the beat in the area, for example. The paper noted "generalized indignation" among residents, and warned that this could be a potentially volatile situation.[22] From their complaints it is clear that residents felt their rights were being abused, and that their only recourse to air their grievances and have them addressed was via the newspapers. Police persecution was an experience acquired early, according to Américo Fluminense's article on Castelo. He observed the *jogo da buraca,* a children's game that consisted of trying to throw a coin into a hole in the ground. Passion for the game would often lead to minor scuffles among the children. However, this was apparently nothing compared to the treatment meted out by policemen on the beat, who would frequently disperse the game by raining blows on the children's heads. In order to avoid discovery, the children would position lookouts on Castelo Square where they could warn of the policeman's arrival (Fluminense 1905, 43). Early experiences of police violence led them to learn precociously how to defend their position on their turf.

Although the police evidently tended to criminalize the neighborhood, a former castelense took grave offense at the chronicler Hermeto Lima's characterization of the neighborhood as "a den of notorious crooks, thieving and mugging, and prostitutes making an infernal din." In a 1930 letter to the *Jornal do Brasil* he identifies himself as Dr M. Elysio de Vasconcellos, a descendant of a family that lived on Morro do Castelo for nearly a century. Castelo, he insists, was a place of hardworking men and women and civil service families who resided near the fort. He chides the chronicler for opining on something about which he clearly had no real knowledge and offending castelense families (*Jornal do Brasil,* January 23, 1930). In the interview with the former residents the siblings also considered Castelo to be a very safe place. From a perspective no doubt tinged with nostalgia, they recalled that violent incidents took place at the bottom of the slopes, or in the city center streets around them. On the Ladeira do Carmo on the corner with São José Street, for example, hoodlums would throw pepper in the faces of passersby to immobilize them as they robbed them: "But that was at the bottom of the slope, they didn't hang around on top of the hill" (Nonato and Santos 2000, 202). The interviewees remember Misericórdia Street—the multiethnic space described by João do Rio—in which Turks, Arabs, and Chinese people who smoked opium lived as "somewhat dangerous." According to the residents castelenses never entered the area where the Chinese lived.

Despite residents' memories of Castelo as a place in which crime was nonexistent, apart from the ubiquitous practice of the *jogo do bicho,* or animal lottery, the conditions under which people were forced to live in cortiços made for complaints about petty thieving and violent altercations. Research carried out by Paixão using police logbooks shows that of the 426 incidents involving Castelo, assaults account for 48 incidents; robberies for 44; assaults between residents for 34; and robberies in residences for 25. In the case of robberies in residences, usually victim and accused shared rooms in casas de cômodos, and the majority of residents who appear in the logbooks lived in this type of housing. Of the 426 incidents and 553 residents identified, however, the majority appear as witnesses, and of the rest 148 are victims, and only 104 are infractors. The logbooks register race too sporadically to draw any firm conclusions—only 147 of the 553 residents appearing in the logs are identified by race—although the preponderance of whites recorded reflects the hillside's demographic. Of the 142 incidents in which the nationality was noted, there are 69 Brazilians,[23] 55 Portuguese, 14 incidents involving Italians, 3 involving Spaniards, and one involving an Argentine (Paixão 2008, 154–57). The *botequim,* or street corner bar, was the site of many police incidents, usually involving disorderly behavior or robbery. For example, in April 1920, Francisco Antonio de Oliveira, "a black [*preto*] native of Rio Grande do Sul," fifty-six years old, with no profession or fixed residence, was accused of stealing a gold watch from the cashier in a bar on number 10, Ladeira do Castelo. The suspected thief was apprehended by the cashier (who also lived locally) with the help of his customers and local residents and taken to the police station. Shootings were also occasionally registered, such as the three bullets fired by the white Brazilian electrician living in Chácara da Pau da Bandeira against the Portuguese driver who lived in the same cortiço (161). The religious festivals for which Castelo was famous were sometimes an occasion for drunken and disorderly behavior, such as two Italians, Ritus Spatermo and Miguel Luciano, fighting at the Festa da Gloria (*A Noite,* August 15, 1911). Castelenses' grievances spilled over outside of the neighborhood too, as with the two Italian immigrants Nicolão Carnavel and Salvador Siciliano fighting on Uruguayana Street "over family matters."[24]

In a curious incident recounted in the press on October 10, 1920, rather than being detained by the police a Castelo resident had to be rescued by them for inciting a crowd. The occasion was a demonstration against the nationalization of the fishing industry. The organizer of the protest, Vicente Ferreira, began the meeting by climbing the stairs of the Teatro Municipal and launching into a ferocious attack on the government. Interestingly, given the general lack of support for the Republic among the city's poor (Carvalho 1999, 29–31), those present in the crowd began to take offense at the intensity of his attack, which was also directed at members of Congress. The crowd began to shout him down and eventually, when he refused to stop his tirade, began to threaten him with violence. The audacious speaker fled first to Carioca Square, and eventually climbed a lamppost there, seeking to continue his harangue, as a crowd of about a hundred people gathered around, booing and threatening to attack him. One press report claimed that a member of the crowd approached Ferreira with a raised fist and shouted: "Shameless Brazilian! You dare to oppose your country's interests?!" At that point Ferreira hurried down, making his way through the punches and kicks of the crowd, and took refuge in the editorial offices of *A Noite* newspaper until the police arrived to disperse the crowd. The chief of police of the 3rd District, Francisco Chagas, advised Ferreira to desist from further meetings and ordered police to escort him to the top of Morro do Castelo, in order to avoid a beating by the crowd.[25] The following year the police would prohibit a protest planned for Carioca Square in which Ferreira planned to speak on the issue of compensation for Brazil for ships torpedoed by the Germans during the First World War. Ferreira insisted on attempting to deliver his speech in the square and was arrested and taken into custody by the police.[26]

The account suggests that castelenses participated actively in the political life of the city, and were no strangers to public protest. Indeed, Ferreira's determination and the confidence with which he appears to have staked a place for his voice to be heard, whether on the steps of the elegant Teatro Municipal on the Avenida Rio Branco or at the top of a lamppost in one of the city's main squares, suggests someone very insistent on claiming his right to the city. Ferreira was recognized in the press as a "popular orator," and was also a protagonist in a protest of the demolition held in Castelo Square the previous month. The large crowd in attendance applauded him enthusiastically as he "energetically protested" the government's demolition plans.[27] This protest meeting was organized by "a group of ordinary folk" as an immediate response to the vote in the municipal council the previous day approving the project (*Gazeta de Notícias*, September 5, 1920). It was not unusual for Ferreira to be directing a passionate invective against the government at the fishing industry protest, as well as expressing outrage at their plans for the demolition. Ferreira was, in fact, a fiery and articulate regular at protests and public meetings across the city, eventually becoming a highly politicized public figure in the black community in Rio de Janeiro and São Paulo. Paulina Alberto describes how he led a committee of four men of color to the offices of *A Notícia* newspaper to express enthusiasm for the paper's call for a monument to the *mãe preta* in the capital city. The proposal, Alberto observes, received broad support from white readers who saw in the figure of the long-suffering slave wet nurse "a reassuring vision of a stable, patriarchal Brazilian society . . . in which women remained in the domestic sphere and people of color and the poor knew their place in the social hierarchy" (2011, 75). Alberto surmises that Ferreira supported the monument on account of its homage to blackness, its echoes with notions of the superiority of the "sentimental" black race espoused in the later writings of positivist philosopher Auguste Comte, and its rejection of doctrinaire scientific racism.[28]

Ferreira would later become a leading member of the Frente Negra Brasileira in São Paulo, a black political organization mobilizing for equal rights and social advancement, with its own newspaper, *A Voz da Raça* (The voice of the race) (see Alberti and Araujo Pereira, 2016). While still in Rio he campaigned for the reputedly *mulato* politician Nilo Peçanha and a report in the *Correio da Manhã* newspaper captures the tone of his impassioned speeches and his positioning as "the soul of the people, who spoke through his lips." He wanted the candidate to know that "this was not a protest initiated by politicians, organized by party leaders. Quite the contrary. Here were the people, the popular masses who had come to greet their cherished candidate. Here were . . . the white camellias of the soul of the people."[29] However, speaking in 1928 as a representative of the Centro Cívico Palmares black social club in São Paulo, at official celebrations of the founding of the city, the tenor of his speech changes to emphasize the contribution and potential of black people in building the country. Ferreira emphasized the "patriotic sentiments of the black Brazilian, whose race labored in the fields [and] wept in the slave barracks, only to emerge smiling in the Republic."[30] In other speeches Ferreira declared that black voters would withhold support for politicians who denigrated "the black race"; spoke regularly in commemorations of the abolition of slavery; and denounced abuse of police power.[31] He experienced the latter firsthand and made a public complaint against the police in the *Correio da Manhã* when he was accused of solicitation. According to Ferreira he was merely conversing with a woman of his acquaintance when he was arrested and held in a cell overnight and the following day among "thieves and vagrants."[32]

Incipient union and civil society organizations against the demolition of

Castelo also kept up the pressure on the government with their protests.[33] In August of 1920, for example, the League of Tenants and Consumers (Liga dos Inquilinos e Consumidores) published an announcement rallying residents to attend a demonstration: "Today at 6:00 p.m. there will be a large popular protest in Castelo Square; residents of Castelo Hill and all interested parties should be present in the aforementioned locale at 6:00 p.m. precisely" (*Jornal do Brasil,* August 25, 1920, 8). The league, recently founded by municipal employees, used a variety of tactics to attempt to hold the government's feet to the fire over the city's housing crisis. In 1920 it sought out the support of the press, wrote to public officials, and proposed a withholding of payment of electricity bills by renters. In January of 1921 they stepped up protest marches against high rental costs, in which they encouraged disturbance of the peace, "since the laws were not made in the people's interests." They encouraged all tenants to drag their furniture out into the nearest public square as a sign of protest, and called for a renters' general strike. The struggle for decent and affordable housing pitted the emerging middle classes and the popular classes against the oligarchs who traditionally held power. Pressing for legal protection for tenants, the leaders of the league declared themselves to be "fed up with suffering the injustices of landlords" (Carone 1978, 182–84).

On December 22, 1921, the government passed a law regulating the rental market and specifying the responsibilities of landlords and tenants. The law (Lei do Inquilinato) was something of a Pyrrhic victory for the league, as it froze rents but offered no protection from eviction. A wave of evictions followed it as landlords sought to have their properties revalued in order to be able to raise rents (Bonduki 1998, 714). In the month after the Centennial World Fair opened the league continued to demand that the government take responsibility for the housing crisis, calling for the construction of houses "that are modest and can be rented out cheaply—not palaces that bring no benefit whatsoever to the people."[34] Indeed, Mayor Sampaio's protestations that there was no money for government housing must have sounded hollow in the extreme in light of the opulent buildings constructed for the exposition. The following year the administration of Alaor Prata made the largely empty, if cruelly ironic gesture of giving away the debris from the Castelo demolition to workers for building homes. Workers had to furnish proof of their employment, and more difficult still, proof of land ownership in order to receive the discarded materials.[35]

If the threat or the experience of eviction was ever present for racialized residents of downtown Rio, popular carnival celebrations frequently represented important cultural-spatial practices that allowed them to temporarily occupy the city center from which they were being ejected. As discussed in chapter 1, the takeover of the streets by carnival groups called *ranchos* and *cordões*, originally formed by Afro-descendants, created transformative moments that momentarily disturbed the city's geographies of domination. These groups transformed public spaces into a battleground for asserting their different regional origins in Africa and their urban neighborhood identities (Leu 2014).

The *Jornal do Brasil* names three carnival ranchos in Castelo that were rivals, given to street brawling: Castello de Ouro, Prazer do Castello, and Filhos do Castello de Ouro (Golden Castelo, Pleasure of Castelo, and the Children of Golden Castelo) (Emygdio 1927). The first two groups were well known throughout the city and competed fiercely in the competition that the newspaper organized and held on the Avenida Rio Branco as a way of showcasing the talent of the city's ranchos. The competition, initiated in 1920 and dubbed the Mi-Carême dos Ranchos, required the associations to parade near the newspaper's offices in front of a committee made up of carnival chroniclers from different newspapers. Carnival societies needed to present a license in order to compete, and the paper functioned as a third party that solicited permits from the police on their behalf (*Jornal do Brasil*, March 2 and March 3, 1920). As patron of this systematized parade the *Jornal do Brasil*, with its offices on the Avenida Rio Branco, became a central location in the cultural geography of Rio's carnival participants. The paper displayed the standards of their clubs in their editorial offices one month before carnival, removing them with due solemnity on the Saturday night before the festival (*O Paiz*, January 31, 1928). A great deal of effort and money were invested in these standards, for which a prize was awarded (won by Prazer do Castello in the inaugural competition in 1920), and which tended to rely on nationalistic themes:

> As well as being beautiful Pleasure of Castelo's standard is patriotic. Inspired by *O Guarany* and the work of Carlos Gomes, the artist wished to pay homage to two important geniuses of Brazil . . . [36] How much did Pleasure of Castelo's carnival revelers spend? Even they have no idea. A lot of money. But money that produces victory is well spent and Pleasure of Castelo was victorious!
>
> The good folk from Golden Castelo also deserve our congratulations. Let's give them their due. And they did everything artistically, without worrying about cost. They spent freely, and they can boast a stunning standard . . . a beautiful and ornate

allegory of our brave heroes of the South American Football Championship. (*Gazeta de Notícias,* February 15, 1920)

The tone of the parades on the days of carnival itself was less reverent, however. In the carnival of 1922 one of the allegorical floats was titled "Fico" (I'm staying) and leveled criticism at the plans to demolish Castelo.[37] Given the nature of the prizes awarded, carnival clubs must have competed for the pride that came in part from the social recognition of their efforts in the press. Casa Adamo, a jewelry store in the Rua do Ouvidor, donated the prizes for the Mi-Carême of 1920. They included a bronze lamp, a statuette of Joan of Arc, a marble goblet, a mirror with a terra-cotta frame made to look like a waterfall, and a pair of marble bookends.[38] The prizes reflected the tastes of the city's elites, but one can hardly imagine more impractical rewards for group winners whose members probably lived in cortiços. While competing and even winning a prize in a parade was a collective achievement, a list of the directorship of the group Afilhados do Castelo de Ouro (Godchildren of Golden Castelo) in the *Jornal do Brasil* reveals a very organized and hierarchical management structure: "João Correa, President; Aires Carneiro Costa, Vice-President; Firmino dos Santos, 1st Secretary; Alvaro Silva, 2nd Secretary; João Vidal Soares, Treasurer; Benjamim Valentim, 1st Financial Officer; Waldemar Silva, 2nd Financial Officer; Waldemar Mesquita, 1st Representative; Antonio Teixeira, 2nd Representative; Francisco de Araújo, Percussion Master" (March 6, 1920). All of the names are Portuguese in origin, suggesting that the *carnavalescos* were Afro-descendants or of Portuguese descent. People of Italian descent are conspicuous by their absence, especially given the demographics of Castelo. Luiz Edmundo describes in rich detail the nighttime parade of a carnival group with their standard to the offices of the *Jornal do Brasil.* A "pretty *mestiça*" would usually carry the standard, followed by black drummers, capoeiristas, and black, *mulata,* and "lively, rowdy white women," all dancing samba and bellowing songs at the top of their lungs (1957, 801–4).

A press account of the rivalry between Castello de Ouro and Prazer do Castello transcribes a conversation between two members in vernacular Portuguese:

> The combat between the two rival contenders was even more serious [than that between partidos], because it involved capoeira moves. The clash that occurred one time, I believe on Misericórdia Street, was one of the bloodiest in memory, with some warrior "Indians" laid out for good![39] In time the remnants of that old

savagery disappeared, and the Avenida Central, cutting through the century old slope, limited the field of action of the fighters who remained. Dejected, they began to move out to Favella and other strategic points.

These street toughs had a way of talking that was original and colorful. A curious observer had the patience to publish some examples of this specialist lingo in a magazine at the time. Two of these rascals bumped into each other after one of these huge brawls and one recounted to the other:

> The brother was geared up for it! So I moved back three steps into the stork pose; I landed my best blow right on the brute's mug; knocked his skull to one side and went for the chompers! Blood everywhere! I didn't give him time to come to, I did an upward move then brought it down on the Bahian. Before my man knew what was happening he'd cracked his block on the edge of the sidewalk!

The other one asked:

> And then?

Then whistles started blowing, the cops turned up with their swords and I wised up and made myself scarce! (Secioso de Sá 1928)

A third party relays the dialogue—a curious onlooker from the middle class or the elites. Indeed, satirical columns and caricatures in the press frequently poked fun at black speech as a way of establishing firm limits of race and class, and reinforcing the superiority of white civilization (Lopes 2006, 74). However mediated, the exchange offers a fascinating glimpse of the wit and verbal agility of black speech in the 1920s. Translating this conversation is something of a challenge because of the highly figurative rendering of ordinary words.[40] For example, the mouth is described as a "guarda-comida," literally a food cupboard or pantry. Similarly, teeth become an "appareio [*aparelho*] mastigante," a "chewing appliance." Vocabulary includes capoeira terms and words are repurposed for idiomatic expression, so that "assentei meus alicerco," whose literal meaning has more to do with strengthening or laying a solid foundation, becomes laying a solid blow. The final consonant ("r") of verbs in the infinitive are elided (*buscá; accendê*), and "l"s are also elided (*appareio/aparelho; carçada/calçada; triáram/trilharam*). The speaker also uses an expression from the regional dialect of the northeast: "tomar tento," meaning to pay attention, or notice something. He describes his rival as a Bahian, indicating that both men are either migrants or descendants of migrants from the northeast. In all likelihood this variant of Portuguese would have been used by blacks addressing other blacks, and would have increasingly disappeared from downtown with the reforms. The article's author notes that the construction of the Avenida limited the space for the activities of rival carnival groups and compelled them to move their battles to the favelas.

Not all groups were rivals, however. Friendly *blocos*, or carnival groups, frequently used performances as occasions to visit a neighboring group. Miséria e Fome (Misery and Hunger), the bloco from the Misericórdia Slope, would occasionally go up to the top of the hill to put on a show (Paixão 2008, 177). Additionally, Castelo's numerous religious festivals afforded many opportunities for cariocas from other parts of the city to visit the neighborhood. One of the key attractions was the weekly mass held by the bearded monks, or *barbadinhos*, of the Capuchin order in the former Jesuit cathedral. The barbadinhos evidently had a keen sense of spectacle and an understanding of the nature of popular religious practice. They turned the church into a place of pilgrimage for the whole city, with penitents down on their luck ascending the hill on Fridays at 4:00 in the morning to pray for favors at the 5:00 a.m. mass (Edmundo 1957, 226–27). The barbadinhos recreated the grotto in which Our Lady of Lourdes was believed to have appeared in France, and encouraged a devotional cult to flourish there. The grotto became one of the most important sites of worship for people of different races, ethnicities, and classes. A photograph showing the crowd outside the grotto from *Careta* magazine shows a mix of black, mixed-race, and white devotees (January 15, 1921). On Fridays "a crowd of ladies and gents from the Rio elite turned up to be blessed by the *barbadinhos*," leaving their luxurious cars and elegantly uniformed drivers at the foot of the hill (Emygdio 1927).

The barbadinhos understood the importance of the visible and the tactile in Brazilian religiosity. They dispelled *maus-olhados* (evil eyes) and *azar* (bad luck), lurking misfortunes over which the individual had little control, with their holy water blessings. This practice usually provoked a veritable stampede, as the faithful sought to catch the holy, beneficial drops (Edmundo 1957, 228–31; Barreto 1987, 116; cited in Nonato and Santos 2000, 97). Others personalized and corporealized their devotion, going so far as to drink holy water left over after the blessing; rub the crucifix and rosary over parts of their bodies; affix ex-votos to the grotto's shrine (Edmundo 1957, 228–31); touch an image of Saint Félix to whom miracles had been attributed; and put on their heads a version of the skullcap that had supposedly belonged to Saint Ubaldo (Edmundo 1957, 228–31; Nonato and Santos 2000, 96). The barbadinhos also made the church central to the city's celebration of its patron saint and the activities surrounding Holy Week. Street toughs used the firework display for the feast of São Sebastião to resolve their differences, starting brawls that would send passersby running for cover (Emygdio 1927). During such feast days, however, Castelo became an important zone of cross-class and cross-racial contact. In Holy Week the church put on a religious play whose central theme was Jesus suffering on the cross, which attracted a crowd from the city below. This theatrical spectacle relied very much on its shock effect, and on immanence, rather than the transcendence suggested by the sacrificial death of Christ. The priest would speak to the faithful as he removed the nails from the hands, knees, and feet of someone playing the role of the Savior. Jesus would then descend from the cross to lie in Our Lady's lap. The drama provoked tears and fainting fits, and was followed by a procession around the whole neighborhood with the coffin of Our Lord, accompanied by Our Lady, the priests, and the congregation (Nonato and Santos 2000, 203–4).

The devotional practices surrounding the church were also syncretic in nature. According to Luiz Edmundo, the faithful would sometimes leave mass and cross over to Castelo Alley to enquire about *macumba* sessions in the *terreiro,* or backyard, of the spiritual leader or *pai-de-santo* João Gambá de Luanda. They would then return at night to make the same pleas they had made in church that morning. Castelo was therefore a site in which the cults of popular Catholicism were sustained and cross-fertilized by Afro-descendant devotional practices. In the terreiro João Gambá presided over a fusion of *gege-nagô* rites that evoked deities such as Ogun, Xangô, Oxalá, São Jorge, São Cosme, São Damião and Santo Onofre. He used "despachos," or offerings made at road crossings, in order to assure that the pleas of devotees were granted. In his minute description of a ceremony, Luiz Edmundo notes "thick-lipped blacks" playing *berimbaus,* and various percussion instruments such as *cuícas, atabaques, ganzás, agogôs,* and *xequerês.* A young "mestiça" woman whom he sexualizes as having "a magnificient figure . . . a firm bosom and wide hips" dances frenetically before falling into a trance. One spirit that inhabits the body of a devotee is a Pernambucan slave, who offers advice and transmits stories of the overseer's lash and the whipping post. Another is a Xingu cacique issuing a call to war (Edmundo 1957, 218–24). The spirits who make an appearance in the ceremony represent suffering and resistance, and are therefore inspiring icons for the humble participants of color. Meanwhile, nearby on Castelo Slope lived three members of a Sebastianist cult. The Sebastianists awaited the reappearance of the Portuguese king Dom Sebastião, who had disappeared in the battle of Alcácer-Quibir in 1578, provoking a crisis in the Portuguese monarchy. They held sessions on Friday nights to pray for his return, believing him to be still alive and imprisoned on an island in the Sargasso Sea (*Correio da Manhã*, September 9, 1928).

Religious festivals with their accompanying secular celebrations seem to have had cross-racial and cross-ethnic appeal. One of the interviewed former Castelo residents who was of Italian descent remembers attending the Penha festival in the north of the city to comply with a religious vow and to picnic with family and friends (Paixão 2008, 178).[41] Penha was originally a religious festival organized by the Portuguese community and held over successive weekends in the month of October. The festival became a regular meeting point for black Bahian migrants after abolition and the inauguration of a train line to the area. The *tias*, or Bahian matriarchs, would arrive early to set up their food stalls; capoeiristas gathered there to participate in *rodas* and engage in combat; and the festival also became one of the most important performing spaces for carnival sambas. The Penha festival was an important substitute for the loss of public space for Afro-descendants in the city center after the reforms (Leu 2014). Within Castelo the interviewees' family also attended the Festa do Divino Espírito Santo (Feast of the Divine Holy Spirit), organized by the Portuguese Azorean community in Chácara da Floresta every year. The patron of the Festa do Divino was Floresta's owner, fulfilling a religious vow. Celebrants prepared a chapel with an icon of the Holy Spirit inside, and decorated with flowers a calf that was allowed to wander through Floresta before being killed and its meat distributed among the poor (Nonato and Santos 2000, 43). Secular live music was performed at night, as was the custom in religious festivals, which sometimes attracted the city's most prominent musicians to perform during or after the religious service. An announcement for the Festa do Divino of 1920 lists the exact order of events: "At 9:30 mass will be celebrated in praise of the Holy Spirit; this will be followed immediately by the blessing of the alms of meat and bread . . . , which will be distributed to those bearing the cards given out earlier; at 3:00 p.m. the auction of items donated by the faithful will begin. . . . The Penha Musical Group will liven up the festival, playing in the bandstand until 11:00" (*Jornal do Brasil*, May 21, 1920).

HETEROGENEOUS SOUNDSCAPES

The Penha Musical Group's performance would have provided one of many different types of music that made up Castelo's diverse soundscape. Castelenses may well have been dancing to sambas and *maxixes* (polka styles fused with Afro-Brazilian rhythms) on the evening of a Portuguese community festival like the Festa do Divino. They had home-grown performers too, like Florêncio da Palma, who lived halfway up Castelo Slope and was also a well-known black tattoo artist used by navy sailors.[42] Castelenses listened to Calado (the acclaimed mestiço classical flautist who had performed for the imperial family) play in the *missa cantata* of another festival, the Grande Festa do Senhor Bom Jesus dos Perdões (Great Feast of Our Lord Jesus of Pardon).[43] Calado had a castelense as his teacher for a short period—the first composer of color sponsored by the Imperial Court to train in Paris, Henrique Alves de Mesquita, a mestiço who was born on Castelo Slope in 1830 (Nonato and Santos 2000, 190). According to one account, Mesquita returned from his time in Paris in 1866 with a great desire to reconnect with his old neighborhood, in spite of its "decadent," ruinous" state, "where he found so many strange people speaking languages he didn't understand; people who came to Brazil to teach locals the music that was popular in their own countries." Why, he wondered, were Brazilians so quick to accept the ideas and cultures of others, but so reluctant to promote their own? As he considered this, the bells in the parish church of São José rang out, confirming his thoughts by playing the most recent melodies of the operettas of Jacques Offenbach. For the maestro this moment represented one more sign of the neglect of the neighborhood and Brazil's patrimony in general (Siqueira 1969, 51).

The influx of European immigrants that Mesquita observed would increasingly lead to Portuguese fado and Italian popular songs competing with each other in the neighborhood's densely occupied living spaces, as in this account from 1928 reminiscing about the neighborhood:

> When in one house someone sang:
>
> Maiannina sta malate
> E soffrendo di dolore.
>
> in another, next door, trying to drown out the regional Italian song, a Portuguese woman bellowed out a mangled version of the "Fado Hilário":
>
> O mar também é casado,
> O mar também tem mulher:
> É casado com a areia
> E dá-lhe beijos quando quer.

> While they danced the *tarantela* in one *cortiço,* next to it others were enthusiastically dancing the *canna verde.*
>
> Bits of operas and Portuguese fados mixed together incomprehensibly, just like the music of the accordions, harmonicas, and guitars, like some kind of strange orchestra. (Emygdio 1927)

This heterogeneous soundscape reflects the crossings, connections, and conflicts of Castelo's interracial and interethnic spaces. It has a story to tell about the comings and goings of people from across the country and across continents that made and remade that place. This chapter has also focused on telling geographical stories. It has explored different ways of organizing and experiencing space from those being imposed by the government at this important moment in the city's urbanization history. The neighborhood's residents resisted destruction as long as they could, inhabiting ruins as the pickaxes and water jets eroded the hill. They mourned the loss of the place they called home that was sacrificed to the national civilizing project. The city and national governments eventually obliterated that space, but as former inhabitants fanned out from the old neighborhood they continued to claim territory beyond the reformed city, on other hillsides downtown and further afield in the suburbs. They multiplied their alternative geographies across urban space in an ongoing process that demonstrates the resilience as well as the suffering of those excluded from the dream of modernity.

Figure 4.1. Bleach advertisement, *Fon-Fon*, September 7, 1922, Biblioteca Nacional Digital Brasil.

4

ERADICATING BLACKNESS FROM THE IDEAL CITY

AN ADVERTISEMENT FOR WHITE BEAR BLEACH appeared in the weekly magazine *Fon-Fon* on September 7, 1922, the day that the nation was marking one hundred years since its independence from Portugal (fig. 4.1). The advertisement shows a little black boy emerging from a bath full of bleach, having turned white from the neck down. The caption in vernacular Portuguese translates as, "Don't you whiten my face now . . . or Pa ain't gonna recognize me!" The aggressive antiblackness of the image and its message not only conveys the desirability of whiteness; it simultaneously takes a swipe at the issue of illegitimacy and the absent black father. The violent cosmetic whitening that the little boy endures is an appropriate metaphor for elite aspirations for the capital city of the nation in its centennial year, and was the underlying impulse behind projects aimed at reclaiming and redistributing urban space. *Fon-Fon* was a publication established in the shadow of the Passos reforms, and a cheerleader for the modernization of the capital, as suggested by its title, which imitated the sound of an automobile's horn. Given widespread illiteracy among the racialized poor, the magazine and the advertisement were aimed at the white, literate middle and upper classes. The advertisement cannily taps into the hopes and fears of the ruling classes with regard to race as the nation commemorated its centenary. In this scenario racial progress is speeded up and realized in time for the showcasing of the country to the world. Hygiene has apparently triumphed to eradicate blackness from the next generation of Brazilians—and with that, presumably, its other signifiers such as sickness, laziness, and ugliness. The little boy's mother appears overjoyed at the prospect of bleaching the stigma of racial degeneracy from her son, thereby facilitating his social advancement. However, the boy seems fearful, as well he might, for he has turned into a curious hybrid whose head remains black.[1] The process is not complete—no matter how white most of his body may appear, the way that he thinks and feels will never be in tune with the ideal social order.

As the nation proclaimed its entry on a modern stage these black characters are the butt of a shared joke in which no amount of social or cultural whitening could make them viable participants in the process. The values and behaviors of modern (white) civilization will never be fully attainable for them. The advertisement also betrays some pessimism about the possibility of European immigration and miscegenation gradually bleaching the population. It suggests that only drastic measures could achieve results—results that are partial and dubious in any case. In her discussion of the soap industry in England during the Victorian era, Anne McClintock observes that soap became signified as a technology of social purification in the context of imperial racism. She analyzes a similar advertisement in which a black child is soaped white as a metaphor for the regeneration of the body politic at a moment of impending crisis of the social order. Like the child in the *Fon-Fon* advertisement, his head remains black, foreshadowing an incomplete imperial metamorphosis that only brings him to the brink of civilization (1995, 211–14). The *Fon-Fon* cartoon taps into a nexus of raced and gendered domination that is profoundly embedded in colonial social relations. The boy exhorts his mother not to whiten his face, so as not to place his paternity in doubt. If the boy's father sees his son thus transformed he will no doubt suspect that he may have been tricked into recognizing the boy as his own. The advertisement's punchline therefore relies on the sexual coercion and violation of black women by white men during slavery and beyond that destroyed black family life.

The bleach advertisement is an enactment in miniature of the national whitening project on display at the world fair that opened that day. In fact, its promotion of this humble domestic product encapsulates the whole spirit of the fair that sought to commodify the desire for modernity and whiteness. The advertisement also probes the concerns and insecurities underlying that desire, but on the whole, the international exposition essayed a jingoistic optimism in the spectacle of a modern nation that it mounted. This provided a much-needed counterweight to the intelligentsia's ambivalence about the Republic and their disappointment that its promise had not been realized (Motta 1992, 26). If the centenary gave cause to agonize over the reasons for the country's backwardness, the exposition felt like an opportunity to prove that Brazil was indeed capable of progress.

There is no doubt as to what progress meant to the organizing committee of the fair, who had Mayor Sampaio as its chair. The mayor's speech inaugurating the Administration Pavilion praised "the huge effort that Brazil, especially in its federal capital, has made to demonstrate to the civilized world that our progress is real, that our culture is not inferior to that of other nations, that our capacity for hard work is proof of the injustice we suffer of being labeled an indolent race."[2] As one contemporary newspaper commentator put it, the fair was "the marvelous triumph of our race over our historical origins."[3] The elimination of the black population and the cultural whitening that became central to the notion of the *raça brasileira* seemed to have culminated for the ruling classes in the spectacle of the fair. Reflecting this, the president of the Republic's speech at a banquet for foreign diplomats consigned slavery very firmly to the past: "Once the consolidation of the Fatherland was realized and its unity guaranteed, we turned to the autonomy of the provinces, prudently granting them decentralization. Immediately we put an end to slave trafficking. Once that wound was staunched, the abolitionist campaign emerged, victorious with the Law of the Free Womb, the freeing of slaves over sixty-five, and shortly thereafter the complete abolition of slavery. With this battle won, we looked to federation and the Republic" (Comissão Organizadora, no. 3–4, September 1922).

The alacrity with which slavery is dispatched in the speech ("Immediately"; "Once that wound was staunched"; "shortly thereafter"; "With this battle won") also suggests an admirable consensus and firmness of purpose, as well as denying any lingering impact for those freed and their descendants. The end of the traffic in slaves and the abolition of slavery, the triumphant discourse suggested, also signaled the end of suffering for the black population. In the potted history of the nation that the speech recounts, these were also the end points of any black presence in the imagined community. In this reinvented history, it is as if the black population had simply disappeared postabolition. The exposition was key to attempting to conjure up this disappearing act that was fundamental to the nation builders' modernizing dreams. The ideal mini-city created for the fair was therefore an exercise both in fulfilling the desire for modernity and in

Figure 4.2. "Morro do Castello," Augusto Malta, March 14, 1922, Biblioteca Nacional Digital Brasil.

Figure 4.3. "Morro do Castello," Augusto Malta, July 9, 1922, Biblioteca Nacional Digital Brasil.

constructing a desired absence—a Rio with some remnants of black culture, perhaps, but ideally without its black population. For this, a symbolic empty space was necessary, a tabula rasa that underlined this monumental act of forgetting. Once most of the hillside was demolished, what was left was a gaping hole in the city center in which a new imagined nation in miniature could be construed (figs. 4.2 and 4.3). In fact, in an article on the fair the American architect J. P. Curtis observed, "Like the plans followed for the World's Fairs in Chicago and San Francisco, foresight was shown in the selection of an *undeveloped* site, so that the plant growths would not be disturbed and fair buildings of permanent construction would remain as part of the city" (1923, 97; my emphasis). It was as though the bustling, historic neighborhood of Castelo had never existed. The rest of this chapter explores the place that the white spatial imaginary of 1920s Brazil built in its place.

CONQUERING THE DARKNESS

The state, the municipality, and the developers sought to present a vacuum for expo construction and for real estate speculation to follow.[4] The new space was produced with the intention of erasing the history of the community that had been rooted above it. However, the entire hillside could not be flattened in time for the fair, which somewhat disturbed the visual illusion of modernity. The image of the fair reproduced in figure 2.17 synthesizes modernity's curious clash of temporalities and its ephemerality. The Pavilion of the Brazilian States seen in the middle foreground is not built in the "new Brazilian" or neocolonial style, but in the already outmoded Belle Époque or French Renaissance style of the Passos reforms. The ruins of Castelo loom over the pavilion like a haunting of the dreams of modernity by the vestiges of the colonial past, as if to indicate that one day it too will be reduced to ruins. In fact, in 1978 the pavilion was demolished, so that from our contemporary viewpoint we are gazing at what Beatriz Jaguaribe calls "the fragility of former utopian projections" that while positing themselves as new, inevitably presage their own demise (2014, 52). This chapter examines the intimate connections between concepts of modernity, urbanization, and racial progress. It explores how the exposition space constructed to house Brazil's first mega-event aimed to nurture the idea of a "Brazilian race" in formation. As discussed in chapter 1, the idea of a "Brazilian race" resulted from the problem of how to construct a nation out of what its leaders and social thinkers considered a racially inferior population. The space of the fair was a racial project. It functioned as an opportunity to stage a whiter city and country. Those who imagined this space sought to materially enact the whitening ideal in the built environment.

Brazil was no stranger to national expositions, having held its first in 1861.[5] However, the Centennial Exhibition was its first world fair, and reflected such events' typical concerns with showcasing the host country's progress. The world fairs held primarily in Europe and the United States in the second half of the late nineteenth century ultimately reinforced imperial superiority and universal progress (Fernández Bravo 2001, 117). For Brazil, the first country on the continent to host a world fair, the event was supremely important as a moment to overcome its feeling of inferiority as regards European and North American standards of civilization, while calling itself into being as a modern nation. The displays therefore reflected a careful balancing act between attempts to establish a unique national brand and aspirations to universality. As a result, the tendency was to present Brazil's renowned tropical exuberance, for example, not as virgin landscapes but as a prolific nature that electricity and modernizing agricultural, transport, and manufacturing practices were taming and harnessing in the march toward progress. Similarly, elements of black popular culture were removed from their contexts in the tenement dwellings and colonial alleys that the urbanizing elites so abhorred, and exhibited at the fair as signs of uniqueness. For example, a "curious festival of regional *carioca* culture" took place in the Music Pavilion some four months after the fair opened, in which a *bloco* of sixty musicians and singing and dancing *baianas* paraded down the reformed Avenida Rio Branco toward the fairgrounds "to demonstrate *batuque* and *samba* to high society and the illustrious foreigners currently visiting us." A lecture that followed praised the agility and strength of the capoeiras who performed the batuque and added that capoeira was superior to boxing and jujitsu. One newspaper stated reassuringly that "even though the members of the *bloco* are devoted to samba they are not troublemakers or social misfits as one might suppose at first glance" (*A Noite*, January 12, 1923, 6). The performance was carefully curated to take place in the city's showpiece boulevard and thence to the distinguished space of the Music Pavilion, and is framed by the lecture that interprets it as the basis for a Brazilian art that is already appropriating and stylizing (in other words, civilizing) these "natural national motifs."

As Thaís Sant'Ana suggests, the appropriation of popular culture for the exposition was couched in a discourse of "cultural unity" geared in part toward encouraging national pride among the poor. This notion also fed into the idea of a common ethnicity of the "Brazilian race" that minimized social contradictions and blackness, making the fair the consummate "festival of the *raça*" (2008, 113). In this scenario the culture of a disappearing black population will be improved upon and whitened in the service of creating a national culture. Here we have an incipient culturalist reification by nation builders that Michael G. Hanchard describes as commodifying and divorcing Afro-descendant cultural practices from their histories and the modes of consciousness that brought them into being (1998, 21). Indigenous peoples had their own display, also described as "curious" in press coverage and also focused on providing evidence of racial progress. The Indian Protection Service exhibited objects, photographs, and statistical studies to demonstrate the "very advanced level of civilization" attained by assimilated indigenous peoples. One newspaper exhorted the public to visit the display in the Industry Pavilion to find "definitive proof of our Indians' capacity for work, their intelligence, and their ease of adaptation to the social life of the civilized world" (*A Noite*, June 14, 1923, 2).

The fair consisted broadly of two sections, foreign and domestic. Thirteen foreign nations participated—nine from Europe, two from Latin America (Argentina and Mexico), the United States, and Japan. Their pavilions occupied land reclaimed from the sea using the soil on which Castelo once stood, as well as some blocks of the densely occupied, interethnic Misericórdia neighborhood that João do Rio describes in chapter 3. The larger exhibition spaces in the domestic section consisted of the Palaces of Festivals, Industries, and Brazilian States, and buildings for hunting and fisheries, statistics, administration, agriculture and transportation, and minor industries. There were also booths in the adapted market front and a number of smaller exhibition buildings, as well as an amusement park (which was only completed in November).

The first in a series of publications by the organizing committee (July 1922) proclaimed that the exhibition was "the expression of economic and social life in Brazil in 1922" and would therefore showcase themes such as education, hygiene, sports, the military, communication, the arts, commerce, and industry. The division and subdivision of sections for the purpose of cataloguing, display, and judging gave organizers the opportunity to (re)define and legitimize various aspects of national life. As a sign of what was at stake in imagining an ideal Brazil in miniature for presentation to the outside world and for the civic education of the population, Sampaio himself designed the layout of the site. The president of the Republic was also involved with minute details of the organization of the event; for example, the planning of the program of events (*Jornal do Brasil*,

April 7, 1921, 8).[6] This participation at the highest level of municipal and federal government can be understood in light of one of the desired outcomes of the fair: to order and unify the idea of the nation at a time of political upheaval and uncertainty. The country had recently been witnessing its first general strikes, and just months before the fair the founding of the Brazilian Communist Party and the rise of the *tenente* movement against the Republic.

Lisa Munro observes that world's fairs introduced regimes of visibility that encouraged new cultural attitudes toward display to flourish and made visual representation an authoritative medium for knowledge transmission (2010, 80). The radical transformation of the landscape of the center of Rio opened it up to the public gaze. That gaze alighted on an exhibition space that evidenced the power of the state and reinforced the social and cultural values it wished to promote, what Álvaro Fernández Bravo calls "a fiction of the state" (2001, 122). Additionally, one of the chief goals of the exposition was to create a spectacle "for the English to see," as the Brazilian idiomatic expression would have it: that is, to impress the outside world and also be hailed as a civilized nation. Organizers must have therefore derived great satisfaction from reports in the *New York Evening Post* that "in the next fifty years Brazil will achieve the huge material gains and development attained by us in the last half century. From the perspective of culture, appreciation of the fine arts, etc., Brazilians are already our equals, and perhaps even our superiors" (*A Noite*, September 8,1922, 1). The social economics display also sought to impress outsiders, highlighting proposals to improve the working conditions and quality of life of the working classes, and distributing information for prospective foreigners interested in working in Brazil (Sant'Ana 2008, 50).

Therefore, despite the city's budgetary crises officials made every effort in the fairgrounds and in related activities to create a lavish display that emphasized light and illumination, evoking the modern and dispelling colonial obscurantism with selective glories of the past. The commemorative *Livro de ouro* (Golden book) of the fair describes an enormous illuminated parade organized by the mayor's office in honor of the heroes of independence with the statues commissioned from Florence: "The impression that the parade produced was dazzling, eliciting the most enthusiastic popular applause. The great historic figures of our independence passed by in effigy borne along in a triumphal march throughout the city and acclaimed by the whole population gathered there" (1923, 325). The Palace of Brazilian States was decorated with forty thousand glass crystals imitating diamonds, rubies, emeralds, and sapphires that powerful searchlights lit up at night. Curtis, the visiting American architect, remarked approvingly that "Rio is abundantly supplied with electricity and at night the Exposition was a brilliant spot, reflected in the inky waters of the bay, and presenting a fascinating spectacle" (Curtis 1923, 103). The panoramas of the city that had been a staple of photographs of Rio (and visual representations of the city in general) since its earliest history became landscapes that were a testament to the triumph of technology over nature.

In her study of the meanings of public illumination in Rio de Janeiro in the early 1900s, Sophia Beal traces how chronicles and photographs imagine the notion of progress as a conquest of darkness (2013, 23–53). She argues that electric street lighting embodied both the practical and aesthetic ideals of the Passos reforms, by purporting to make the city safer and more beautiful (24). Beal's readings of these chronicles emphasize the link between the determination to conquer darkness and the desire to whiten the city: "The first decade of the twentieth century was a time of measurable efforts to make Rio de Janeiro lighter: the installation of the first electric streetlights, a wide straight boulevard replacing dark narrow streets, and the facilitation of white European immigration" (35). As she observes in her analysis of the chronicle "O bebê de tarlatana rosa," by João do Rio, for the reformers the conquest of darkness involved imposing dominant notions of the good, the civilized, and the orderly on chaos, ugliness, and blackness (51). As the reforms attacked the supposed ugliness of the city, she argues, they attacked its Afro-descendant population.

As Beal demonstrates, the illumination of the pavilions at the National Exposition of 1908 dazzled and seduced João do Rio. As he strived to capture this visual experience in words his chronicle "Noturno policromo" resorts to ornate, hyperbolic language to express the wonder that these spectacular displays of electricity provoked in the contemporary observer (42–49). The more sardonic writer Lima Barreto refuses to be won over, however. In his *folhetim* published in the *Correio da Manhã* in 1905, *O subterrâneo do Morro do Castelo,* Lima Barreto condemns the installation of electricity in the caverns under Castelo Hill in search of the fabled wealth of the Jesuits. For him electricity's presence is irreverent and profane in the sacrosanct space of the nation's patrimony ([1905] 1997, 85–86). As Beal notes, Lima Barreto links electric lighting to the destruction and elitism that he condemns in the reforms. She observes that in his novel *Recordações do escrivão Isaías Caminha* (1909) the obsession with eliminating darkness had a decidedly racialized goal: "The Haussmanns swarmed. Avenues were designed; squares arose in the plans, palaces were delineated, and, as a complement, they also wanted a quaint, tidy, elegant, and white population: impeccable coachmen, shoe shiners in livery, blond, blue-eyed maids in the uniform seen in fashionable English newspapers" (quoted in Beal 2013, 32).

On the whole, locals and those who traveled to the capital to witness the spectacle of the centennial celebrations were extremely curious about the multifarious events and displays of the fair, though it is very difficult to glean insights into whether the "popular applause" mentioned earlier was for the dazzling modernity of the light show, pride in the national heroes, or both. Were popular subjects interested in the messages intended for their enlightenment and edification, or did they simply enjoy the entertainment? What was their experience of being in or around the area of the fair? Because of the primary sources available, it is difficult to assess how individuals may have understood the city's monumental centennial effort. In attempting to imagine the experience of city dwellers during the commemorations, as well as explore the ideological agenda of the organizers this chapter must rely on newspaper reports, visual records, and the catalogs and literature published by the organizing committee and other commemorative publications.

VISITING THE FAIR

The fair opened on Independence Day, September 7, 1922, and closed on July 24 the following year. Contemporary newspapers record in detail the official program of the inaugural days, with a gala at the Teatro Municipal (featuring the Romantic Indianist opera *O Guarany*), civic ceremonies such as parades by the military and schoolchildren, formal dinners and balls with the city and presidential administrations, diplomats, and foreign politicians, as well as the great and good of *carioca* society. Foreign visitors were suitably impressed, including Mexico's then secretary of education José Vasconcelos, ideologue of the concept of the "cosmic race." Vasconcelos's influential notion praised a superior Hispanic spirituality that overcame the prejudice of race through race mixing and had a civilizing influence on populations of color. The Rio de Janeiro that Vasconcelos saw in his carefully guided tours was that of a quasi-aristocratic, white society that recalled the Mexico City of the Porfirian middle classes (Tenorio-Trillo 1996, 219). Another Mexican visitor, Alfonso del Toro, a delegate to the Twentieth International Congress of Americanists, which concluded just before the exhibition opened, was able to dispel the perceptions of his countrymen about the city's racial makeup: "This beautiful Brazilian city was recently so little known by Mexicans that there was no shortage of well-educated people who, on learning of my trip, had commented: "But why on earth are you going to Rio de Janeiro if it's just a city full of blacks?" In fact, del Toro assures his readers: "And actually, those blacks that other people mentioned are really very few; you don't see many of them, and you'd surely see more in any American city, no doubt about it. And since we're on the subject of blacks, I can tell you that while they are a real headache for our neighbor, they are not a problem in Brazil; since they're treated just like whites their numbers are dwindling by the day, because they're incorporating themselves and dissolving into the white population, which doesn't happen in the United States because of their concerns with race" ("La bella ciudad brasileña," *Revista de revistas,* October 20, 1922, 11).

Del Toro's perceptions seem to bear out the success of the exposition in disappearing the black population from valorized areas of the city, at least on his presumably guided tours. He also explicitly references the whitening ideal that dominated elite thinking on race in Brazil as elsewhere on the continent. His comments echo those of other analysts of race in Brazil who implied that segregation in the United States had made the "negro problem" impossible to solve there through miscegenation.

Thousands of cariocas flocked to the fair—according to a report in the *Correio da Manhã,* twenty-two thousand people visited on September 9, and one hundred thousand on September 10 (*Correio da Manhã,* September 9, 1922, 1; September 10, 1922, 1). By the time it was over nearly four million people had visited (Tenorio-Trillo 1996, 200). In addition to all the formal events mentioned above, newspapers list many other forms of celebration on the exhibition site, and in theaters and cinemas. Even entertainment spaces that were not part of the official circuit held centenary shows and entire "centenary seasons." Interestingly, despite the fair's overwhelming concern with presenting Brazil as a white country, the legendary band the Batutas, whose members had recently returned home from Paris, performed within the fairgrounds. The US ambassador was reputedly a fan and invited them to play at the General Motors Pavilion, as well as the US embassy, where they entertained visitors with a transnational repertoire that included Charlestons and foxtrots. Despite the outcry that had greeted the presence of a band with black musicians in one of Rio's most elegant cinema theaters in 1919, the Batutas enjoyed the support of a wealthy white patron.[7] He financed their six-month stint in Paris, and while the prospect of Brazilian music being represented in France by black performers had dismayed members of the elite, their success in Paris as part of the "Negro vogue" conferred considerable prestige on the group on their return to Brazil (Vianna 1999, 82–83; Seigel 2009, 107).

From official programs and the coverage of events in the press, we know that special activities were planned for the wider public, many of which did not take place within the fairgrounds, such as fireworks displays, open air concerts, "popular shows" in the city's theaters, and "popular dances" in its parks (*Jornal do Brasil*, September 8, 1922; September 9, 1922, 1; *Correio da Manhã*, September 8, 1922). Organizers also planned a free-entry day and party for poor children with a distribution of toys for September 10, but they postponed the event and announced no alternative (*Correio da Manhã*, September 10,1922, 1; September 11, 1922, 1). Entry to the exposition was briefly free in the days after the inaugural ceremony. During that time an "enormous popular mass" overcame attempts by the police to regulate the crowd and invaded the space. However, during this period all the pavilions remained closed (apart from the Japanese pavilion, which opened briefly) and the only entertainment available to those who managed to enter the grounds was a light show. The price of entry was sufficient to prompt the organizers to hold a lottery with tickets as prizes (*O Paiz*, September 7, 1922). The lottery raised funds for defraying the expenses involved in constructing the site. It also served as a means of advertising the fair widely to the public, as organizers had expressed concern that the public might be indifferent to the event, as had been the case for the 1908 national fair (Sant'Ana 2008, 43). Newspapers suggest curiosity, but also confusion on the part of the public with regard to access to the fairgrounds:

> By 3:30 in the afternoon it was difficult to move near the Monroe Palace. And some curious visitors enquired of others: "Do I need an invitation to enter the Exposition?" "Do I need a special ticket?"
>
> Individuals who looked like rural types from the interior gathered around the large entry gate on Beira-Mar Avenue. A clever young lad stationed there awaited a lucky break. He promptly enquired of anyone with a ticket:
>
> "Are you going in alone, sir?"
>
> "No, with my family, why?"
>
> "Well, if you were on your own you could take me in with you . . ."
>
> Finally, breaking through a large crowd of men with grave countenances dressed completely ridiculously with top hats and tails, we are at the Exhibition gate. A doorman awaits us, serious and rotund, dressed in green, sweating from his ticket collecting exertions: "Your ticket, please?" And on catching sight of the precious pass: "Very good, you may enter, sir." (*Correio da Manhã*, September 8, 1922, 1)

Despite their uncertainty about whether they would be able to enter the exhibition space, people from the countryside—those whom their urban compatriots would have dubbed as hicks—traveled to the capital to witness the commemorations for themselves. Their presence outside the imposing entrance gate, where they stood out as "rural types from the interior," confused about whether they merited access to the official space, speaks to the segregating impulse of the centennial fair and its related urban reforms, and also to their interest in being included in the imagined national community celebrating the centenary. Ironically, while rural folk wondered if they were allowed into the fair, their stereotype, Jeca Tatu, became an attraction inside at the Festival Palace the following June. As part of a variety show billing "six colossal stars" advertisements promised that "the splendid Jeca Tatu" would entertain the audience with "his amazing repertoire of anecdotes" (*A Noite*, June 11, 1923, 2; June 14, 1923, 2).[8]

Confusion definitely featured in popular reaction to aspects of the commemorations, as well as to the newly urbanized city. The day after the fair opened Silveria Fortunata, an Afro-descendant woman who claimed to be 135 years old, visited the offices of the *Correio da Manhã* newspaper to talk about her life. Fortunata claimed to have met the former prince regent Dom Pedro I as a young man, and to have been a witness to his proclamation of independence on the banks of the Ipiranga river. Fortunata was a washerwoman who had once lived in Rio and was at the time living in São Paulo. Despite her advanced years, she continued to make her living taking in washing and ironing. Seized with a desire to see the federal capital during the celebrations, she took a train from the Luz Station in São Paulo and arrived in Rio de Janeiro after a tedious and uncomfortable journey. On arrival, however, she was entirely overwhelmed by the city until a sailor from the naval dockyard, noticing her confusion, took it upon himself to guide her to downtown. What emboldened Fortunata to travel to Rio and visit the paper's offices in order to recount her life story to them? Despite being a poor, elderly, black woman, she felt that her story merited attention. In fact, the journalist notes that she would have stayed for hours recounting her past, had her gallant guide, the sailor, not reminded her that it was time to go out into the city and enjoy the celebrations. Fortunata goes to some lengths to ensure that she emplots herself into the national narrative. She makes herself an agent of one of the most significant moments in the country's history, at a time when the official memorializing of the exhibition organizers was defining a past that represented the black population as "good slaves" but never citizens (to borrow Clóvis Moura's notion [1977, 47]).

Figure 4.4. *Independência ou Morte* (*Independence or Death*), or *O Grito de Ipiranga* (*The Cry of Ipiranga*), Pedro Américo, 1888.

In fact, Fortunata also visually embeds herself in one of the most ubiquitous icons of the centennial commemorations. The painting *O Grito do Ipiranga* (*The Cry of Ipiranga*; 1888), also known as "Independence or Death," by Pedro Américo, was heavily reproduced by the organizers in publications, publicity, souvenirs, and on the lottery tickets for the exhibition (Sant'Ana 2008, 114–15). With the image in such heavy circulation, references to the "grito" would have immediately conjured up the scenario portrayed in Américo's work (see fig. 4.4). The painting shows Dom Pedro on the banks of the Ipiranga river, sword aloft as he issues the revered cry, surrounded by noblemen and soldiers of the empire. In the left foreground of the painting, a figure that looks like a *caboclo* leading his oxen witnesses the solemn act. His appearance contrasts greatly with the other figures in the scene; his clothes are ragged, exposing parts of his body, in contrast to the ostentatious uniforms of the soldiers. He represents the humble people of the new nation, echoing the trend in late nineteenth-century historiography to see the rustic *paulista* of Portuguese and indigenous blood as the foundation for the formation of a strong Brazilian race. There is a distinct hierarchy between the martial air of the men on horseback and the caboclo witnessing the historic moment on foot, engaged in the prosaic act of transporting logs on his beasts of burden. By inserting herself in this profoundly masculine scene, Fortunata feminizes and also blackens the founding iconography of the nation.

Fortunata's act of memorializing from below challenges the silences of the dominant historical narrative. She emerges from the anonymous mass of slaves and their descendants glossed over in exhibition discourse, and seizes an opportunity for social visibility, with the solidarity of the seaman—probably Afro-descendant himself, given the racial demographic of the navy since the period of the empire. The symbolic repertoire that Fortunata activates in the process of her subjectification for the newspaper is based in part on expectations for black women at the time, even as it challenges them. She has labored her whole life, and continues to do so despite her age, in menial, physically demanding work, but "is not resentful." Debate surrounding the African American colonizing syndicates who wished to settle in Brazil drew comparisons between a resigned acceptance of their lot on the part of Brazilian blacks, as opposed to the aggressiveness and assertiveness of US blacks (Ramos 1996, 67). Fortunata may claim to lack resentment (perhaps in order to seize the possibility of address offered by the newspaper article), but she is vocal and proactive. Indeed, after she makes the front page of the paper the day after the fair opens, she returns to thank journalists for telling her life story and to give some impressions of her visit. She declares herself "astonished" by so much progress in a city she once knew as colonial. She does not mention visiting the fairgrounds or other attractions but declares that the new area created by the landfill seems somewhat unnatural, "spreading its huge mass over the water" and giving that part of the city the appearance of being "wrenched from the sea." Instead, she maps her own memoryscapes, visiting places in the city she knows well from the pre-Republican era—the site of the imperial palace in São Cristóvão and the Passeio Público (the first urbanized area of the city). Without her good Samaritan guide from the day before, Fortunata confesses that she set off for the newspaper's offices in the morning but only managed to arrive at 2:00 in the afternoon, having spent hours lost in the newly reformed streets of the city.

There is little information about what new immigrants made of the centennial celebrations. During the intermission of a burlesque operetta at the Teatro República, European immigrants to the interior of the country were the butt of a humorous sketch called "The Centenary Exposition seen by a German and an Italian sharecropper." The comedian was a visiting caricaturist from Lisbon, and we do not know the content of his jokes that reportedly made the theater erupt in laughter. However, it is probably safe to say that they reflected prevailing stereotypes and the perceptions held by landowners of these plantation contract workers as demonstrating "a lack of ambition, of social progress, of elegance, of body posture, of a sense of opportunity and progress, of boldness, of perceptiveness, of wisdom" (Alves Teixeira quoted in Lesser 2013, 40). On the inaugural day of the fair a recent immigrant was the target of ire rather than humor during the solemnities of the opening ceremonies. One novelty of the fair was the transmission by radio of events taking place in one location to other points around the site via loudspeakers. Organizers broadcast the inaugural speeches taking place in the Pavilion of the Brazilian States with national and foreign dignitaries present, followed by the national anthem. According to one newspaper report "everyone stood up and uncovered their heads. One swarthy young man with mediocre manners, however, kept his hat on his head. Irritated protests immediately rained down upon him: 'Take your hat off!' 'It's the national anthem!' 'Take your hat off!' Faced with people's insistence, the young man eventually took their advice and removed his hat. Shortly afterward all was explained: he was Syrian, having arrived in the country only days before, and still didn't recognize the national anthem" (*Correio da Manhã*, September 8, 1922, 1).

As Munro has argued, world's fairs frame the relationship between ordinary citizens and the government and provide a sacred space for public rituals. The rural folk wondering how to enter that space were pushing up against the exposition's role in reinforcing classed and raced hierarchies of power. Faced with her disorientation in the city of the future, Fortunata represents herself as a guardian of its most glorious past and therefore a citizen par excellence, rather than the obsolete pastness to which official discourse relegates her. The newly arrived Syrian immigrant gets his first, memorable lesson in civic pride, appropriate social behavior, and national cultural values at the fair; one that will serve him well in advancing socially in the host country.

Although the humble folk described above appeared to embrace the prospect of commemorating the centennial, on the whole, press coverage of popular participation is conflicting. The *Jornal do Brasil*, a consistent critic of the Republican government, featured a small article on the lively alternative commemorations in the city's cabarets, and observed the public's lack of interest in the official events: "Anyone wandering the city on Wednesday night could not have been optimistic about popular sentiment [about the centennial], except for the odd, scanty group in celebratory mood. Serious citizens and fervent patriots lamented this lack of public vigor and enthusiasm. Again one had the impression, you could say, that the civic festivities were official commemorations from which the general public remained absent" (*Jornal do Brasil*, September 8, 1922, 4).

However, the *Correio da Manhã* reported cars full of passengers on the Central do Brasil train line from the suburbs, neighborhoods to which the Passos reforms had displaced the poor. In all likelihood, these people were traveling into the city center to attend the free events. The paper reported on the "humble masses" attending these shows; for example, the free concerts performed by an army band, and by the Torreblanca Orchestra sponsored by the Mexican consul (*Correio da Manhã*, September 3 and September 8, 1922). The *Jornal do Brasil* reported 14,821 visitors to the fair during a period of three hours even on one rainy night (September 10, 1922). The commemorative magazine of the fair's organizing commission claimed that "all the social classes fraternally participated in the commemorative celebrations for the great event." It further claimed that half a million spectators (nearly half of the city's population!) gathered for the military parade on September 7 (Comissão Organizadora September 1922, no. 3–4).[9] In a scathing critique of the pointless pomp of the commemorations, Lima Barreto observes that there may have been popular interest in the parades, light shows, and sporting events, but the meaning of the historic event was rightfully met with indifference and incomprehension. Humble cariocas, he opined, were no doubt wondering, "'What good are [historical figures] José Bonifacio, Pedro I, Alvares Cabral, the Amazon, the gold of Minas, the Rio World Fair . . . if I spend my life counting pennies to survive?' That state of mind doesn't lend itself to patriotic enthusiasm" (*Careta*, September 30, 1922).

Many photographs documenting the event tended to focus on the grandeur of the pavilions or on panoramas of the site rather than individuals in the fairgrounds and its vicinity. Cinema also played a major role in the visual record of the exhibition, with a special centennial committee that commissioned films from all the states of the country (Martins 2013, 27). However, the guidelines of the organizing committee to filmmakers were so rigid and detailed as to make creativity challenging. As a result, surviving footage features many static cameras, panoramas, and lengthy descriptions of the workings of a particular machine or the importance of a certain product (Morettin 2011, 144). After all, filmmakers were commissioned by government and private entities to represent their coherent vision of the modernizing nation. Cinema of the centenary was called upon to play a civic role, and the films produced for the event therefore produce a kind of visual monument to progress (Morettin 2013, 157). Newspapers announced film showings such as "Parque Centenário," "A exposição do centenário," and films of the military parades, some of which were shown across the country (*O Paiz*, July 13, 1920, and September 10, 1922). Generally, films commissioned for the fair aimed to show the "history, geography, nature and civilization of Brazil, its landscapes, customs and types, dress and dwellings, key aspects of rural and urban life, such as beauty, culture, and progress" (Commissão Organisadora, July 1922, no. 1, 27). However, films made for or about the fair that survive today do offer glimpses of anonymous visitors to the site, and of people at work on the products showcased on screen. Luciana Martins demonstrates how the film *No paiz das Amazonas*, by Silvino Santos, a Portuguese immigrant living in Manaus, uses closeups and continuity editing to highlight the dynamics of people laboring and producing the featured goods (2013, 27–28). While in Rio to exhibit his film at the fair Santos filmed life in the city, footage from which was remounted and made into two shorts by Roberto Kahané and Domingos Demasi in 1970, *Fragmentos da terra encantada* and *1922: A Exposição da Independência*. The first of these, *Fragmentos*, takes us on a tour of downtown, featuring some of the areas that underwent reform during the Passos mayorship, as well as the older middle-class suburb of Botafogo and the emerging neighborhood of Copacabana. In this film the camera captures passersby, pedestrians, and travelers of different classes and races moving about the city. The short *1922* also produces this mobile visuality. As Martins has observed, in the film even when the camera is static it is capturing people moving all around the exhibition site enjoying the entertainment on offer (2013, 33). The fluid movement through the city was facilitated by the increasing availability of electricity and the expansion of the tram system that created new standards and expectations for circulating in urban space (Mascarenhas 2012).

Film footage that captures images of the public at close to medium range within the exhibition grounds shows overwhelmingly white and very well-dressed visitors (see stills in Noronha 1987). In theater performances commemorating the centenary the police were obliged to request that women in the balconies remove their elaborate hats during performances so as not to obscure the view for other patrons (*Correio da Manhã*, September 1, 1922, 5). White women were a significant presence within the fairgrounds, indicating that the event was considered an acceptable space for them to circulate, perhaps because the entrance fee was prohibitive for the city's poor. The dominant presence of white visitors to the fair makes a scene from Santos's *1922* somewhat unusual. In it a black boy appears from inside a large ceramic pot. Other pots are lined up in the background, apparently part of a display of national products. How to explain the presence of this boy in a space that organizers sought to purge of blackness except for narratives of pastness, or moments of culturalist reification? Did they ask him to pose in the display in this way in order to emphasize the impressive size of the pots? Martins reads this moment as a knowing allusion by Santos to the invisibility of the black population in the spectacle of the modern city (2013, 33–34). Regardless of any intention Santos may have had in filming and including the scene, the effect is to surprise the onlooker. This element of surprise comes from beholding this usually disavowed black body among and within the desirable products of the exhibition space. The boy becomes part of the display, consumable by the gaze of curious visitors just like the products on show. However, since official exposition discourse evoked the black population in the context of a slaving past that the country was in the process of eliminating, his presence here suggests a primitivism that Brazil's progress is overcoming.

In "exhibiting alterity" (Andermann 2007, 61) in this way, the display temporally distances blackness from the nation's modernizing present and future.[10] The visual arrangement that juxtaposes the black body signified as belonging to the colonial era to the mass-produced pots of an emergent capitalism constructs otherness and "denies coevalness" (Fabian 1983). It is also a kind of image-narrative that synthesizes the ideology and trajectory of modernization as whitening. The display frames the black body using what Jens Andermann describes in the context of indigenous peoples and the 1882 Brazilian Anthropological Exhibition as a politics of concealment, or "a disappearing act of museum magic" (2007, 73). Blackness was generally absent from the space of the fair except in the contexts previously mentioned, and on this rare occasion where it appears integrated into a display the body is concealed within the product on show. Johannes Fabian observes that museum displays imagine objects within a temporality of disappearance rather than emergence. The object, thus displayed, has a pastness that contrasts with the present time of the observer and that also implies oppositions between subject and object, and civilized and uncivilized (1991, 197). However, although the pot is so large that it can entirely conceal the boy, his performance for the camera is not one of disappearing but of emerging. The display inscribes and frames the black body as a disappearing act, but the camera captures the boy performing a reappearance. Andermann argues that photography of the Brazilian Anthropological Exhibition created new visual objects by revealing the invisible process of naturalization at work in the displays. In other words, images of the exhibitions add another level of framing and objectification to the display that calls attention to the tensions and contradictions involved in the making of objects. In exposing this process photographs exact a kind of revenge of the object (2007, 81). This is precisely what is happening in this scene from Santos's film in which the metonymic black population that the whitening project is supposedly eliminating suddenly reappears and smilingly reasserts itself. In a way, this sequence is a counterpoint to the advertisement that opens this chapter. Instead of the black boy emerging from the bath bleached white for the centennial, in this film the boy emerging from the pot represents a resurgent blackness that will not be so easy to eradicate.

THE ARCHITECTURE OF "THE LUSITANIAN RACE"

The mini-city constructed to host the pavilions of the world fair offers us a glimpse of the ideal city envisaged by Rio's elites. The exposition city also represents a highly significant moment in the history of the architectural profession in Brazil. The early 1920s marked a concerted attempt by the nation's architects to have their work officially recognized and valorized (Levy 2007, 1; Atique 2010, 4). The year preceding the centennial saw the creation of two professional organizations, the Instituto Brasileiro de Arquitetos and the Sociedade Central de Arquitetos (Levy 2007, 4).[11] The magazine *Arquitetura no Brasil* was also established in 1921, and functioned as the mouthpiece of these two associations and as part of the campaign for the acknowledgment of the profession. In its pages Rio's architecture was roundly condemned as having "traditional deformities that disfigure our urbanization projects," echoing the negative appraisal of colonial architecture during the Passos era. However, the magazine also directed its displeasure at the latter reforms, which it described as lacking in proportion, high-quality construction, and artistic qualities (6, 3, 2). It behooved the city's architects—in the face of what the magazine dubbed the "public calamity" that was Rio's urbanization—to come up with a homogenous vision for the city (3, 4). Architects seized their chance to play a civic role in filling the new spaces of the city with monumental buildings onto which the dreams of the country's future could be projected.

No one was more vigorous in championing this vision and the cause of Brazilian architects than the medical doctor and artistic patron José Marianno Filho. Marianno Filho agitated strongly for the kind of city he wished to see in the highest circles of influence in which he circulated. A concerted campaign and direct appeals to the mayor's office had the desired effect when it announced that the competition for building projects for the fair would require all projects to be designed and submitted by qualified architects. This vote of confidence in the profession was a defining moment, and made Mayor Sampaio into a kind of patron of Brazilian architects, who was repeatedly praised in the pages of *Arquitetura no Brasil* (Atique 2010, 4; Stuckenbruck 1996, 73; Levy 2007, 6). Marianno Filho's vision strongly influenced the style that eventually dominated the exhibition pavilions designed by local architects (Atique 2010, 5). As it turned out, the vision for the modern, cosmopolitan city that Marianno Filho championed ended up drawing heavily on colonial styles. Of the fourteen exposition buildings designed by local architects, six were visibly neocolonial, and another four mixed colonial baroque elements with traces of eclecticism (Kessel 2002, 102). Ironically, municipal authorities had razed to the ground some of the city's oldest surviving colonial buildings with their finely wrought Plateresque and Manueline details in order to construct new ones inspired by colonial architecture.

The anachronistic architectural imaginary of the fair stood in stark contrast to the wholesale rejection of colonial urban aesthetics that had characterized the Passos reforms. During the Bota-Abaixo elites bemoaned the backwardness resulting from colonialism, and berated the ugliness and insalubriousness of colonial urban design. In 1922, for those involved in designing the ideal capital city of the future, however, it was necessary to look to the past. Curtis notes in his article on the fair for *Art and Architecture* that, "as intended, the Exposition awakened national interest and the talk and enthusiasm was [*sic*] toward things national—to find something that would give a national stamp to the buildings. The Centenary dating back to colonial times, it was natural that 'Portuguese colonial' would appear in the Exposition architecture. Old drawings, engravings, and pictures were diligently sought and studied" (1923, 1999). Indeed, Curtis described the Palace of Industries, a remodeled complex of colonial buildings, as "a semi-museum of [the] neo-colonial" (1923, 100).[12]

Why were so many of the buildings intended to showcase the modernity and cosmopolitanism of Rio neocolonial in style? Why did Rio seem to be embracing its Portuguese legacy at precisely the time when progressive cultural sectors in other parts of the country were rejecting it and embracing Modernism? Andermann notes that such "modern archaic" style was deployed by Latin American exhibitors at world's fairs as a way of reconciling exotic perceptions of their countries within a modern architectural idiom (2007, 338, 357). The architecture of the Centenary Exhibition, intended as a large-scale international event, exemplified this tendency to produce the archaic while asserting its modernity. In fact,

Fernando Atique points out that the recuperation of colonial design reflected a cosmopolitan trend in evidence across the continent (2010, 6). From Marianno Filho's perspective, the neocolonial represented a way of recovering the form and aesthetic sensibility of colonial Brazil, but for a modern age and with the benefit of technological advances in construction and civil engineering. Shortly after the fair he dispatched a group of newly qualified architects (Lúcio Costa among them) to visit the colonial cities of Minas Gerais to document and later distribute typical aspects of "Brazilian style." Proponents of the style rejected the term *neocolonial*, preferring instead "traditional Brazilian architecture" (Atique 2010, 14, 6). This was not surprising considering that *colonial* generally invoked slavery in social thought at the time. The insistence on the Brazilianness of colonial architecture also represents a creative recasting of the power balance in the metropolis-colony relationship. The presence of the baroque suggests a Brazilianizing of colonial style; in other words, a cultural relationship that involved creative and specifically local reinvention, rather than simply borrowing or imitation. Rather than functioning simply as a "semi-museum of [the] neocolonial," therefore, the design, building, and ultimately the spectacle of structures like the Palace of Industries represented a dynamic process of reimagining the nation. The architecture of the fair reinforced the organizing committee's official message that Brazil had inherited the racial and cultural superiority of the former mother country, and that its progress since independence made it Portugal's equal in a twentieth-century community of nations. According to Marianno Filho, the country's adoption of foreign styles over the nineteenth century had subdued the full expression of the "Brazilian race." He called for a recuperation of the forms and sensibilities of the colony, but in modern times (Atique 2010, 6).

This message was explicitly transmitted in the commemorative publications of the fair's organizing committee. The prime minister of Portugal honored the event and the country with a visit on the occasion of the centenary, which generated a discourse that privileged the "Lusitanian race"—the "race of heroes, artists and intellectuals"—as the bedrock of Brazil. This was clearly a counterdiscourse to contemporary theories of Latin degeneracy that predicted that Brazil would never achieve the highest levels of development because its history began with colonization by the inferior Portuguese (Skidmore 1993, 62–63). The visit of the Portuguese leader, dubbed the "Ambassador of Our Race," was proof that "once the relationship of political subordination had ended," it had been replaced by a fraternal friendship based on "one shared race," moral values and language (Comissão Organizadora, October 1922, no. 6–7). This discourse recasts the country's colonial racial legacy, reducing its population of color to mere traces and to spectacle. Vestiges of the indigenous were represented, for example, in the Romantic Indianism of the opera *O Guarany*, performed for the occasion of the centenary at the Teatro Municipal and broadcast around the city. Visitors to the fair also confronted immobile Tapuia, Guarani, and Tupi figures with bows and arrows interspersed with national fruit and flora in sculptural friezes on the enormous main entrance gate (Sant'Ana 2008, 76).[13] Their contemporary counterparts, the semiassimilated groups portrayed in the display by the Indian Protection Service, only had a place in the nation imagined by the fair as evidence of racial progress; that is, in a spectacle of their own destruction.

In fact, what was curious about the world fair was that it produced a space of neocolonial dominion that disavowed the real, contemporary presence of the dominated. "Indians" gave the nation their lives, blacks their labor. The black body is no longer needed for labor, so at the fair it is signified in different ways. The sixty *sambistas* performing in the Festival Pavilion become "a spectacle of the other"—part of a "racialized regime of representation" that taps into global stereotypes about happy natives who sing and dance to entertain white folks (Hall 1997, 245). This is an incipient moment in the fashioning of a symbolic universe of representations of black and popular identity in Brazil associated with carnivalesque exuberance, dance, and festivity. In the 1930s this ensemble of racial meanings would acquire full force in tandem with the consolidation of the ideology of racial democracy. In the context of the Centennial World Fair these black bodies were visually read as part of a disappearing breed, but as a resource for future, more sophisticated expressions of national culture. Like the "Indians," they would be sacrificed in the pursuit of modernity, but leave traces to be reified in imagining the nation. This is why the list of exhibits of musical instruments in the serial publication of the organizing commission makes no mention of instruments of Afro-Brazilian origin. The catalogue plays a role in legitimizing certain forms of culture and producing knowledge about the nation that its elites envisioned. When official speeches and publications acknowledged blackness at all they consigned it to the past as a folklorized and historical blackness. In an article titled "Our Folklore" above a photo showing the destruction of Castelo, Afro-descendant cultural heritage appears as part of Brazil's triad of races. Quoting Olavo Bilac's foundational poem, the anonymous author reiterates that a truly Brazilian folkloric expression was *mestiça,* the "blossoming love of three sad races" (Flôr amorosa de três raças tristes). The writer hastens to add, however, that in the future Brazil's definitive racial type would be dominated by the appearance and intelligence of the white man. The mestiço, he adds, is evolving that way due to laws of adaptation and natural selection, and the country's population should one day represent the ideal human type, "concentrating in its blood the tenacity of the yellow race, the emotion of the black race, and the intelligence of the white race" (Comissão Organizadora, August 1922, no. 2, 28–30; July 1922, no. 1, 14). Elsewhere in the publication, the point is made even more forcefully that *mestiçagem* should not be a desirable end goal but a stop on the way to a better, whiter future. In a commentary on Brazil's demography the author assures readers that although Brazil had not received as many immigrants as the United States or Argentina, they should trust in the future when blackness would be "diluted by the great fusion," and Brazil would become a white country. He categorically dismisses the "absurd" idea of some sociologists that the mestiço represents the best of all races (Comissão Organizadora, July 1922, no. 1, 20–21).

"WHITE AND DAZZLING"

In a short history of the city published in a lavishly illustrated book to accompany the fair, blackness is similarly consigned to the past, part of an unhappy chapter that progress and modernity have transcended. According to the author the city richly deserves the moniker of the "marvelous city" that amazed visitors had been conferring upon it. The article also reproduces an homage by poet Murillo Araujo that imagines centennial Rio as the "golden city." For the poet the promise of urbanization is a "dazzlingly white" capital. An enduring dreamscape of marble has replaced the leaden city of the past. The latter is symbolized by blackness and disease, both inextricably linked in the image of Death and Pestilence dancing duets as "black as the night." The place that was once dominated by mournful slave quarters heralding death is transformed into "radiant . . . white columns / porticos of gold and glory . . . luminously white architraves" (*Livro de ouro* 1923, 376-H). According to issue number 2 of the organizing committee's commemorative serial publication, one of Brazil's key achievements was the "extinction of racial prejudice" (Comissão Organizadora, August 1922, 12). This poem demonstrates that what had been extinguished was blackness itself—symbolically, at least. As the author who complained about sociologists' fixation with mestiçagem made clear, the centennial year provided a moment for the state, municipal authorities, and Rio elites to project into the future the city, and the Brazil of their dreams. They made use of this large, international spectacle to attempt to reinvent the capital's symbolic patrimony and that of the nation (Jaguaribe 2011, 329).

In his essay on the image that Argentina presented to the world at the 1889 Paris Universal Exposition, Álvaro Fernández Bravo asks: "What consequences, surviving effects, and remainders of this image are present in the cultural patrimony?" It is true that it is not the monumental centennial effort that dominates the year 1922 in Brazil's cultural memory but the Week of Modern Art in São Paulo. It was there that an intellectual elite imagined a different expression of modernity that appropriated a very present and pervasive Afro-descendant culture. In the decade following the Week of Modern Art it was modernist, not neocolonial architecture, that prevailed among urbanizers (Kessel cited in Motta 1992, 53). As a discourse of deracination it was mestiçagem, not whitening, that disavowed the black population and dominated the myths of national identity in the decades to come. Additionally, the exposition space did not enjoy its ideal city status for very long after the event was over. Publications like the *Revista da Semana* that had previously praised Sampaio's initiative now expressed their disappointment in its lack of a holistic vision, with the haphazard placement of buildings obstructing the construction of roads in the new area opened up by the destruction of Castelo (Levy 2007, 9–10). As Sant'Ana notes, in the last months that the fair remained open the spectacle was already decaying and falling into oblivion (2008, 35).

Pressure to destroy Castelo based on real estate speculation had relied on the spike in the value of land surrounding the new Avenida Central constructed during the Bota-Abaixo reforms (Abreu 1986, 76). However, Sampaio's much-touted sale of lots on the landfill to replenish the city's coffers did not materialize. Even in 1930 two auctions organized by the city for thirty-nine lots on very favorable terms in "a delightful location" that was "soon to be one of the most beautiful parts of the city" failed to produce any buyers (*Jornal do Commercio*, March 10–11, 1930, 16). The city conceded half a dozen lots to former property owners on Castelo, no doubt prompted by complaints registered by the likes of businessman Antônio Seabra. Seabra had agreed to receive a particular lot in the new area in compensation for land he had given up to the city for the reform, but saw his promised compensation advertised for auction in 1930 (*Jornal do Commercio*, March 20, 1930, 13). The city managed to auction off three lots, but the vast majority of the land remained unsold (*Diario da Noite*, July 10, 1930). In 1930 officials even offered the use of the land to produce vendors required to vacate the Municipal Market. However, the vendors protested that the space was totally inadequate—lacking in shade, running water, and other necessary amenities (*A Noite*, May 17, 1932; *Diario da Noite*, May 29, 1930; July 28, 1930; August 1, 1930; *Jornal do Brasil*, March 13, 1930; *A Noite*, December 30, 1930). From the end of the world fair until the mid-1930s the newly baptized Castelo Esplanade became an ad hoc site for individual tragedy in the form of two suicides, and for large-scale events such as a mass to commemorate the founding of the city and a historic rally in support of Getúlio Vargas's campaign for the presidency (*O Jornal*, January 3 and January 1, 1930). In this period various permanent uses were suggested for the space, including as a site for the headquarters of the different Brazilian states, and for the University Students Association (Casa do Estudante do Brasil); land concessions to build foreign embassies; and heavily subsidized sale for the construction of a private theater (*A Noite*, August 24, 1931; *Diario da Noite*, July 4, 1930; August 1, 1930; May 23, 1930). Meanwhile, the city's most disadvantaged inhabitants were already reclaiming this new area only three years after the fair ended. In 1926, at a Rotary Club meeting focused on generating ideas for the remodeling of the capital, the influential doctor and civic leader João Augusto de Mattos informed the mayor that its members were "declaring war on the favelas" (*O Jornal*, November 27, 1926). He had already complained bitterly about the spread of favelas across the city, arguing that it was necessary "to erect a protective barrier against the overwhelming invasion of the beautiful mountains of Rio de Janeiro by the scourge of 'favelas'—an aesthetic leprosy, that emerged there on the hillside between the Central railway road and the Port Avenue and has been spreading everywhere, filling the newest neighborhoods where nature is most prodigiously beautiful with dirt and poverty: the hillsides of Leme, Copacabana, and Ipanema . . . and even the new lots near the site of the Centenary Fair!" (speech at the Rotary Club, November 12, 1926; quoted in Stuckenbruck 1996, 86).

This rapid reterritorializing of part of the exhibition area suggests that city officials faced quite a challenge in their attempts to invisibilize blackness in urban space. Republican elites overwhelmingly retained their faith in the whitening ideal as the country celebrated its centenary of independence, despite concerns about regression, and even as the viability of whitening became questionable and a goal that seemed ever more difficult to realize demographically. Urbanization was an important element of the racial project to bleach the capital. Blackness unsettled the vision of the city that the nation builders imagined and so they sought its removal from the showpiece city being produced by the reforms. At the fair they constructed a fantasy of cosmopolitanism and progress that represented the majority of the country's population as disappearing. In this simulacrum space they attempted to imagine into existence their ideal city of the future.

Despite the ephemerality of aspects of the fair, the way that nation was imagined in the monumental Centennial Exposition of 1922 continues to reverberate in society and space in urban Brazil. The black population still lives with the consequences of a celebration of a common Brazilian ethnicity that became the national ideology par excellence. One of the many effects of this has been the continued disruption and destruction of the lives of people of color without enough attention paid to the raced dimension of these abuses. The epilogue that follows this chapter will reflect on a recent example of this. The ruination of Morro do Castelo in the 1920s and of communities like Vila Autódromo today in the name of modernization and mega-events points to urbanization as an enduring tool for maintaining racial hierarchies in the city. Large-scale urbanization ventures have been central to concepts of nation building. They connect twenty-first-century development with an urbanization history that is inseparable from the laying to waste of racialized subjects. Such spatial histories repeat themselves and come to constitute a racialized geographic present. We must unpack these histories in order to understand what George Lipsitz calls "the full force and pernicious power of the white spatial imaginary" (2011, 20). Today, these peoples and places continue to suffer violence and loss in the name of a national project that is being refashioned in the context of neoliberal flows of capital and culture. The spectacle of the mega-event has drawn to a close, but the fallout of early twentieth-and twenty-first-century urbanization is plain to see in the ruination of the lives of black and blackened city dwellers today.

EPILOGUE

MEGA-EVENTS, RUINATION, AND THE POLITICS OF STAYING PUT

No way did we ever want to leave. . . . They told us to go, but people didn't want to. We residents left little by little as they demolished the hill. When they started using the water bombs things got really bad. They took water from the sea to make enormous bombs. . . . We only left the hill the day before the area where we lived was destroyed.

—**Florinda Alói and Francisco Moreno, former residents of Castelo (Nonato and Santos 2000, 234)**

None of us wanted to leave there. The mayor's office used guerrilla tactics to force us out, making access to the neighborhood difficult, imposing a series of obstructions. Life became very difficult, they were suffocating us.

—**Former resident of Vila Autódromo (*O Globo*, May 14, 2015)**

THE STATE-SANCTIONED RUINATION of the Vila Autódromo community in preparation for the 2016 Olympic Games hosted in Rio de Janeiro allows us to consider once again how twentieth- and now twenty-first-century urbanization has functioned as one of the most important tools in creating and maintaining racialized and spatialized hierarchies of power in the city, while articulating the modernizing desires of municipal and federal governments. The city conducted its first radical social engineering experiment that aimed to remove undesirable social groups from downtown in 1903–1906. A postabolition whitening ideology underpinned these official attempts to produce space and eliminate the black population from the city center. Such early twentieth-century projects set a standard for urban policy then and since. Like other low-income settlements in Rio and Brazil's other big cities, Vila Autódromo is a racialized space. Overall, Afro-descendants make up the majority of residents of Brazil's informal communities (IPEA 2011). It is not difficult to discern a racialized subtext at work in the arguments that city officials employed to discredit residents in their attempts to displace them from their neighborhood.

One such argument emphasized that security at the Olympic Village being constructed next door would be compromised unless the community was removed. This despite the fact that the community had very low levels of crime and no established drugs trade. Another argument portrayed residents as bad stewards of the land and polluters of the lake that bordered it. In fact, residents refuted this claim by pointing to the sewage treatment system that they themselves organized and installed without help from the city (Associação de Moradores e Pescadores da Vila Autódromo 2012, 7). Yet another portrayed those who refused to leave as land speculators, trying to extract the highest compensation from the city, denying them any right to participate to their advantage in the real estate market. These arguments portrayed Vila Autódromo's residents as dangerous, irresponsible, and not eligible for inclusion in the material benefits and bonanzas of mega-event development. In other words, they presented an obstacle to modernization, and indeed as black or blackened subjects, were seen as fundamentally incompatible with it.[1] As discussed in chapter 1, in Brazil race injustice occurs because blackness and whiteness indicate distinct kinds of modern subjects. The bodies and the spaces inhabited by people of color are signifiers of illegality, while white bodies and spaces of whiteness signify the notions of universal equality and freedom (Silva 2001, 427). In the case of Vila Autódromo, the placing of such neighborhoods on the other side of legality explains why the municipality could ignore legal titles that some residents held to the land and justify their removal.

As with Castelo, the dispossession of Vila Autódromo allows us to consider the process of ruination as a violent accrual of colonial aftermaths (Stoler 2013, 2). Ruination connects twenty-first-century development with an urbanization history in which black and less than white subjects are produced as either bounded by space—assigned and reassigned to their "proper" place—or else simply ungeographic—incapable of making, transforming, and developing profound affective ties to space (see McKittrick 2006, x–xi). The discourse and publicity material of municipal authorities repeatedly articulated Vila Autódromo as uninhabitable and negated the labor of residents who developed the site and made it home.[2] Those who laid waste to the neighborhood were a public-private collaboration consisting of the municipality in partnership with large construction firms. Although some of the residents of Vila Autódromo were legal occupants of the land, under the guise of Olympic preparation municipal agents used intimidation and fear to remove them and attempt to reclaim the area. As frequently occurs with mega-event development, pressure to deliver in time for the Olympics and very vocal and widely covered criticism by the Olympic committee led to aggressive and illegal territorializing on the part of the municipality in the service of capital (Gaffney 2010). Ultimately, such projects are both a continuity and a reformulation of urban governance that seeks to forcefully manage people's bodies and lives according to naturalized racial hierarchies.

A little over a year before the Olympics began, residents had abandoned 590 out of a total of 760 homes in Vila Autódromo. Those who remained faced "guerrilla tactics" to remove them, such as cuts to water and electricity services that made for extremely difficult living conditions. Additionally, as individual property owners or occupants left, the city immediately demolished their homes and business places, meaning that those left behind were surrounded by rubble. As the built environment and people's lives were reduced to debris, however, the residents holding out in Vila Autódromo became more than mere witnesses to what seemed like the inevitable topocide (Porteous 1989, 230) of their community. Even as the city sought to annihilate the material objects, memories, spatial practices, and geographical stories involved in place making, people also invented varied forms of refusal when confronted with the threat of ruination.[3]

Amid the decomposition of their surroundings, the family in the photograph reproduced here has fashioned a place of relaxation and fun with their young child during a hot Rio summer (fig. E.1). The intimate, domestic time-space of leisure they have created around the pool disturbs the unrelenting march of the destruction of the neighborhood. It somehow suspends or holds at bay the spatial and temporal encroachment of the demolition. This snapshot of family life also has an affective and critical charge that communicates what is at stake for communities of color that lie in the path of such development projects, as well as their resourcefulness in the face of their destruction. Their refusal to leave tells yet another story of the struggle of Afro-descendants to defend their claims to territory and their right to home. While residents also mobilized collectively in defense of their community through various forms of public protest, this photograph reminds us of the myriad private fashionings of place that presented

Figure E.1. Vila Autódromo family, January 2015. Courtesy of Catalytic Communities—*Rio On Watch*.

obstacles to the state's technologies of destruction. The image also contributes to the disputed meanings of the value of the space of Vila Autódromo: land that the developers and the city devalued as unsanitary and degraded, but that had speculative value on the real estate market and in the context of mega-event planning, becomes revalued in this image as a space of social reproduction for poor families of color. This space of refusal represents a black microgeography that challenged the municipality's proposed landscape of development. These "defiant geographies" are forms of spatial production that counter attempts to violently eradicate a black presence from the city. They also trouble the city's and the nation's narratives of modernization based on whitening. These forms of space and place making may be more enduring physical occupations, or may be ephemeral and contingent places and practices, but they demonstrate a resilient capacity for visibilizing Afro-descendant bodies in disputed spaces.

TELLING GEOGRAPHICAL STORIES

> This is a struggle born out of love. Love of my history, love of the land, love of my rights.
>
> —Maria da Penha Macena, Vila Autódromo resident[4]

In 2012 residents published their own alternative to the city's development plan, the Plano Popular da Vila Autódromo. This document resulted from a collaboration between the Residents' Association, members of the community, and a team of planners from two Rio universities. The stories that residents tell about their community in this document reiterate themes of collective mobilization, territorial conquest, and resistance. They are counternarratives of social lives that are frequently displaced and rendered ungeographic. They talk back to practices and discourses that treat and represent them as unable to make and transform space. In carving out fora in which to tell their stories, residents asserted their presence as agents of history and producers of geographical knowledge. That such knowledge is produced in the context of struggle points to a history of black subject making in Brazil.

The potted history of the community in the Plano Popular is titled "Vila Autódromo: Uma história de luta" (Vila Autódromo: a history of struggle), and the text represents the plan as a continuation of the fight to remain. The community began as a former fishermen's village, located alongside the Jacarepaguá lagoon in the west zone of Rio. Residents' oral histories dated the growth of the community to the 1960s and the occupation of the land by local fishermen. However, the Plano Popular's history of the neighborhood begins tactically in the 1980s, with the official relocation of families there by the city. In 1975, the construction of the Autódromo de Jacarepaguá racetrack commenced directly adjacent to the small neighborhood. As construction and development accelerated in Jacarepaguá in the 1980s, many low-income workers sought residence closer to the jobs they generated and settled in the area. The Association of Residents and Fishermen of Vila Autódromo (AMPVA) was founded in 1987 to represent the interests of local residents. In the association's plan the residents narrate how they managed to establish roads and basic infrastructure such as electricity, water, telephone services, and septic tanks without government support (Associação de Moradores e Pescadores da Vila Autódromo 2012).

Although it began as a peri-urban neighborhood, by the runup to the Olympics Vila Autódromo was part of the rapidly expanding western part of the city.

As the city grew, the community became surrounded by luxury condominiums in the upper- and middle-class neighborhood of Barra da Tijuca. As a result, the growth of Vila Autódromo over time was directly tied to real estate development in the Barra da Tijuca area (Magalhães 2014). Barra was developed in the 1970s, emerging out of the demand for a suburban lifestyle and coastal properties based in enclaves of gated condominiums and luxury high-rises and houses. Barra expanded from a population of forty-five thousand in 1980 to a quarter million by the early 2000s as people sought out its social exclusivity (Herzog 2013, 119). The location of Vila Autódromo near Barra was an important source of economic opportunity for residents, providing direct access to construction and service sector jobs in local commercial and residential developments.

In 1997 a portion of the community of Vila Autódromo (140 families) received legal title from the state government of Rio de Janeiro. The following year, households living on the lagoon's edge received a ninety-nine-year legal concession of land use. However, the course of Vila Autódromo's history shifted with the announcement in 2009 that the adjacent racetrack would be one of the central development sites for the 2016 Olympic Games. While Vila Autódromo had survived previous eviction threats dating back to 1992, and more recently in 2007 in the context of preparations for the Pan-American Games, the potential scale of displacement for the Olympics escalated the treat of evictions within the community. In October 2009, Mayor Eduardo Paes announced that at least 3,500 families in the city would be relocated as part of the urban and environmental legacy of the Olympic Games. This formed part of a goal of reducing areas occupied by favelas in Rio de Janeiro by 3.5 percent through the removal of at least 119 favelas (Bastos and Schmidt 2010). The campaign targeted Vila Autódromo as one of the communities to be removed, which led to immediate organization and resistance to the municipal government's plans from local residents.

POLITICAL MOBILIZATION IN VILA AUTÓDROMO

The city's and the developers' attempts to destroy Vila Autódromo resulted in the splintering of the community, with the majority of the residents abandoning or pressured into abandoning their homes. Despite this gradual, unrelenting process of annihilation new forms of politics were activated in the refusal of this public-private project of ruination. The community had a history of resistance, as they made clear in the Plano Popular. The residents' association, AMPVA, had played a central role over the past twenty years in community organization and activism to contest removal. In this latest struggle they were more vocal and more visible, certainly due in part to the internet and social media, than at any time in their history. Along with the leadership of AMPVA, residents maintained a lively public debate about the community, and to sympathizers across the city and beyond they came to symbolize popular resistance to neoliberal urbanization projects. When developers demolished the building serving as the headquarters of the organization, remaining residents painted "Residents' Association of Vila Autódromo" on their houses to demonstrate that the association was the community, not the building, and that the struggle would continue. The residents' repertoire of narratives, articulated not just in the Plano Popular but in interviews, placards, banners, and shouted opinions expressed during protests, resisted Brazil's modernization discourse of development for the sake of the few. They substituted that discourse with the notion that modernization should be democratic and collaborative, respecting the right to the city of all social groups, and prioritizing this right over the courting of transnational investment capital. As their community was being reduced to rubble around them, those who did not wish to leave continued to very publicly imagine and articulate a future for Vila Autódromo that involved its reurbanization and coexistence with the Olympic Village and luxury condominiums intended to replace it.[5]

The right to stay was also articulated as resistance to an erasure of their local histories, as in a newspaper editorial penned by the president of the residents' association: "The community has been here for nearly 40 years, people have a life and a history here. We also have the right to live in this city" (Freitas 2012). The association emphasized collective mobilization as a counter to the city's refusal to negotiate with residents collectively. Leaders used residents' meetings to keep the community up to date on developments within City Hall, in order for all neighbors to be well informed about relocation offers. When the mayor overrode the negotiation process with a decree on March 19, 2015, announcing the expropriation of houses for the purpose of public works, residents took to the streets, stopping traffic at a nearby avenue and temporarily suspending construction work. In addition to public protests, residents collaborated with the Rio de Janeiro Committee against the World Cup and the Olympics to use the latter's established internet presence to denounce their deterritorialization. Collaboration with nonprofits and activist organizations who supported their right to stay helped them to maintain visibility for their campaign, and the city's public defender's office leveled pointed criticisms at the mayor's office for illegal attempts to evict residents. Mayor Eduardo Paes described this coalition of

Figure E.2 "We Want the Popular Urbanization Plan!" 2014. Courtesy of Sara McTarnaghan.

support as a "gang" that compelled the city to offer market value compensation sums to some holdouts in the community (Berta 2015).

In a creative partnership with architects and planners from local universities Vila Autódromo developed alternative visions and proposals for integrated in situ urban development through the creation of the Plano Popular. The plan demonstrated that urbanization of the site would cost less than 20 percent of the anticipated costs for removal and relocation. It affirmed the right of Vila Autódromo residents to stay in place and the right to urban, economic, social, and cultural development associated with the urbanization of their neighborhood (Plano Popular 2012, 5). The plan's objective was to propose bottom-up alternative solutions that could be developed alongside the Olympic Park construction (Silvestre and Gusmão de Oliveira 2012, 208). The residents mobilized rights-based discourse from the 2001 city statute to argue against their removal in the plan: "We are not a threat to the environment, nor the landscape, nor anyone's security. We are only a threat to those who do not recognize the social

Figure 5.3 Annotated maps at the Residents' Association, 2014. Courtesy of Sara McTarnaghan.

function of property and the social function of the city. We threaten those who wish to violate our constitutional right to housing. We are only a threat to those who wish to speculate with the land and to the politicians who serve their interests" (Silvestre and Gusmão de Oliveira 2012, 10).

The process of producing the plan involved participatory research methods in a collaboration between the residents and planning scholars at the Universidade Federal do Rio de Janeiro and the Universidade Federal Fluminense. First, a community-needs assessment was conducted through neighborhood mapping and public meetings. Based on this initial process, residents created proposals for a wide range of projects in housing, sanitation, environment, transportation, and basic services. The team working on the plan presented a preliminary draft on December 18, 2011, to a full assembly of local residents. Five additional community assemblies were held to refine the proposal and gain community consensus (Associação de Moradores e Pescadores da Vila Autódromo 2012). The maps tacked to the walls of the residents' association were therefore the materialization of the community's place making and life making, its memories and its imagined futures. They are forms of geographical knowledge based on lived experience, emotional ties, and cross-society collaborations that conflict radically with geographies of "accumulation by dispossession" (Harvey 2004).

BLACK TERROR AS THE PRICE OF MODERNITY

> The truth is that the city of Rio de Janeiro is trying to terrorize us psychologically. That terror is nothing new, in fact it's ancient. It just happens to be intensifying at the moment.
>
> —**Pedro Berto, Vila Autódromo resident (quoted in Gonzalez 2015)**

Municipal authorities ignored the plan and continued exerting pressure on residents to leave with relocation offers and intimidation. On June 3, 2015, two homes were identified for demolition under the terms of the mayor's March decree authorizing forcible relocation. The inhabitants of the two dwellings had refused to accept the compensation proposed by the municipality, and negotiations conducted by a court official failed to convince them to abandon their homes. The official called for shock troops of the Municipal Guard to remove them and their neighbors who had formed a human chain around the properties in question. According to residents, faced with their refusal to withdraw, the troops began beating them with batons and using pepper spray. In response, residents threw rubble from the demolitions and were eventually subdued with rubber bullets and percussion grenades (Watts 2015).

Residents posted images with their faces bruised and bloodied on social media to denounce the violence. The public defender's office criticized the mayor's office for the use of force and residents succeeded in gaining a temporary halt to the evictions. The struggle to save Vila Autódromo from the bulldozers pitted residents against the violence of the city government. This violence was met with determined, fierce resistance on the part of residents. In the end, the city succeeded in destroying the existing neighborhood and decimating the community. However, twenty families managed to remain in Vila Autódromo on the condition that the city destroy their houses and install them in new ones, which were hurriedly, shoddily constructed in time for the opening of the Olympics.

This book has sought to highlight the racialized nature of the struggle over space in Rio de Janeiro, focusing on the country's first mega-event development project. The city's recent international events are part of a continuum that seizes such opportunities to spatially organize racial inequality. In her study of black women's struggle for land in northeastern Brazil, Keisha-Khan Perry comments that out of police violence emerges black people's "agency and political will to survive, their determination to defy individual and collective death" (Perry 2013a, 131). This book has aimed to spotlight this defiance. As in Vila Autódromo authorities were unable to completely destroy Castelo by the time the world fair opened, due in part to the intransigence of property owners and residents. As the former residents of Castelo Florinda Alói and Francisco Moreno mentioned, their family refused to leave their home until the day before demolition began. Cláudia Paixão notes the death of a child due to demolition work in December of 1922, meaning that people continued to live on the hillside months after the opening of the world fair in September (2008, 165). Those compelled to leave temporarily occupied precarious, unsanitary shacks built by the government outside of the downtown area that had no access to water. Former residents eventually resettled without government assistance on other hillsides in or near downtown, defying the intention to eject them from the city center. The interviewees expressed their sadness as they experienced the ruination of their community and its physical toll on residents, not only in the difficult living conditions created by the demolition, but in the injuries and worse caused by explosions and falling construction materials (Nonato and Santos 2000, 198; Paixão 2008, 42, 183, 157).

Living in ruins among noise and debris, under constant pressure from the city, and losing friends and family, according to Pedro Berto, the Vila Autódromo resident quoted in this section's epigraph, placed a huge psychological weight on remaining residents. Yet his family stayed put, in a home damaged by bulldozers that continued to function for as long as possible as a space of worship for the community's *candomblé* practitioners. Pedro Berto's family, in particular his mother, Heloísa Helena Berto, a *mãe de santo,* or spiritual leader, experienced particularly egregious harassment. When they refused to leave, officials enclosed their home within the construction site of the Olympic Park and cut them off from the rest of Vila Autódromo. They were required to show a special pass in order to enter the site and gain access to their own house. Visitors were prohibited and their electricity and water services were suspended. Dona Heloísa became a prominent advocate and spokesperson for the community, suffering death threats, and physical and emotional distress.[6] Her determination to remain and practice her religion, the use of debris to defend a neighbor's house from agents of the municipality, the family discussed earlier creating a moment of fun amid the destruction, all demonstrated an "active and ongoing engagement with ruins" (Rao 2013, 316). They articulated a sense of belonging, as well as political resentments that questioned the technologies of terror of the city government.

The city targeted Vila Autódromo for topocide. They succeeded in radically altering the space and seizing most of the neighborhood's land, but they did not succeed entirely in the killing of place. Vila Autódromo's few remaining residents and their supporters inaugurated an open-air museum on May 18, 2016, that provided a counternarrative to official accounts of modernization and mega-events. The organizers of the Museum of Removals aimed to chronicle evictions and resistance to them by Vila Autódromo, as well as other communities past and present. In their first exhibition they used rubble from demolished buildings to create seven art installations on an open-air site to memorialize the neighborhood. The sculptures were built in collaborative workshops in which residents participated alongside architecture students from a local university. In one of them a kitchen chair and a bicycle lie atop a pile of debris—broken concrete slabs and rocks, and the twisted guts of iron and plumbing. In front of it they tagged a large piece of gaily painted galvanized iron roofing with the words "Residents' Association," a key site from which they had organized their protests (McKay 2016).[7]

The installations included photographs and videos, and sought to honor key places and people in the history of the community. One of the former residents honored in the inaugural display was Dona Heloísa. As she recalled that the residents of the well-off area of Barra never accepted having a candomblé temple so close to their neighborhood, she highlighted both the racialized nature of her displacement and the importance of memory to struggle: "The people of Barra da Tijuca would not stand for the sound of the *atabaque* drums, nor the sight of black people dressed in white unless it was to serve them as nannies or caregivers. The house and temple are gone, but I continue to struggle for the goals of religious and racial equality, I continue to fight for all of that. And the Museum of Removals ensures that people are remembered for the struggles they fought" (Peregrino 2016). Castelo Hill is also gone, but memories of that struggle echo down through the years and are remembered here, pushing back against geographies of dispossession and intimidation.

NOTES

INTRODUCTION

1. Historians Marly Silva da Motta (1992), Thaís Sant'Ana (2008), and Cláudia Quelhas Paixão (2008) have conducted important studies of the exposition and the attendant destruction of Morro do Castelo (Castelo Hill). Motta's work is particularly useful with regard to social thinking on the nation in the 1920s; Sant'Ana's master's thesis provides rich details of the exposition site; and Paixão's master's thesis imagines daily life in Castelo before its destruction.

2. The census of Rio de Janeiro in 1906 and the national census of 1920 did not record race, although they do list the national origins of immigrants.

3. As a point of comparison, only about a third of Rio's favela population was white around the time that Castelo was destroyed (Fischer 2008, 4).

4. "Salada da Semana: Na Capital," *Revista da Semana* 446 (1911): 41.

5. See Leu 2014 on black spaces of cultural expression in early twentieth-century Rio de Janeiro.

6. A significant body of scholarship exists on the Passos reforms; see, for example, Abreu 1986, 1997; Benchimol 1992; Brenna 1985; Meade 1999; Pechman and Fritsch 1985; Rocha and Carvalho 1986; Needell 1987; Sevcenko 1993.

7. Overall, in research on urban Brazil class has tended to overwhelm race in studies of disadvantaged communities (Ramos 2007, 188). For example, of the 668 publications on favelas listed in the bibliographical guide published in 2003 by Valladares and Medeiros, only 9 have race as an explicit focus. Exceptions in terms of thinking about race and the production of space in post-abolition Brazil include Moura (1983); Velloso (1988, 1990); Oliveira (1996); Cunha et al (2007); and Campos (2005). A body of recent scholarship on twenty-first-century racialized space has also emerged from scholars of cultural anthropology; for example, Vargas (2010, 2013); Alves (2012, 2014, 2018); Perry (2013a); and Smith (2016). In a foundational article on race thinking in Brazil in the late nineteenth and early twentieth centuries, Dain Borges observes that the urban reforms of 1903–1906 were "in the broad sense 'racial,'" motivated by the idea that modernization could bring about racial progress (1993, 249).

8. In *Trabalho, lar e botequim* (1986), although not focusing on the reforms, Sidney Chalhoub uses press accounts and police documents to explore racial and ethnic rivalries between poor city dwellers of Rio around this time, particularly conflicts between Afro-descendants and European immigrants.

9. See, for example, Mbembe 2003; Hartman 1997; McKittrick 2006; Iton 2008; and in the Brazilian context Vargas 2010; Alves 2012, 2014; Perry 2013a; Smith 2016.

10. For example, see in *Careta* the articles "Megalomania," August 28, 1920; "O Prefeito e o Povo," January 15, 1921; "Reliquias, ossos, e colchões," January 28, 1922; "Hotel 7 de Setembro," August 5, 1922; and "O Centenário," September 30, 1922.

11. For instance, Robin Sheriff (2001) grounds her ethnography in the particularities of an

informal community in Rio de Janeiro to demonstrate that outside of scholarly and activist circles Brazilians also understand themselves and others in terms of black and white. Her study concludes that while people described themselves using a wide range of terms relating to color in certain social situations, they ultimately identified according to a racial binary that they understood as underpinning the subordination of nonwhites. The more pragmatic and etiquette-driven discourse, using color descriptively or as polite euphemisms, spoke to a "culturally articulated yearning to escape from all that is negatively associated with blackness." Sheriff demonstrates that euphemisms and semantic ambiguity are forms of linguistic agency that ultimately comment on the implicit understanding that "there are only two races" (2001, 31, 58).

12. See Peter Fry, "Why Brazil Is Different," *New York Times Literary Supplement,* December 8, 1995; and Fry, "Race Is Too Hard to Identify in Brazil," *New York Times,* March 29, 2012; also Yvonne Maggie, "Looking to the U.S. Has Been a Mistake," *New York Times,* March 29, 2012. The publication of political scientist Michael Hanchard's book (1998) on black consciousness movements in Brazil ignited intense debate over this issue. Two non-Brazilianists, the French sociologists Pierre Bourdieu and Loïc Wacquant, critiqued Hanchard's book and what they saw as his presumption at reading race in Brazil through a dichotomous black/white lens (1999, 44). This, they argued, imposed an alien, US model on a society where the entire notion of race makes no sense because of Brazilians' well-documented tendency to describe race using a color continuum (45). In turn, Brazilianist historian John D. French issued a detailed critique of what he called their "caricature" of Hanchard's analysis that did not acknowledge the latter's insistence on the plurality of racisms across the diaspora (2000, 109, 113). More recently, in the context of contemporary black women's neighborhood activism, anthropologist Keisha-Khan Perry wonders, "Why are scholars fascinated with the supposed Brazilian plurality of racial identities, when it is not key to how black women in Brazil see themselves?" (2016, 107). Citing the feminist scholar Sônia Beatriz dos Santos, she continues:

> The argument persists that racial identity in Brazil is ambiguous and that there are at least 135 categories of self-identification that have produced a vast color gradient unlike any other nation in the Americas ([Santos 2006,] 34). Santos highlights the absurdity of this ambiguity:
>
> > Brazilian intellectuals declare themselves unable to decipher who is black in Brazil, even though the police, the justice system, public and private employers, the media (especially television), and other social groups and institutions can instantly identify blacks when physically and symbolically attacking them, denying them jobs for which they are qualified, and punishing them more severely than their white counterparts for committing crimes of equal or comparable gravity. ([2006,] 37)

13. The work of social scientist Gilberto Freyre represents an important moment in the valorization of *mestiçagem.* Freyre's best-known text, *Casa-grande e senzala* (published in Portuguese in 1933; first published in English in 1946 as *The Masters and the Slaves*), is a nostalgic excursion into Brazil's slaving past by a descendant of planter families from the northeastern state of Pernambuco (Freyre 1956). Freyre makes the case that Afro-Brazilian social and cultural practices have influenced virtually all aspects of Brazilian society, and that this influence and the *mestiço* cultural heritage it produces should be acknowledged and celebrated. As Needell and others have pointed out, within this founding fiction of racial and sexual dominance and subordination Freyre tends to objectify slave women as passive, sensual, willing, and accessible (Needell

1995, 70). In Freyre's work the predominant feature of master-slave intercourse comes across as creative, rather than coercive. His account of the benefits of racial mixing ultimately proved palatable to those who held the whitening ideal dear. In the decades that followed mestiçagem has proven itself to be an effective national narrative for disavowing blackness in Brazil despite revisionist critiques (Leu 2010, 78).

14. Based on the most recent census of 2010 (IPEA 2011).

15. José de Alencar's *O Guaraní* (1857) and *Iracema* (1865) are two of the best-known examples of this kind of Indianist literature.

16. Alberto notes that censuses from the 1940s onward only occasionally included the category of *indígena* and folded the category of *caboclo* into *pardo* (mulatto), which meant that people of partial indigenous descent became indistinguishable from those of partial African descent. This demonstrates an increasing narrowing of racial descriptions to a black-white spectrum (2011, 11).

17. Respectively, "darkie" (connotations with slavery), "inky black," "dark-skinned," "light-brown," "mulatto," and "freckled-white."

18. In apparent deference to this status, when a family member had Lima Barreto committed to the National Mental Asylum in 1914 on account of delusions relating to his alcoholism, his race was recorded as "white." Five years later, when interned again, this time brought to the asylum by the police with other, anonymous internees, and in a worse physical state than before, he appears in its records as *pardo*, or mulatto (Schwarcz 2017b, 273, 390–91).

19. In the original Portuguese Lima Barreto actually uses the term *pretinho*, the diminutive form of *preto*. "Preto" refers to the actual color black and, as Paulina Alberto observes, was less injurious than "negro," a term that activists in the early twentieth century began to reclaim (2011, 22).

20. As an example of this complexity of this paradigm, Jeffrey Lesser (1999) has explored the concern to represent Arab and Japanese immigrants as white in early twentieth-century Brazil.

21. There is one interview available with two residents of Castelo Hill, a brother and sister of Italian descent, reminiscing about the neighborhood some six decades after its destruction began (see chapter 3).

1. RACE, ETHNICITY, AND URBANIZATION

1. The song was called "Olh'Abacaxi," a samba whose title and repeated refrain were based on the cries of street vendors selling pineapples. Its composer was F. Soriano Robert, a pianist and maestro working in Rio de Janeiro between 1916 and 1923 (Lago 2002, 1–59).

2. "Encontro de um cadaver nas escavações do morro do Castello," *Jornal do Brasil*, June 26, 1921.

3. Keisha-Khan Perry also connects urban development to the national whitening project in Brazil (2013, 43).

4. The actions of the municipality were generally oriented by the demands of the federal government (Silva 2003, 29). National and city affairs were closely interlinked, with federal regulation of most urban services, from sanitation to local police and the courts (Conniff 1981, 61).

5. I am evoking the phrase by anthropologist Raimundo Nina Rodrigues (1977, 1).

6. See Skidmore (1993, 271n35) on the writer Lobato's private despair that "race is everything and . . . we have no race."

7. An article in the magazine *Eu Sei Tudo* describes residents of Castelo as "lacking civic education" and creating a "bestial" confusion in the Avenida Rio Branco when they occupied it for carnival. E. Felix, "O berço da cidade," January 1919.

8. Dávila (2003, 3) observes that Brazilian elites throughout the first half of the twentieth century tended to believe that the nonwhite and the poor were overwhelmingly degenerate.

9. "O Kysto do Rio: Deverá arrasar-se o morro do Castello?: A 20 metros da Avenida Rio Branco! Civilisação versus Barbaria," *Revista da Semana*, December 2, 1916, 14.

10. See Cunha ([1902] 2002) on the development of techniques of criminal identification used in police archives since the late nineteenth century, with a particular focus on 1927–1942. In the context of the 1890 decree ordering the destruction of documents relating to slavery in Brazil, Cunha sees police records as playing an important role in producing people of color in the postabolition nation as dangerous and morally condemnable.

11. Immigration played a central role in government policy from at least 1850, when it became clear that slavery would not exist for much longer (Lesser 1999, 7).

12. "Belleza brasileira: As mais lindas moças do Brasil," *Revista da Semana*, January 15, 1921.

13. "As mais lindas moças do Brasil: Concurso de belleza regional," *Revista da Semana*, June 11, 1921.

14. See Schwarcz (1999, 268) on a combined "hard" and "soft" understanding of eugenics by Bahian physicians in the mid 1920s: one sector of the population could perhaps be cured, but another was beyond help, and extreme measures were needed to allow degenerates to reproduce among themselves and extinguish themselves through sterility and juvenile mortality. She also discusses proposals for sterilization in medical journals, and doctors in Rio de Janeiro arguing for the introduction of sterilization for the "diseased sectors" of society (291, 296).

15. João Rialto was the pseudonym of the humorist Edigar Barbosa de Barros.

16. L. H. Stinson, a physician from Augusta, Georgia, who also visited in 1920, even declared: "The higher class Brazilian is very desirous of colored North Americans settling in Brazil. They look upon the North American negro as being far advanced in civilization and intelligence" (Hellwig 1992, 45). The vision of a Brazil in which "any Negro or mulatto who shows himself fit is without question given the place to which his abilities entitle him," also received widespread publicity through Theodore Roosevelt's article "Brazil and the Negro" in the *Outlook* magazine, February 21, 1914, 409–11.

17. For more on Robert Abbott's visit to Brazil see Seigel (2009, 192–205).

18. With regard to the urban poor in general, according to Fischer, after 1930 families began to build a legal existence by managing to lay claim to some degree of permanence in urban space (2008, 7).

19. According to music historian José Ramos Tinhorão, troubadours of Portuguese descent increasingly left the streets to perform in the drawing rooms of the wealthy after the eighteenth-century gold rush that animated the social life of Brazil's well-off families. Those without access to high society continued the tradition of the street serenade, and early accounts (with derogatory racialized overtones) describe them as wily mulattos pedantically attempting to emulate the refinement of salon music (1976, 10).

20. My discussion of the cordões draws on Leu 2014, 185–86.

21. Lima and Hochman (2000, 323) also point out that another catchphrase of Macunaíma's "Pouca saúde e muita saúva, os males do Brasil são" (Poor health and too many ants, those are the great problems of Brazil) represents a satirical swipe by Mário de Andrade on the sanitation campaigns. The author Lima Barreto, a trenchant critic of the Republican government, also has a

patriotic Republican character's ambitions undone by armies of ants as he attempts to prove the fertility of Brazilian soil on his countryside estate ([1915] 1997).

22. Today the term *caboclo* is generally understood to refer to rural inhabitants of Amazônia. On the diverse meanings and uses of the word *caboclo* in Amazônia see Lima (1999).

23. Pereira's phrase was one of the first sparks to ignite the sanitation campaign (Lima and Hochman 1996, 24). He also described caboclos as "incapacitated, defeated, worn down by hookworm and malaria; ruined and beaten down by Chagas disease; eaten away by syphilis and leprosy; devastated by alcoholism; exhausted by hunger, ignorant" (quoted in Lima and Hochman 2000, 316).

24. Skidmore's research demonstrates that privately Lobato continued to entertain doubts about the potential of the "Brazilian race" (1993, 271n35).

25. "A guitar in such a respectable household!" exclaim neighbors of the extreme patriot Policarpo Quaresma when he begins to take guitar lessons (Barreto [1915] 1997, 10).

26. The phrase "for the English to see" comes from Brazil's on the surface conformity to an 1831 ban on the slave trade to mollify the British, while continuing to import slaves into the country. Caulfield mentions that at least three popular songs of 1920 critiqued the fuss made over the royal visit (2000, 68).

27. Sinhô's brother's nickname was "Caboclo" (Alencar 1981, 19).

28. In the 1920s nearly 840,000 European immigrants arrived in Brazil (Marques 1994, 87). Instituto Brasileiro de Geografia e Estatística (IBGE) immigration to Brazil in 1884–1939: Spain, 581,718; Italy, 1,412,263; Portugal, 1,204,394 (Oliveira 2006, 43).

29. For more on female immigrants working as seamstresses see the Immigration Museum of the State of São Paulo, accessed March 3, 2017, http://museudaimigracao.org.br/conhecendo-o-acervo-vitrine-mulheres-imigrantes; also Pinsky and Pedro (2012). On Italian immigrant women who worked as seamstresses and were anarchist leaders in the struggle for improved rights for women workers in the early twentieth century, see Minardi (2008).

30. Interestingly, this period covers exactly the same time frame that Oliveira (2006, 8, 26) identifies as encompassing eight key waves of immigration to Brazil, with the most intense flow between 1880 and 1920.

31. Jair de Souza Ramos also discusses hopeful African American colonists as "racial undesirables" (1996, 64).

32. See Chalhoub (1986, 99) for a photograph of a basement rented out to a family of six in a *casa de cômodos* in 1910.

33. Sampaio (1924, 45) also asserts in his memoir that 470 buildings were destroyed without a single complaint from their owners about their appropriation. He does not comment on the situation of those who had occupied, rather than owned, the buildings.

34. See historian Carlos Kessel's *A Vitrine e o Espelho* for a detailed account of Sampaio's career that explores his involvement with urban reform in Rio since 1887 (2001). Sampaio's engineering firm benefited from several concessions during the Passos reforms of 1903–1906, no doubt owing at least in part to the fact that his business partner was Paulo de Frontin, the engineer in charge of the construction of the Avenida Central, as well as other projects during the Passos mayorship. Kessel also examines the ideologies and politics of Sampaio's mayorship and his vexed relationship as an appointee of the country's president with a municipal council looking to establish its autonomy from the federal government.

35. Kessel cites Sampaio describing his extensive role in the centenary celebrations: "I was the one who came up with the ideas, who chose the site, who prepared and even created part of that site, who gave instructions for its general contours . . . who decided on the different palaces and pavilions and engaged different, distinguished architects to design them, who resolved the various problems surrounding the creation of roads, gardens, landscaping, water supply, sewage, telegraph, telephone, transport, and lighting" (2001, 74).

36. Sueann Caulfield observes that the police took the opportunity afforded by the king and queen's visit to purge downtown streets of prostitutes and anarchist militants in order not to disturb the image of the city that the government wished to present (2000, 63–67).

37. Maurício Abreu notes that Sampaio's mayorship represents a period in which land value began to figure explicitly in municipal planning and projects (1997, 78).

38. See Lima Barreto's critique of the demolition in "Megalomania," *Careta*, August 28, 1920. Even the general secretary of the Instituto Histórico e Geográfico Brasileiro, charged with preserving the history of the city, supported the demolition for the sake of modernity (Motta 1992, 63).

39. Motta notes that the *Jornal do Brasil* did consistently protest the lack of respect for the country's historical patrimony (1992, 59–63).

40. Other perspectives include those of artists and writers involved in the modernist cultural movement officially launched in São Paulo in 1922. For them the city was a complex reality that produced a fragmented poetics, and they attempted to express the spatial and temporal contradictions and overlaps between tradition and modernity.

41. "O novo símbolo," *Careta*, November 20, 1920; "Os últimos dias do Castello," *Revista da Semana*, June 16, 1921; "Pelo molde da civilização," *Careta*, July 31, 1920.

42. Thousands of people attended the final mass in the Igreja de São Sebastião. According to the *Correio da Manhã*, November 3, 1921, the church was "constantly visited by the population, of all social classes, the expression of a common faith making all the pilgrims equal."

43. See Paixão 2008, 166–73, on interviews with Carlos Soares Pereira (November 13, 1984) and José de Oliveira Reis (October 2, 1985) for the Museu da Imagem e do Som, Projeto Arquivo Vivo. In Reis's *O Rio de Janeiro e seus prefeitos* (1977), residents are completely absent from the text (Paixão 2008, 171).

44. Given the makeup of the navy and army, many of the occupants of the cortiço João do Rio describes would have been Afro-descendant. Since the period of the empire the navy had functioned as a form of penal servitude for Afro-descendants convicted, accused, or suspected of criminal activity. The targets of conscription were often capoeiras, runaway or rebellious slaves, delinquent adolescents, and *desprotegidos*, the unprotected and vulnerable of society who had no patron to intercede on their behalf. The navy continued to be used by Republican authorities as a means of dealing with the problems of social disorder and vagrancy that thwarted their civilizing project (Beattie 1999, 847–78). In addition, military service was intended to take "criminals" off the streets and instill discipline and respect for authority, thereby cleansing the urban environment. (Schneider 2004, 21).

45. At least one favela also sprang up there shortly after the fair (see chapter 4).

46. They were described thus by the influential doctor João Augusto de Mattos in a 1926 speech to the Rotary Club, in which he complained bitterly about the spread of favelas across the city (cited in Stuckenbruck 1996, 86). See Rafael Soares Gonçalves (2013) for a detailed analysis of official language concerning favelas.

47. See for example a scathing critique in *O Paiz,* December 30, 1922, titled "Wholesale Devastation," which accuses Sampaio of reducing not just the historic neighborhood to ruins but the municipality's finances, too.

2. RACE, ETHNICITY, AND VISUALITY

1. Contemporary art critic Gonzaga Duque (2001, 37–40) identifies the figures who appear in this plane.

2. See Brand (2006) on the staging of sovereign power through temporary sets during the residence of the Portuguese court in Rio de Janeiro.

3. The city purchased Monteiro's painting just a year after its execution, and Emperor Pedro II sponsored his travel to Europe (Moreira 2016, 39–41). The painting still hangs in the Palácio Pedro Ernesto of the Câmara Municipal in Rio de Janeiro.

4. Contemporary orthography conventionally wrote *Castello* instead of *Castelo.*

5. In this brief account of lithography in Brazil and the work of Johann Steinmann I draw largely on the work of Renata Santos (2008, 46–71).

6. See Santos for more information on this lithograph (2008, 61, 66, 84, 85); this paragraph draws on her work in recounting its production and trajectory.

7. "Na litografia de J. Steinmann, Rua do Ouvidor, no 199, vendem-se as seguintes obras: vistas do Rio de Janeiro e das províncias do Brasil, relatos dos índios etc., negros em fundo, e colorido" (*Jornal do Commércio,* May 24, 1852, cited in Santos 2008, 84).

8. See Sela on the market for the highly valued iconography of Rio de Janeiro at this time and complaints by travelers about exorbitant prices (2008, 164–65). See also Zenha (2004) on the market for city views during the empire.

9. Sela suggests that consciously or not, in copying Rugendas Steinmann may have been reinforcing the vision of German Romanticism evident in Rugendas's representations of humans and animal integrated into a beautiful landscape that was the cradle of a new civilization in the tropics (2008, 170). If so, the frame of the lithograph both echoes that vision and shows its terrible flip side.

10. As discussed in chapter 1, after the Passos urban reforms in 1904–1906, which Castelo survived despite losing one of its slopes, black communities were ejected from the downtown area and reestablished themselves in the surrounding suburbs (Moura 1983; Carvalho 2013).

11. The term "pessoal da lyra" references regulars on the carnival and samba scene. The expression comes from the hit carnival march (*marchinha*) "Ô Abre-Alas," by Chiqiunha Gonzaga (1899), an ode to the musical talent of the Rosa de Ouro *cordão* (black carnival group). The phrase "Eu sou da lira" in the song came to mean "to be a carnival reveler, a bohemian, a performer" (Efegê 1978, 222).

12. According to Herman Lima the *bombacha* provoked a series of humorous caricatures by men lamenting women's adoption of the masculine style (1963, 452).

13. The population of Canudos probably numbered about thirty-five thousand at its height in 1895 (Levine 1995, 16). See Levine's *Vale of Tears* (1995) for one of the most important and detailed studies of Canudos.

14. See Edwards (2009), who discusses amateur photographic projects in Britain in the late nineteenth century, noting that they were "part of a broader cultural matrix concerned with the ethnographic and archaeological delineation of the racial and cultural origins of the British people" (71). Although Malta's photography was a harbinger of destruction rather than following a preservationist impulse, he also delineates what should be excluded or eliminated in imagining a "Brazilian race."

15. See James Green on the influence of Cesare Lombroso's criminal anthropology on thinking race, sexuality, and criminality in Brazil in the 1930s and 1940s (1999, 107–46).

16. For Malta's social standing see Ermakoff (2009, 18, 34, 37, 39).

17. Stoler observes that this endeavor "may involve forced removal of populations and new zones of uninhabitable space, reassigning inhabitable space and dictating how people are supposed to live in them" (2013, 21).

18. The comment perhaps refers to the crisis of statistical production in the capital exemplified by crippling problems of training, structure, and resources in the Diretoria Geral de Estatística, the government statistical agency, which Bulhões did not head until 1907, but which had garnered severe criticism for its failure to generate the reliable demographic information needed for the urban reforms (Senra 2009, 388–89). The Diretoria Geral de Estatística had also presided over the fiasco of the 1900 census (Loveman 2009, 452).

19. "A Avenida Central," *Jornal do Brasil*, September 8, 1904.

20. Reasons for the overrepresentation of Afro-descendants in the navy include attempts to gain freedom during slavery; press-ganging by the police postabolition; the need for food and lodging; and the possibility of mobility and migration to the capital city (Almeida 2012, 16). Over 90% of Brazil's navy was nonwhite (50% "negros," 30% "mulatos," 10% "caboclos") according to the personal observation of a contemporary former lieutenant cited in Almeida (2012, 16). Using information from a 1908 publication of the Gabinete de Identificação da Armada, Almeida herself estimates that the Afro-descendants made up close to 70% of the navy, with another 10.4%"morenos," and that the majority of sailors (65.6%) were from the north or northeast of Brazil (17).

21. "A demolição do morro do Castello," *O Malho*, August 20, 1921.

22. See Purbrick (2017) on pictorial analogues and photographic performances of industrial capital in her detailed and sensitive analysis of images of nitrate mining in the Atacama Desert. My analysis of this image is inspired by her readings.

23. Noel Rosa in *O Debate*, Belo Horizonte, May 9, 1935 (cited in Nonato and Santos 2000, 304).

24. Jacobina and Tapajós, *Organização e administração do Ministério da Justiça no império* (cited in Nonato and Santos 2000, 69).

25. Carneiro Leão, Honório Hermeto, "Relatório do Ministério da Justiça de 1832, apresentado à Assembléia Geral Legislativa, na sessão ordinária de 1833" (cited in Nonato and Santos 2000, 69).

26. The novel is based on life in Castelo shortly before its demolition.

3. ALTERNATIVE GEOGRAPHIES AND SPATIAL PRACTICES

1. As Jeffrey Needell (1987) observed, this and other main cultural institutions constructed during the reforms possessed merely the façade of fine Belle Époque architecture that concealed an unremarkable interior.

2. The caption of a photograph accompanying a December 2, 1916, article in the *Revista da Semana* titled "O Kysto do Rio: Deverá arrasar-se o morro do Castello?" read: "Just 20 meters from the Avenida Rio Branco! Civilization versus Barbarity" (14).

3. The evening daily *A Noite* speculated that thieves might steal works of art from the Fine Arts School by entering from Castelo Hill without being seen (August 31, 1911).

4. "O Rio civiliza-se!" was the rallying cry launched by the newspaper *Gazeta de Notícias* in 1904 at the start of the Passos reforms. Teresa Meade's *"Civilizing" Rio* (1997) explores this elite concern with civilizing the city and the reactions of the popular classes.

5. Luiz Edmundo de Melo Pereira da Costa wrote under the name Luiz Edmundo, and I will follow the convention in Brazilian academic writing to refer to him as such.

6. See Schneider (2004) on how the revolt by mainly Afro-descendent sailors challenged ideas of citizenship in the first Republic.

7. The children were named as: "Ricardina (8, white) and Hernani (4), children of Honorio Batista Leal and Maria Monteiro Leal" (*O Paiz*, November 24, 1910). Former residents stated in interview that the whole community was affected by the deaths, and that rebel leader João Cândido himself had warned *castelenses* to evacuate. Reflecting the generally sympathetic popular perception of Cândido as discussed by Schneider, the interviewee observes: "He went up there, to the hill afterwards, because he never wanted that to happen, although he was a revolutionary, he never wanted that to happen" (quoted in Nonato and Santos 2000, 113).

8. "Grande desastre: Uma familia soterrada," *O Malho*, April 1, 1911, Revista 446.

9. As Paulina Alberto notes, employers frequently used the term *nationals* as a derisive synonym for undesirable black workers (2011, 57).

10. "Os ultimos dias do Castello: Um passeio à collina historica, antes da demolição." *Revista da Semana*, July 16, 1921. According to former Castelo residents and siblings Florinda Alói and Francisco Moreno, Castelo attracted Italians like their parents because there was already "an Italian enclave on the hill, so immigrants were drawn towards the place" (Nonato and Santos 2000, 198).

11. According to an article published in the *Revista da Semana* Cova da Onça led to one of the great mysteries of Castelo—the entrance to the underground caverns where the Jesuits had supposedly buried their wealth before being expelled from Brazil in 1759. "Os ultimos dias do Castello: Um passeio à collina historica, antes da demolição," July 16, 1921.

12. Incidentally, the Santa Casa was one of the biggest property owners in Castelo (Nonato and Santos 2000, 76).

13. An article in the *Jornal do Brasil* claimed that Castelo had a population of six or seven thousand by the time it was demolished: "the majority were Italians from Calabria and Portuguese from the Açores" (Emygdio 1927).

14. Despite this, there were clearly people in dire straits living in flimsy self-built shacks in Chácara, like the family buried in the mudslide in 1911.

15. *Partido* can mean political party; in samba a *partido(-alto)* can be a duel in song; and *tomar o partido de* means "to side with." Moura Square was located in the Misericórdia neighborhood at the foot of Castelo; the Povo do Castello could be referencing the street or square of the same name; Santa Luzia was the beach frequented by castelenses at the foot of the hill and the street that ran along it.

16. This incredibly rich and detailed account was written by one Antonio Secioso de Sá (1928), who mentions that his late father worked as a doctor in the area and used to protest energetically to the authorities against the "barbarity" of the skirmishes.

17. Although rivals in the job market and the workplace in the early twentieth century (Chalhoub 1986, 36), in the late nineteenth century Portuguese men are known to have joined the predominantly black and mulatto capoeira gangs belonging to competing "nations" (*nagoas* or *nagôs*). In the nineteenth century the parish of São José in which Castelo was located had been a well-known domain of capoeira gangs belonging to these rival "nations" (Farias et al. 2006, 81).

18. "Ferido à bala sem saber por quem?" *Correio da Manhã*, April 11, 1920; "Um popular tomba," *Gazeta de Notícias*, April 11, 1920.

19. According to the *Gazeta de Notícias* (April 11, 1920, 3), Silva was about to rest near the São

Zacharias Hospital, when he noticed that he was being followed and quickened his step before being accosted by the soldier.

20. "Grave accusação contra um soldado de policia," *Jornal do Brasil*, April 11, 1920.

21. Before the victim died in hospital, he described his attacker as "a soldier with dark skin, stocky build, short" (*Gazeta de Notícias*, April 11, 1920, 3).

22. "No Morro do Castello: Queixas e mais queixas," *Jornal do Brasil*, April 2, 1920.

23. Paixão notes that some of these had Italian names, or were noted as "filhos de portugueses," but were recorded as "Brazilian."

24. "O Carnavel rompeu a Alleluia," *Jornal do Brasil*, April 4, 1920.

25. "Comicio que não se realiza: A indignação popular contra um orador," *Jornal do Brasil*, October 10, 1920, 12; "A nacionalização da pesca," *Correio da Manhã*, October 10, 1920.

26. "Meetings, correrias e prisões," *Correio da Manhã*, March 18, 1921.

27. "Contra o arrasamento do Morro do Castelo!" *Correio da Manhã*, September 6, 1920, 3.

28. Drawing on an interview with a key figure of the black press in São Paulo conducted by the poet Cuti (Luiz Silva; Leite 1992), Alberto remarks that Ferreira could read, but not write, and therefore gave unscripted speeches. He attended public lectures on philosophy and politics, and felt sufficiently empowered to dictate a letter to then president Washington Luís soliciting his view on the *mãe preta* campaign. *A Notícia* duly published the president's warm words of support. Despite his public visibility, Ferreira lived precariously, sleeping in rooming houses or relying on the kindness of friends (Alberto 2011, 82–83). As discussed, news coverage of the protest against the nationalization of the fishing industry in October 1920 reports that his place of residence at the time was on Castelo Hill. Ferreira moved to São Paulo in 1927, where he continued to advocate for some form of commemoration of the *mãe preta* (Alberto 2011, 92).

29. "Um discurso do Professor Vicente Ferreira," *Correio da Manhã*, November 6, 1921.

30. "Ainda a commemoração do anniversario da fundação de São Paulo," *Correio da Manhã*, January 26, 1928.

31. "O meeting de hontem," *Correio da Manhã*, September 1, 1921; "Ainda é vivo o Professor Vicente Ferreira!" *Correio da Manhã*, October 6, 1929; "Ainda a commemoração do anniversario da fundação de São Paulo," *Correio da Manhã*, January 26, 1928; "As manifestações populares e alguns abusos das autoridades policiais," *Correio da Manhã*, January 22, 1922.

32. "Queixa contra a policia,"*Correio da Manhã*, April 26, 1922.

33. See for example the *Jornal do Brasil* on protests by the Centro dos Operarios da União (August 31, 1920, 9).

34. "Casas! Casas! Casas!" *Jornal do Brasil*, October 13, 1922.

35. "Em favor dos operarios," *Gazeta de Notícias*, September 22, 1923.

36. José de Alencar, the author of the Romantic Indianist novel *O Guarani* (1857), which inspired Carlos Gomes's opera (first performed in 1870 in the Teatro Alla Scalla in Milan).

37. "Carnaval," *O Paiz*, March 1–2, 1922.

38. "Ecos do carnaval," *Jornal do Brasil*, March 2, 1920.

39. The "Indian" was a stock character of traditional carnival. "Indians" usually led the parade to deliver the standard to the *Jornal do Brasil's* offices (Edmundo 1957, 799, 802).]

40. The conversation between the two men in the original Portuguese is as follows:

— O "nêgo" veiu feito! Ahi arredei tres "pé" pr'a traz no passo do jaburu'; assentei meus "alicerco" na tampa do guarda-comida do bruto; levei a caveira de lado e fui "buscá" o "appareio" mastigante do poeta! O veneno espirrou. Não dei tempo pr'a o bruto "accendê" a lamparina, fiz uma figuração "purriba" e abaixei em baixo no bahiano. Quando o camarada tomou tento, tinha ido "amarrotá" a tampa do juizo no fio da "carçada!"

Perguntava o outro:

— E "aspois"?

— Aspois, "triáram" os "apito"; méganha veiu chegando com escova de paizano e eu tomei tento e fui ganhando "arage"!

41. One of the first films to be made in Brazil was Italian immigrant Pascoal Segreto's *As Festas da Penha* in 1900.

42. Florêncio da Palma was covered in tattoos himself, including one of Jesus Our Savior, an image that was extremely commonplace on the bodies of black males at the time, according to João do Rio (2005, 103; Edmundo 1957, 212).

43. Joaquim Antônio da Silva Calado was classically trained and was appointed to Brazil's Conservatório de Música in 1871. He is best known in Brazilian music history, however, as a key figure in the development of the popular *choro* genre, a complex style of playing that mixes structures of European dance forms like polkas and waltzes with African-influenced rhythms. He would have, therefore, been equally at home playing popular music for the secular part of the festival which also included an auction and fireworks display (*Gazeta de Notícias*, July 11, 1878, 4).

4. ERADICATING BLACKNESS FROM THE IDEAL CITY

1. His racial hybridity recalls Macunaíma, "the hero without a character" and protagonist of modernist writer Mário de Andrade's eponymous novel ([1928] 2008) who starts life black, but turns white by bathing in an enchanted pool. Or perhaps the little boy's predicament is more similar to Macunaíma's brother Manaape, who bathes in the puddle too, in an attempt to whiten himself, but only finds enough water there to whiten parts of his body.

2. "Homenagem prestada pelos servidores da municipalidade ao Prefeito Exmo. Sr. Dr. Carlos Sampaio, no dia da inauguração do Pavilhão do Distrito Federal a 20 de setembro de 1922." *Typ do Jornal do Comércio*, 1922, 19; quoted in Sant'Ana 2008, 101.

3. Costa Rego, "O Centenário," *Correio da Manhã*, June 5, 1920, 2.

4. It was during the Sampaio administration that real estate value began to figure explicitly in municipal projects and planning (Abreu 1997, 78).

5. See Sant'Ana (2008, 27–31) for a summary of Brazil's national exhibitions before the Centenary.

6. The Ministry of Justice and the Interior had oversight of the fair, with the Ministry of Agriculture, Industry and Commerce in charge of overall organization, and the mayor's office responsible for necessary urban reforms and managing preparation of the exposition site. *Regimento Interno da Comissão Executiva da Comemoração do Primeiro Centenário da Independência Política do Brasil* (quoted in Sant'Ana 2008, 47n124).

7. See Larry Crook on the interest of members of Rio's elites in the musical folk traditions of the country in the early twentieth century. Their interest took the form of patronage of various kinds, and the organization of conferences and festivals on regional folklore (2005, 243–46).

8. Jeca was no stranger to the stage. Earlier that year, for example, the Troupe Sertaneja, a touring musical group originally from Pernambuco, performed at the Cinema Central in Rio with the singer Juvenal Fontes performing as Jeca Tatu (*A Noite*, February 15, 1923).

9. According to the 1920 census the population of the Federal District of Rio de Janeiro was around 1.1 million (Meade 1999).

10. Eduardo Morretin has noted that a figure that São Paulo elites would identify as a *caipira* appears in the exposition film *Companhia Fabril de Cubatão* (João de Sá Rocha 1922). This Jeca Tatu is frozen in a tableau in the middle of "virgin forest" as a vestige of the past with no link whatsoever with the progress represented by the factory portrayed in the film (2013, 152–53).

11. Levy mentions that this society had a more open membership policy, accepting architects without diplomas as well as members in related professions, such as draftsmen and watercolorists (2007, 4).

12. Brazil's National History Museum, created in 1922 in the context of the fair, originally occupied part of this complex, and still stands on the site today.

13. According to Sant'Ana (2008, 76) one of the architects, Edgar Vianna, was inspired by ceramics brought back from Pará by exploratory missions.

EPILOGUE. MEGA-EVENTS, RUINATION, AND THE POLITICS OF STAYING PUT

1. In a diasporic context, see Iton (2008, 16, 201) on the incompatibility of blackness in the United States with modernity; Gilroy (1993, 191) on modernity's ambivalence toward black subjectivities; and McKittrick (2006, xx) on how the discourse of modernity is underwritten by slavery and its legacies.

2. See for example the video "Vida Nova no Parque Carioca" (A New Life in Carioca Park, https://www.youtube.com/watch?v=cIQ-dMxUtgc), uploaded to YouTube by then mayor Eduardo Paes's office. Carioca Park is the housing development built for former residents of Vila Autódromo, and the video features a mother who states that she was unable to live "decently" in the old community due to complete lack of basic sanitation. The identical, boxlike apartments of the new development are officially sanctioned by contrast as an appropriately habitable space.

3. See Chari (2013) and Collins (2008; 2013) on political refusal in situations of ruination.

4. Maria da Penha Macena occupies one of the twenty new homes built by the city in Vila Autódromo (Peregrino 2016).

5. The Olympic athletes' accommodations became part of a condominium development infelicitously named Ilha Pura (Island of Purity). A publicity video for the new neighborhood shows a near monochromatically white population as the target residents of the complex. See "Ilha Pura - Na Voz de Fernanda Montenegro," uploaded September 18, 2014, by robinson lima, https://www.youtube.com/watch?v=smlSkgQ8KXQ.

6. D. Heloisa wrote and published two articles on her intimidation and humiliation by municipal officials in the community reporting news site *Rio On Watch*: "Candomblecista da Vila Autódromo Descreve o Terror do Processo de Remoção," September 17, 2015, and "Ameaça à Vida da Mãe de Santo Luizinha de Nanã da Vila Autódromo," February 23, 2016.

7. On May 18, 2017, at a ceremony in the National History Museum in Rio de Janeiro, Vila Autódromo residents donated their archive of materials on the history of the community and its struggle against removal. The museum plans to mount a permanent exhibition of the materials (Lígia Souto 2017).

BIBLIOGRAPHY

PERIODICALS CONSULTED

Agência Brasil
A Noite
Almanaque (Almanak) Laemmert
Correio da Manhã
Fon-Fon
Guardian
Jornal do Brasil
Jornal O Cidadão
Kosmos
Latin Correspondent
O Globo
O Jornal
O Malho
New York Times
Revista da Semana
Revista de Revistas
Rio On Watch

SOURCES

Abreu, Maurício de Almeida. 1986. *O Rio de Janeiro e a sua evolução urbana*. Rio de Janeiro: Zahar.

Abreu, Maurício de Almeida. 2003. "Da habitação ao habitat: a questão da habitação popular no Rio de Janeiro e sua evolução." *Revista Rio de Janeiro* 10: 210–34.

Alberto, Paulina. 2011. *Terms of Inclusion: Black Intellectuals in Twentieth-Century Brazil*. Chapel Hill: University of North Carolina Press.

Alberti, Verena, and Amilcar Araujo Pereira, eds. 2016. *Histórias do movimento negro no Brasil: Depoimentos ao CPDOC*. Rio de Janeiro: Pallas.

Alencar, Edigar de. 1981. *Nosso Sinhô do samba*. Rio de Janeiro: FUNARTE.

Alencar, José de. (1857) 1982. *O Guaraní*. Reprint, São Paulo: Ática.

Alencar, José de. (1921) 2006. *Iracema*. Reprint, Fortaleza: UFC Edições.

Almeida, Sílvia Capanema P. de. 2012. "Corpo, saúde e alimentação na Marinha de Guerra brasileira no período pós-abolição, 1890–1910." *História, ciências, saúde—Manguinhos* 19, suppl. 1: 15–33.

Alves, Jaime. 2012. "Macabre Spatialities: The Politics of Race, Gender and Violence in a Neoliberal City." PhD diss., University of Texas at Austin.

Alves, Jaime. 2014. "From Necropolis to Blackpolis: Necropolitical Governance and Black Spatial Praxis in São Paulo, Brazil." *Antipode* 46, no. 2: 323–39.

Alves, Jaime. 2018. *The Anti-Black City: Police Terror and Black Urban Life in Brazil.* Minneapolis: University of Minnesota Press.

Andermann, Jens. 2007. *The Optic of the State: Visuality and Power in Argentina and Brazil.* Pittsburgh: University of Pittsburgh Press.

Andrade, Mário de. (1928) 2008. *Macunaima: o herói sem nenhum caráter.* Reprint, Rio de Janeiro: Agir.

Associação de Moradores e Pescadores da Vila Autódromo (AMPVA). 2012. *Plano popular da Vila Autódromo: Plano de desenvolvimento urbano, econômico, social e cultural.* Rio de Janeiro: AMPVA.

Atique, Fernando. 2010. "A presença americana na Exposição Internacional do Centenário da independência do Brasil: antecedentes e repercussões." Paper presented at the Tenth International Congress of the Brazilian Studies Association (BRASA), Brasília, July 22–24.

Azevedo, Aluísio. (1890) 1980. *O Cortiço.* Reprint, Belo Horizonte: Itatiaia.

Andrews, George Reid. 1991. *Blacks and Whites in São Paulo, Brazil, 1888–1988.* Madison: University of Wisconsin Press.

Andrews, George Reid. 2004. *Afro-Latin America, 1800–2000.* Oxford: Oxford University Press.

Andrews, George Reid. 2016. *Afro-Latin America: Black Lives, 1600–2000.* Cambridge, MA: Harvard University Press.

Backheuser, Everardo. 1906. *Habitações populares: Relatório apresentado ao Exm. Sr. Dr. J. J. Seabra, Ministro da Justiça e Negócios Interiores.* Rio de Janeiro: Imprensa Nacional.

Barreto, Lima. (1905) 1997. *O subterrâneo do Morro do Castelo.* Rio de Janeiro: Dantes.

Barreto, Lima. (1915) 1961. *Numa e a ninfa: Romance.* Reprint, São Paulo: Brasiliense.

Barreto, Lima. (1915) 1997. *Triste fim de policarpo quaresma.* Reprint, Madrid: ALLCA XX/Scipione Cultural.

Barreto, Lima. (1948) n.d. *Clara dos Anjos.* Reprint, Rio de Janeiro: Ediouro.

Barreto, Lima. 1961. *Diário íntimo: Memórias.* São Paulo: Brasiliense.

Barreto, Luís Muniz. 1987. *Observatório Nacional, 160 anos de história.* Rio de Janeiro: Edição MCT/CNPQ/ Observatório Nacional/ABC/Secretaria de Ciência e Tecnologia do Estado do RJ.

Bastos, Isabela, and Selma Schmidt. 2010. "Prefeitura Removerá 119 Favelas até fim de 2012." *O Globo,* January 7.

Beal, Sophia. 2012. "The Substance of Light: Literature and Public Space in Belle Époque Rio de Janeiro (1894–1914)." *Luso-Brazilian Review* 49, no. 2: 5–27.

Beal, Sophia. 2013. *Brazil under Construction: Fiction and Public Works.* New York: Palgrave Macmillan.

Beasley-Murray, Jon. 2010. "Vilcashuamán: Telling Stories in Ruins." In *Ruins of Modernity,* edited by Julia Hell and Andreas Schönle, 212–31. Durham, NC: Duke University Press.

Beattie, Peter. 1999. "Conscription versus Penal Servitude: Army Reform's Influence on the Brazilian State's Management of Social Control, 1870–1930." *Journal of Social History* 32, no. 4: 847–79.

Benchimol, Jaime Larry. 1985. "A modernização do Rio de Janeiro." In *O Rio de Janeiro de Pereira Passos: Uma cidade em questão II,* edited by Giovanna Rosso Del Brenna, 599–611. Rio de Janeiro: Index.

Benchimol, Jaime Larry. 1992. *Pereira Passos: Um Haussmann tropical: A renovação urbana da cidade do Rio de Janeiro no início do século XX.* Rio de Janeiro: Secretaria Municipal de Cultura, Turismo e Esportes, Departamento Geral de Documentação e Informação Cultural.

Benjamin, Walter. 1982. "The Work of Art in the Age of Mechanical Reproduction." In *Modern Art and Modernism: A Critical Anthology*, edited by Francis Frascina, Charles Harrison, and Deirdre Paul, 217–20. Boulder, CO: Westview.

Berta, Ruben. 2015. "Apesar de indenizações milionárias, prefeitura não consegue acabar com a Vila Autódromo." *O Globo*, May 14, 2015.

Bletz, May. 2010. *Immigration and Acculturation in Brazil and Argentina: 1890–1929*. New York: Palgrave Macmillan.

Bonduki, Nabil Georges. 1998. "Origens da habitação social no Brasil: Arquitetura moderna, lei do inquilinato e difusão da casa própria." *Análise Social*, 4th series, 29, no. 127: 711–32.

Borges, Dain. 1993. "'Puffy, Ugly, Slothful and Inert': Degeneration in Brazilian Social Thought, 1880–1940." *Journal of Latin American Studies* 25, no. 2: 235–56.

Bourdieu, Pierre, and Loïc Wacquant. 1999. "On the Cunning of Imperialist Reason." *Theory, Culture and Society* 16, no. 1: 41–58.

Brand, Diane. 2006. "Sets and Extras: Ephemeral Architecture and Urban Ceremony in Rio de Janeiro (1808–1821)." *Journal of Latin American Cultural Studies* 15, no. 3: 263–79.

Burns, E. Bradford. 1980. *A History of Brazil*. New York: Columbia University Press.

Campos, Andrelino. 2005. *Do quilombo à favela: A produção do "espaço criminalizado" no Rio de Janeiro*. Rio de Janeiro: Bertrand Brasil.

Carone, Edgard. 1978. *A república velha*. Vol. 1, *Instituições e classes sociais, 1889–1930*. São Paulo: Difel.

Carvalho, Bruno. 2013. *Porous City: A Cultural History of Rio de Janeiro (From the 1810s Onward)*. Liverpool: Liverpool University Press.

Carvalho, José Murilo de. (1990) 2003. *A formação das almas: O imaginário da república no Brasil*. Reprint, São Paulo: Companhia das Letras.

Carvalho, José Murilo de. 1999. *Os bestializados: O Rio de Janeiro e a República que não foi*. São Paulo: Companhia das Letras.

Carvalho, Marco. 2014. *Uma ladeira para lugar nenhum*. Rio de Janeiro: Record.

Caulfield, Sueann. 2000. *In Defense of Honor: Sexual Morality, Modernity, and Nation in Early-Twentieth-Century Brazil*. Durham, NC: Duke University Press.

Certeau, Michel de. 1984. *The Practice of Everyday Life*. Berkeley: University of California Press.

Chalhoub, Sidney. 1986. *Trabalho, lar e botequim: O cotidiano dos trabalhadores no Rio de Janeiro da belle epoque*. São Paulo: Brasiliense.

Chalhoub, Sidney. 1996. *Cidade febril: Cortiços e epidemias na corte imperial*. São Paulo: Companhia das Letras.

Chari, Sharad. 2013. "Detritus in Durban: Polluted Environs and the Biopolitics of Refusal." In *Imperial Debris: On Ruins and Ruination*, edited by Ann Laura Stoler, 131–61. Durham, NC: Duke University Press.

Coaracy, Vivaldo. 1955. *Memórias da cidade do Rio de Janeiro*. Rio de Janeiro: Livraria José Olympio.

Collins, John. 2008. "But What if I Should Need to Defecate in Your Neighborhood, Madame?: Empire, Redemption, and the Tradition of the Oppressed in a Brazilian World Heritage Site." *Cultural Anthropology* 23, no. 2: 279–328.

Collins, John. 2013. "Ruins, Redemption, and Brazil's Imperial Exception." In *Imperial Debris: On Ruins and Ruination*, edited by Ann Laura Stoler, 162–93. Durham, NC: Duke University Press.

Comissão Organizadora. 1922. (July, August, September, October). *A Exposição de 1922*. Rio de Janeiro: Litho-Typographia Fluminense.

Conniff, Michael L. 1981. *Urban Politics in Brazil: The Rise of Populism, 1925–1945*. Pittsburgh: University of Pittsburgh Press.

Corrêa, Felipe Botelho. 2012. "The Readership of Caricatures in the Brazilian Belle Époque: The Case of the Illustrated Magazine *Careta* (1908–1922)." *Patrimônio e Memória*: 71–97.

Crenshaw, Kimberlé, Neil Gotanda, Gary Peller, and Kendall Thomas, eds. 1995. *Critical Race Theory: The Key Writings That Formed the Movement*. New York: The New Press.

Crook, Larry N. 2005. *Brazilian Music: Northeastern Traditions and the Heartbeat of a Modern Nation*. Santa Barbara: ABC-CLIO.

Crouch, David. 1998. "The Street in the Making of Popular Geographical Knowledge." In *Images of the Street: Planning, Identity and Control in Public Space*, edited by Nicholas R. Fyfe, 160–75. New York: Routledge.

Cruls, Gastão. 1952. *Aparência do Rio de Janeiro: Noticia histórica e descriptiva da cidade*, vol. 1. Rio de Janeiro: José Olympio.

Cunha, Euclides da. (1902) 2002. *Os sertões: Campanha de Canudos*. Reprint, São Paulo: Alteliê.

Cunha Jr., Henrique Antunes, Maria Estela Rocha Ramos, and Antonia dos Santos Garcia, eds. 2007. *Espaço urbano e afrodescendência: Estudos da espacialidade negra urbana para o debate das políticas públicas*. Fortaleza: UFC Edições.

Curtis, John P. 1923. "Architecture of the Brazil Centennial Exposition." *Art and Architecture* 5: 95–104.

Dávila, Jerry. 2003. *Diploma of Whiteness: Race and Social Policy in Brazil, 1917–1945*. Durham, NC: Duke University Press.

Dealtry, Giovanna. 2009. "Margens da *Belle Époque* carioca pelo traço de Calixto Cordeiro." *Alceu* 9, no. 18: 117–30.

Del Brenna, Giovanna Rosso, ed. 1985. *O Rio de Janeiro de Pereira Passos: Uma cidade em questão II*. Rio de Janeiro: Index.

Directoria Geral de Saúde Pública. 1906. Prefeitura do Distrito Federal, Arquivo Geral da Cidade do Rio de Janeiro, Códice 44.2.12.

Duque, Gonzaga. 2001. *Impressões de um amador: Textos esparsos de crítica (1882–1909)*. Edited by Vera Lins and Júlio Castañon Guimarães. Rio de Janeiro: UFMG.

Edmundo, Luiz. 1957. *O Rio do Janeiro do Meu Tempo*. Rio de Janeiro: Conquista.

Edwards, Elizabeth. 2009. "Salvaging Our Past: Photography and Survival." In *Photography, Anthropology and History*, edited by Christopher Morton and Elizabeth Edwards, 67–88. Farnham: Ashgate.

Efegê, Jota. 1978. *Figuras e Coisas da Música Popular Brasileira*. Vol. 1. Rio de Janeiro: FUNARTE.

Emygdio, Carlos. 1927. "Era uma vez um bairro alto . . ." *Jornal do Brasil*, September 25, 1927.

Engel, Magali Gouveia. 2001. *Os delírios da razão: Médicos, loucos e hospícios (Rio de Janeiro, 1830–1930)*. Rio de Janeiro: Fiocruz.

Ermakoff, George. 2009. *Augusto Malta e o Rio de Janeiro, 1903–1936*. Rio de Janeiro: G. Ermakoff.

Fabian, Johannes. 1983. *Time and the Other: How Anthropology Makes Its Object*. New York: Columbia University Press.

Fabian, Johannes. 1991. "Culture, Time, and the Object of Anthropology." In *Time and the Work of Anthropology: Critical Essays, 1971–1991*, 191–206. Amsterdam: Harwood.

Fanon, Frantz. 1967. *Black Skin, White Masks*. New York: Grove.

Farias, Juliana Barreto, Flávio dos Santos Gomes, and Carlos Eugênio Líbano Soares. 2006. *Cidades negras: Africanos, crioulos e espaços urbanos no Brasil do século XIX*. São Paulo: Alameda.

Fausto, Bóris. 1976. *Trabalho Urbano e Conflito Industrial, 1890–1920.* São Paulo: Difel.

Fernández-Bravo, Alvaro. 2001. "Ambivalent Argentina: Nationalism, Exoticism, and Latin Americanism at the 1889 Paris Universal Exposition." *Nepantla: Views from South* 2, no. 1: 115–39.

Ferreira, Aurélio Buarque de Holanda. 1971. *Pequeno dicionário Brasileiro da língua portuguesa—ilustrado.* 11th ed. Rio de Janeiro: Gama/Civilização Brasileira.

Ferreira, Aurélio Buarque de Holanda and José Baptista da Luz. 1987. *Pequeno dicionário brasileiro da língua portuguesa.* Rio de Janeiro: Civilização Brasileira.

Ferreira, Orlando da Costa. 1994. *Imagem e letra: Introdução à bibliologia brasileira: A imagem gravada,* vol. 10. São Paulo: Editora da Universidade de São Paulo.

Fischer, Brodwyn M. 2008. *A Poverty of Rights: Citizenship and Inequality in Twentieth-Century Rio de Janeiro.* Palo Alto, CA: Stanford University Press.

Fleetwood, Nicole. 2011. *Troubling Vision: Performance, Visuality, and Blackness.* Chicago: University of Chicago Press.

Florentino, Manolo, and Cacilda Machado. 2002. "Imigração portuguesa e miscigenação no Brasil nos séculos XIX e XX." In *Os lusíadas na aventura do Rio moderno,* edited by Carlos Lessa, 91–116. Rio de Janeiro: Record.

Fluminense, Américo. 1905. "O Morro do Castelo." *Revista Kosmos* 2, no. 10: 43.

Freitas, Guilherme. 2012. "Temos o Direito de Morar Nesta Cidade." *O Globo,* August 25, 2012.

French, John D. 2000. "The Missteps of Anti-imperialist Reason: Bourdieu, Wacquant and Hanchard's *Orpheus and Power.*" *Theory, Culture & Society* 17, no. 1: 107–28.

Freyre, Gilberto. 1956. *The Masters and the Slaves: A Study in the Development of Brazilian Civilization.* Translated by Samuel Putnam. New York: Alfred A. Knopf.

Fridman, Sergio, and Roberto Menezes de Moraes. 1999. *Morro do Castelo: Seus aspectos numa rara coleção de cartões-postais.* Rio de Janeiro: Arte Maior Gráfica e Editora.

Gaffney, Christopher. 2010. "Mega-events and Socio-spatial Dynamics in Rio de Janeiro, 1919–2016." *Journal of Latin American Geography* 9, no. 1: 7–29.

Gilroy, Paul. 1993. *The Black Atlantic: Modernity and Double Consciousness.* Cambridge, MA: Harvard University Press.

Godoy, Silvana Alves de. 2014. "Martim Afonso Tibiriçá. A Nobreza Indígena e Seus Descendentes nos Campos de Piratininga no Século XVI." *Recôncavo: Revista de História da UNIABEU* 4, no. 7: 191–212.

Gomes, Thiago de Melo. 2003. "Para além da casa da Tia Ciata: Outras experiências no universo cultural carioca, 1830–1930." *Afro-Ásia* 30: 175–98.

Gonçalves, Rafael Soares. 2013. *Favelas do Rio de Janeiro: História e direito.* Rio de Janeiro: Pallas.

Gonzalez, Elma. 2015. "To Make Way for 2016 Olympics, Rio de Janeiro Removes Favelas," *Latin Correspondent,* June 8, 2015.

Gordillo, Gastón. 2014. *Rubble: The Afterlife of Destruction.* Durham, NC: Duke University Press.

Green, James N. 1999. *Beyond Carnival: Male Homosexuality in Twentieth-Century Brazil.* Chicago: University of Chicago Press.

Guerra Amorim, Carlos Eduardo, Carolina Carvalho Gontijo, and Silviene Fabiana de Oliveira. 2012. "Migration in Afro-Brazilian Rural Communities: Crossing Historical, Demographic, and Genetic Data." In *Causes and Consequences of Human Migration: An Evolutionary Perspective,* edited by Michael H. Crawford and Benjamin C. Campbell, 473–98. Cambridge: Cambridge University Press.

Hall, Stuart. 1997. *Representation: Cultural Representations and Signifying Practices.* London: SAGE.

Hanchard, Michael G. 1998. *Orpheus and Power: The Movimento Negro of Rio de Janeiro and São Paulo, Brazil 1945–1988.* Princeton, NJ: Princeton University Press.

Harris, Marvin. 1964. *Patterns of Race in the Americas.* New York: Walker.

Harris, Marvin. 1970. "Referential Ambiguity in the Calculus of Brazilian Racial Identity." *Southwestern Journal of Anthropology* 26, no. 1: 1–14.

Harrison, Faye V. 2014. "Reflections on the AAA Die-in as a Symbolic Space of Social Death." *Savage Minds,* December 12. https://savageminds.org/2014/12/12/reflections-on-the-aaa-die-in-as-a-symbolic-space-of-social-death/.

Hartman, Saidiya. 1997. *Scenes of Subjection: Terror, Slavery, and Self-Making in Nineteenth- Century America.* New York: Oxford University Press.

Harvey, David. 2004. "The 'New' Imperialism: Accumulation by Dispossession." *Socialist Register* 40: 63–87.

Hasenbalg, Carlos. 1985. "Race and Socioeconomic Inequalities in Brazil." In *Race, Class and Power in Brazil,* edited by Pierre-Michel Fontaine, 25–41. Los Angeles: University of California Press.

Hellwig, David J. 1992. *African-American Reflections on Brazil's Racial Paradise.* Philadelphia: Temple University Press.

Herzog, Lawrence A. 2013. "Barra da Tijuca The Political Economy of a Global Suburb in Rio de Janeiro, Brazil." *Latin American Perspectives* 40, no. 2: 118–34.

Holloway, Thomas. 2009. "O Calabouço e o Aljube do Rio de Janeiro no Século XIX." In *História das Prisões no Brasil,* edited by Clarissa Nunes Maia, Flávio Neto, Marcos Costa, and Marcos Luiz Bretas, 1:253–81. Rio de Janeiro: Rocco.

Instituto da Pesquisa Econômica Aplicada. 2011. *Retrato das Desigualdades de Gênero e Raça.* 4th ed. Brasília: IPEA.

Iton, Richard. 2008. *In Search of the Black Fantastic: Politics and Popular Culture in the Post-Civil Rights Era.* New York: Oxford University Press.

Jaguaribe, Beatriz. 2011. "Imaginando a 'cidade maravilhosa': Modernidade, espetáculo e espaços urbanos." *Revista FAMECOS* 18, no. 2: 327–47.

Jaguaribe, Beatriz. 2014. *Rio de Janeiro: Urban Life through the Eyes of the City.* New York: Routledge.

Jaguaribe, Beatriz, and Maurício Lissovsky. 2009. "The Visible and the Invisibles: Photography and Social Imaginaries in Brazil." *Public Culture* 21, no. 1: 175–209.

Jorge, Marcelo Gonczarowska. 2010. "As pinturas indianistas de Rodolfo Amoedo." *19&20* 5, no. 2.

"Plano Popular da Vila Autódromo Ganha Premio Internacional de Urbanismo." 2013. *Justiça Global,* December 4.

Kessel, Carlos. 2001. *A vitrine e o espelho: O Rio de Janeiro de Carlos Sampaio.* Rio de Janeiro: Prefeitura da Cidade do Rio de Janeiro.

Kessel, Carlos. 2002. "Entre o pastiche e a modernidade: Arquitetura neocolonial no Brasil." PhD diss., Universidade Federal do Rio de Janeiro.

Kessel, Carlos. 2008. *Tesouros do Morro do Castelo: Mistério e história nos subterrâneos do Rio de Janeiro.* Rio de Janeiro: Zahar.

Klein, Herbert S., and Francisco Vidal Luna. 2009. *Slavery in Brazil.* Cambridge: Cambridge University Press.

Lago, Manoel Aranha Corrêa do. 2002. "Brazilian Sources in Milhaud's 'Le Boeuf sur le Toit': A Discussion and a Musical Analysis." *Latin American Music Review* 23, no. 1: 1–59.

Leite, José Correia, and Cuti [Luiz Silva]. 1992. *E disse o velho militante José Correia Leite.* São Paulo: Secretaria Municipal de Cultura.

Lesser, Jeffrey. 1999. *Negotiating National Identity: Immigrants, Minorities, and the Struggle for Ethnicity in Brazil.* Durham, NC: Duke University Press.

Lesser, Jeffrey. 2013. *Immigration, Ethnicity, and National Identity in Brazil, 1808 to the Present.* Cambridge: Cambridge University Press.

Leu, Lorraine. 2010. "Performing Race and Gender in Brazil: Karim Ainouz's *Madame Satã.*" *Race/Ethnicity: Multidisciplinary Global Contexts* 4, no. 1: 73–95.

Leu, Lorraine. 2014. "Deviant Geographies: Black Spaces of Cultural Expression in Early 20th-Century Rio de Janeiro." *Latin American and Caribbean Ethnic Studies* 9, no. 2: 177–94.

Levine, Robert M. 1995. *Vale of Tears: Revisiting the Canudos Massacre in Northeastern Brazil, 1893–1897.* Berkeley: University of California Press.

Levy, Ruth. 2007. "A Exposição do Centenário como Marco para a Profissão do Arquiteto." *19&20* 3, no. 2: 4.

Lígia Souto. 2017. "Museu Histórico Nacional Recebe Acervo de Remoção da Vila Autódromo," *Agência Brasil,* May 20, 2017.

Lima, Deborah Magalhães. 1999. "A construção histórica do termo caboclo: Sobre estruturas e representações sociais no meio rural amazônico." *Novos Cadernos NAEA* 2, no. 2: 5–32.

Lima, Herman. 1963. *História da caricatura no Brasil.* Rio de Janeiro: José Olympio.

Lima, Nísia Trinidade, and Gilberto Hochman. 1996. "Condenado pela Raça, Absolvido pela Medicina." In *Raca, Ciência e Sociedade,* edited by Marcos Chor Maio and Ricardo Ventura Santos, 23–40. Rio de Janeiro: Fiocruz.

Lima, Nísia Trinidade, and Gilberto Hochman. 2000. "Pouca saúde, muita saúva, os males do Brasil são . . . Discurso médico-sanitário e interpretação do país." *Ciência e Saúde Coletiva* 5, no. 2: 313–32.

Lipsitz, George. 2011. *How Racism Takes Place.* Philadelphia: Temple University Press.

Livro de Ouro Commemorativo do Centenário da Independência do Brasil e da Exposição Internacional do Rio de Janeiro. 1923. Rio de Janeiro: Almanak Laemmert.

Lobato, José Bento Monteiro. (1919) 1946. *Urupês.* Reprint, São Paulo: Editora Brasiliense.

Lobato, José Bento Monteiro. (1918) 2010. *Problema Vital, Jeca Tatu e Outros Textos.* Reprint, São Paulo: Globo Livros.

Lobato, José Bento Monteiro. (1920) 1965. "Não Arrasem o Morro do Castelo." In *Rio de Janeiro em Prosa e Verso,* edited by Manuel Bandeira and Carlos Drummond de Andrade, 412–14. São Paulo: José Olympio.

Lopes, Antonio Herculano. 2006. "Um forrobodó da raça e da cultura." *Revista Brasileira de Ciências Sociais* 21, no. 62: 69–83.

Loveman, Mara. 2009. "The Race to Progress: Census Taking and Nation Making in Brazil (1870–1920)." *Hispanic American Historical Review* 89, no. 3: 435–70.

Lugo-Ortiz, Agnes. 2012. "Material Culture, Slavery, and Governability in Colonial Cuba: The Humorous Lessons of the Cigarette Marquillas." *Journal of Latin American Cultural Studies* 21, no. 1: 61–85.

Machado de Assis, Joaquim Maria. (1904) 1988. *Esaú e Jacó.* Reprint, Rio de Janeiro: Livraria Garnier.

Magalhães, Luiz Ernesto. 2014. "Favela Vila Autódromo Também tem Casas de Classe Media." *O Globo*, March 15, 2014.

Malamud, Samuel. 1988. *Recordando a Praça Onze*. Rio de Janeiro: Kosmos.

Marques, Vera Regina. 1994. *A medicalização da raça: Médicos, educadores e discursos eugênicos*. Campinas: Unicamp.

Martins, Luciana de Lima. 2013. *Photography and Documentary Film in the Making of Modern Brazil*. Manchester: Manchester University Press.

Mascarenhas, Gilmar. 2012. "A Modernidade das Redes Técnics e as Temporalidades em Contraste: a Produção do Abandono na Area Central do Rio de Janeiro (1890–1930)." Paper presented at Simposio Internacional Globalización, Inovación y Construcción de Redes Técnicas Urbanas en América y Europa, 1890–1930. Universidad de Barcelona, Facultad de Geografia y Historia, January 23–26.

Matos, Cláudia. 1982. *Acertei no milhar: Malandragem e samba no tempo de Getúlio*. Rio de Janeiro: Paz e Terra.

Mbembe, Achille. 2003. "Necropolitics." Translated by Libby Meintjes. *Public Culture* 15, no. 1: 11–40.

McKay, Rhona. 2016. "Vila Autódromo Inaugura Museu das Remoções," *Rio On Watch*, May 24, 2016.

McKittrick, Katherine. 2006. *Demonic Grounds: Black Women and the Cartographies of Struggle*. Minneapolis: University of Minnesota Press.

McKittrick, Katherine, and Clyde Woods. 2007. *Black Geographies and the Politics of Place*. Toronto: Between the Lines.

McClintock, Anne. 1995. *Imperial Leather: Race, Gender, and Sexuality in the Colonial Conquest*. New York: Routledge.

Meade, Teresa. 1997. *"Civilizing" Rio: Reform and Resistance in a Brazilian City, 1889–1930*. University Park: Pennsylvania State University Press.

Meade, Teresa, and Gregory Alonso Pirio. 1988. "In Search of the Afro-American 'Eldorado': Attempts by North American Blacks to Enter Brazil in the 1920s." *Luso-Brazilian Review* 25, no. 1: 85–110.

Menezes, Lená Medeiros de. 1996. *Os indesejáveis: Desclassificados da modernidade: Protesto, crime e expulsão na Capital Federal (1890–1930)*. Rio de Janeiro: EDUERJ.

Mignolo, Walter D. 2007. "Delinking: The Rhetoric of Modernity, the Logic of Coloniality and the Grammar of De-coloniality." *Cultural Studies* 21, no. 2/3: 449–514.

Minardi, Ines. 2008. "Trajetória de Luta: Mulheres Imigrantes Italianas Anarquistas." In *Texto integrante dos Anais do XIX Encontro Regional de História: Poder, Violência e Exclusão*. ANPUH/SP-USP. São Paulo.

Mitchell, Don. 2000. *Cultural Geography: A Critical Introduction*. Oxford: Blackwell.

Mirzoeff, Nicholas. 2011. *The Right to Look: A Counterhistory of Visuality*. Durham, NC: Duke University Press.

Moreira, Giovana Loos. 2016. "A Construção da História Nacional pelo Pintor Firmino Monteiro entre 1879 e 1884." MA thesis, Universidade Federal de Juiz de Fora.

Moreno, Francisco, and Florinda Alói. 2000. "Transcribed Interview by Former Residents of Castelo for Projeto Arquivo Vivo by the Rio de Janeiro Museum of Image and Sound." In *Era Uma Vez o Morro do Castelo*, edited by José Antonio Nonato and Nubia Santos, 198–204. Rio de Janeiro: Ministério da Cultura, Instituto do Patrimônio Histórico e Artístico Nacional.

Morettin, Eduardo. 2011. "A Exposição Internacional do Centenário da Independência em 1922 e 1923." *Novos Estudos* 89: 137–48.

Morettin, Eduardo. 2013. "O Cinema e a Exposição Internacional do Centenário da Independência do Brasil." *Artcultura* 15, no. 27: 145–57.

Mota, André. 2003. *Quem é bom já nasce feito: Sanitarismo e eugenia no Brasil*. São Paulo: DP&A.

Motta, Marly Silva da. 1992. *A nação faz cem anos: A questão nacional no Centenário da Independência*. Rio de Janeiro: Fundação Getúlio Vargas.

Moura, Clóvis. 1977. *O Negro, de bom escravo a mau cidadão?* Rio de Janeiro: Conquista.

Moura, Roberto. 1983. *Tia ciata e a pequena África no Rio de Janeiro*. Rio de Janeiro: FUNARTE.

Munro, Lisa. 2010. "Investigating World's Fairs: An Historiography." *Studies in Latin American Popular Culture* 28, no. 1: 80–94.

Nascimento, Abdias do. 1989. *Brazil, Mixture or Massacre?: Essays in the Genocide of a Black People*. Dover: The Majority Press.

Needell, Jeffrey. 1984. "Making the Carioca Belle Epoque Concrete: The Urban Reforms of Rio de Janeiro under Pereira Passos." *Journal of Urban History* 10, no. 4: 383–422.

Needell, Jeffrey. 1987. *A Tropical Belle Epoque: Elite Culture and Society in Turn-of-the-Century Rio de Janeiro*. Cambridge: Cambridge University Press.

Needell, Jeffrey. 1995. "Identity, Race, Gender and Modernity in the Origins of Gilberto Freyre's Oeuvre." *American Historical Review* 100, no. 1: 51–77.

Neves, Margarida de Souza. 1986. *As vitrines do progresso: O Brasil nas Exposições Internacionais*. Rio de Janeiro: PUC-Rio.

Nixon, Rob. 2013. *Slow Violence and the Environmentalism of the Poor*. Cambridge, MA: Harvard University Press.

Nonato, José Antonio, and Nubia Melhem Santos. 2000. *Era Uma Vez o Morro do Castelo*. Rio de Janeiro: Ministério da Cultura, Instituto do Patrimônio Histórico e Artístico Nacional.

Noronha, Jurandyr. 1987. *No tempo da manivela*. Rio de Janeiro: EMBRAFILME.

Oliveira, Josivaldo Pires de. 2009. "Cosme de Farias e os Capoeiras na Bahia: Um Capítulo de História e Cultura Afro-Brasileira." *Sankofa (São Paulo)* 2, no. 4: 51–66.

Oliveira, Lúcia Lippi. 2006. *Nós e eles: Relações culturais entre brasileiros e imigrantes*. Rio de Janeiro: FGV.

Oliveira, Ney dos Santos. 1996. "Favelas and Ghettos: Race and Class in Rio de Janeiro and New York City." *Latin American Perspectives* 23, no. 4: 71–89.

Oliveira Vianna, Francisco José de. 1938. *Raça e Assimilação: I. Os Problemas da Raça. II. Os Problemas da Assimilação*. São Paulo: Companhia Editora Nacional.

Paixão, Cláudia Míriam Quelhas. 2008. "O Rio de Janeiro e o Morro do Castelo: Populares, Estratégias de Vida e Hierarquias Sociais (1904–1922)." MA thesis, Universidade Federal Fluminense, Niterói.

Pechman, Sérgio, and Lilian Fritsch. 1985. "A reforma urbana e o seu avesso: Algumas considerações a propósito da modernização do Distrito Federal na virada do século." *Revista Brasileira de História* 5, no. 8/9: 139–95.

Peregrino, Miriane. 2016. "Museu das Remoções é Inaugurado na Vila Autódromo," *O Cidadão*, May 26, 2016.

Perry, Keisha-Khan Y. 2013a. *Black Women against the Land Grab: The Fight for Racial Justice in Brazil*. Minneapolis: University of Minnesota Press.

Perry, Keisha-Khan Y. 2013b. "State Violence and the Ethnographic Encounter: Feminist Research and Racial Embodiment," In *Rewriting the African Diaspora in Latin America and the Caribbean,* edited by Robert Lee Adams Jr., 129–48. Abingdon: Routledge.

Perry, Keisha-Khan Y. 2016. "Geographies of Power: Black Women Mobilizing Intersectionality in Brazil." *Meridians* 14, no. 1: 94–120.

Pinsky, Carla Bassanezi, and Joana Maria Pedro. 2012. *Nova história das mulheres no Brasil.* São Paulo: Editora Contexto.

Poole, Deborah. 1997. *Vision, Race, and Modernity: A Visual Economy of the Andean Image World.* Princeton: Princeton University Press.

Porteous, J. Douglas. 1989. *Planned to Death: The Annihilation of a Place Called Howdendyke.* Manchester: Manchester University Press.

Purbrick, Louise. 2017. "Nitrate Ruins: The Photography of Mining in the Atacama Desert, Chile." *Journal of Latin American Cultural Studies.* 26, no. 2: 253–78.

Rao, Vyjayanthi. 2013. "The Future in Ruins." In *Imperial Debris: On Ruins and Ruination,* edited by Ann Laura Stoler, 287–321. Durham, NC: Duke University Press.

Ramos, Jair de Souza. 1996. "Dos Males que Vêm com o Sangue: As Representações Raciais e a Categoria do Imigrante Indesejável nas Concepções Sobre Imigração da Década de 1920." In *Raça, Ciência e Sociedade. Rio de Janeiro,* edited by Marcos Chor Maio and Ricardo Ventura Santos, 59–82. Rio de Janeiro: FIOCRUZ.

Ramos, Maria Estela Rocha. 2007. "Origens da Segregação Espacial da População Afrodescendente em Cidades Brasileiras." In *Espaço urbano e afrodescendência: Estudos da espacialidade negra urbana para o debate das políticas públicas,* edited by Henrique Antunes Cunha Jr., Maria Estela Rocha Ramos, and Antonia dos Santos Garcia, 97–120. Fortaleza: UFC Edições.

Resende, Beatriz. 2000. "Brazilian Modernism: The Canonised Revolution." In *Through the Kaleidoscope: The Experience of Modernity in Latin America,* edited by Vivian Schelling, 199–218. Rio de Janeiro: Verso.

Ribeiro, Gladys Sabina. 1994. "'Por que você veio encher o pandulho aqui?' Os portugueses, o antilusitanismo e a exploração das moradias populares no Rio de Janeiro da República Velha." *Análise Social* 29, no. 127: 631–54.

Rio, João do. (1904) 2006. *As religiões no Rio.* Rio de Janeiro: José Olympio.

Rio, João do. 2005. *A alma encantadora das ruas.* São Paulo: Companhia das Letras.

Rocha, Oswaldo Porto, and Lia de Aquino Carvalho. 1995. *A era das demolições: Cidade do Rio de Janeiro, 1870–1920.* Rio de Janeiro: Prefeitura da cidade do Rio de Janeiro.

Rodrigues, Raimundo Nina. 1932. *O problema da raça negra na américa portuguesa.* Sao Paulo: Brasiliana.

Rodrigues, Raimundo Nina. 1977. *Os africanos no Brasil.* 5th ed. São Paulo: Companhia Editora Nacional.

Roediger, David R. 2006. *Working toward Whiteness: How America's Immigrants Became White: The Strange Journey from Ellis Island to the Suburbs.* New York: Basic Books.

Rolnik, Raquel. 1989. "Territórios Negros nas Cidades Brasileiras. (Etnicidade e Cidade em São Paulo e Rio de Janeiro)." *Estudos Afro-Asiáticos* 17: 29–41.

Rose, Gillian. 2016. *Visual Methodologies: An Introduction to Researching with Visual Materials.* London: Sage.

Ryan, James R., and Joan M. Schwartz. 2003. *Picturing Place: Photography and the Geographical Imagination.* London: I. B. Tauris.

Sant'Ana, Thaís Rezende da Silva de. 2008. "A Exposição Internacional do Centenário da Independência: Modernidade e Política no Rio de Janeiro do Início dos Anos 1920." MA thesis, Universidad Estadual de Campinas.

Santos, Renata. 2008. *A imagem gravada: A gravura no Rio de Janeiro entre 1808 e 1853*. Rio de Janeiro: Casa da Palavra.

Sampaio, Carlos. 1924. *Memória histórica: Obras da prefeitura do Rio de Janeiro: 8 Junho de 1920 a 15 de novembro de 1922*. Lisbon: Lumen.

Schneider, Ann. 2004. "The 1910 Sailors' 'Revolt Against the Lash': The Military, Politics, the Body, and Rights in Brazil." University of Chicago Pozin Center Ignacio Martín-Baró Human Rights Essay Competition, Chicago, Illinois.

Schwarcz, Lilia Moritz. 1999. *The Spectacle of the Races: Scientists, Institutions, and the Race Question in Brazil, 1870–1930*. New York City: Hill and Wang.

Schwarcz, Lilia Moritz. 2017a. "Clara dos Anjos e as Cores de Lima." *Sociologia & Antropologia* 7, no. 1, 125–55.

Schwarcz, Lilia Moritz. 2017b. *Lima Barreto: Triste visionário*. São Paulo: Companhia das Letras.

Schwarz, Roberto. 1992. *Misplaced Ideas: Essays on Brazilian Culture*. Translated by John Gledson. New York: Verso.

Scorer, James. 2017. "Photography and Latin American Ruins." *Journal of Latin American Cultural Studies* 26, no. 2: 141–64.

Secioso de Sá, Antonio. 1928. "Os valentões e originaes do Morro do Castello." *Correio da Manhã*, September 9, 1928.

Seigel, Micol. 2009. *Uneven Encounters: Making Race and Nation in Brazil and the United States*. Durham, NC: Duke University Press.

Sela, Eneida M. 2008. *Modos de ser, modos de ver: Viajantes europeus e escravos africanos no Rio de Janeiro (1808–1850)*. Campinas: Unicamp.

Senra, Nelson de Castro. 2009. "Na Primeira República, Bulhões Carvalho legaliza a atividade estatística e a põe na ordem do Estado." *Boletim do Museu Paraense Emílio Goeldi. Ciências Humanas* 4, no. 3: 387–99.

Sevcenko, Nicolau. 1993. *A revolta da vacina: Mentes insanas em corpos rebeldes*. São Paulo: Scipione.

Seyferth, Giralda. 1990. *Imigração e cultura no Brasil*. Brasília: Universidade de Brasília.

Seyferth, Giralda. 1996. "Construindo a Nação: Hierarquias Raciais e o Papel do Racismo na Política de Imigração e Colonização." In *Raca, Ciência e Sociedade*, edited by Marcos Chor Maio and Ricardo Ventura Santos, 41–58. Rio de Janeiro: FIOCRUZ.

Seyferth, Giralda. 2003. "German Immigration and Brazil's Colonization Policy." In *Mass Migration to Modern Latin America*, edited by Samuel L. Baily and Eduardo José Míguez, 227–44. Wilmington: Scholarly Resources.

Sharpe, Christina. 2010. *Monstrous Intimacies: Making Post-Slavery Subjects*. Durham, NC: Duke University Press.

Sheriff, Robin. 2001. *Dreaming Equality: Color, Race, and Racism in Urban Brazil*. New Brunswick, NJ: Rutgers University Press.

Silva, Denise Ferreira da. 1998. "Facts of Blackness: Brazil is Not Quite the United States . . . and Racial Politics in Brazil?" *Social Identities* 4, no. 2: 201–34.

Silva, Denise Ferreira da. 2001. "Towards a Critique of the Socio-logos of Justice: The Analytics of Raciality and the Production of Universality." *Social Identities* 7, no. 3: 421–54.

Silva, Denise Ferreira da. 2009. "No-bodies: Law, Raciality and Violence." *Griffith Law Review* 18, no. 2: 212–36.

Silva, Lúcia. 2003. *História do urbanismo no Rio de Janeiro: Administração municipal, engenharia e arquitetura dos anos 1920 à ditadura Vargas.* Rio de Janeiro: E-papers.

Silva, Nelson do Valle. 1985. "Updating the Cost of Not Being White in Brazil." In *Race, Class and Power in Brazil*, edited by Pierre-Michel Fontaine, 42–55. Berkeley: University of California Press.

Silvestre, Gabriel, and Nelma Gusmão de Oliveira. 2012. "The Revanchist Logic of Mega-Events: Community Displacement in Rio De Janeiro's West End." *Visual Studies* 27, no. 2: 204–10.

"Sinhô." 2017. Diccionário Cravo Albin da Música Popular Brasileira. Accessed March 14, 2017. http://dicionariompb.com.br/sinho/biografia.

Siqueira, Baptista. 1969. *Três vultos históricos da música brasileira: Mesquita–Callado–Anacleto.* Rio de Janeiro: Araújo.

Skidmore, Thomas. (1974) 1993. *Black into White: Race and Nationality in Brazilian Thought.* Reprint, Durham, NC: Duke University Press.

Skidmore, Thomas E. 1993. "Bi-racial U.S.A. vs. Multi-racial Brazil: Is the Contrast still Valid?" *Journal of Latin American Studies* 25, no. 2: 373–86.

Smith, Christen. 2016. *Afro-paradise: Blackness, Violence, and Performance in Brazil.* Urbana: University of Illinois Press.

Sodré, Nelson Werneck. 1977. *História da imprensa no Brasil.* Rio de Janeiro: Graal.

Sommer, Doris. 1993. *Foundational Fictions: The National Romances of Latin America.* Berkeley: University of California Press.

Steinmann, João [Johann]. (1835) 1944. *Souvenirs du Rio de Janeiro.* Reprint, São Paulo: Livraria Martins.

Stepan, Nancy. 1991. *"The Hour of Eugenics": Race, Gender, and Nation in Latin America.* Ithaca, NY: Cornell University Press.

Stoler, Ann Laura. 2013. *Imperial Debris: On Ruins and Ruination.* Durham, NC: Duke University Press.

Stuckenbruck, Denise Cabral. 1996. *O Rio de Janeiro em questão: o Plano Agache e o ideário reformista dos anos 20.* Rio de Janeiro: Observatório de Políticas Urbanas.

Süssekind, Flora. 1997. *Cinematograph of Words: Literature, Technique, and Modernization in Brazil.* Stanford, CA: Stanford University Press.

Tagg, John. 1988. *The Burden of Representation: Essays on Photographies and Histories.* Amherst: University of Massachusetts Press.

Tenorio-Trillo, Mauricio. 1996. *Mexico at the World's Fairs: Crafting a Modern Nation.* Vol. 35. Berkeley: University of California Press.

Tinhorão, José Ramos. 1998. *História social da música popular brasileira.* São Paulo: Editora 34.

Tinhorão, José Ramos. 1976. *Música popular: Os sons que vem da rua.* São Paulo: Edições Tinhorão.

"Toada." 2015. Enciclopédia Itaú Cultural. Last modified December 2, 2015. http://enciclopedia.itaucultural.org.br/termo14244/toada.

Turazzi, Maria Inez. 1995. *Poses e trejeitos: A fotografia e as exposições na era do espetáculo (1839–1889).* Rio de Janeiro: FUNARTE.

Turazzi, Maria Inez. 2006. "Paisagem construída. Fotografia e memória dos "melhoramentos urbanos" na cidade do Rio de Janeiro." *Varia História* 22, no. 35: 64–78.

Valladares, Lícia do Prado, and Lídia Medeiros. 2003. *Pensando as favelas do Rio de Janeiro, 1906–2000: Uma bibliografia analítica*. Rio de Janeiro: Relume Dumará.

Valladares, Lícia do Prado. 2005. *A invenção da favela: Do mito de origem a favela.com*. Rio de Janeiro: FGV.

Vargas, João H. Costa. 2006. "When a Favela Dared to Become a Gated Condominium: The Politics of Race and Urban Space in Rio de Janeiro." *Latin American Perspectives* 33, no. 4: 49–81.

Vargas, João H. Costa. 2010. *Never Meant to Survive: Genocide and Utopias in Black Diaspora Communities*. Lanham, MD: Rowman and Littlefield.

Vargas, João H. Costa. 2013. "Taking Back the Land: Police Operations and Sport Megaevents in Rio de Janeiro." *Souls: A Critical Journal of Black Politics, Culture, and Society* 15, no. 4: 275–303.

Vasconcelos, José. (1925) 1979. *La raza cósmica*. Translated by Didier T. Jaén. Los Angeles: Centro de Publicaciones, Department of Chicano Studies, California State University, Los Angeles.

Vaz, Lilian Fessler. 1994. "Dos cortiços às favelas e aos edifícios de apartamentos—a modernização da moradia no Rio de Janeiro." *Análise social* 29, no. 127: 581–97.

Vaz, Lilian Fessler. 2000. "Diferentes olhares sobre a cidade: O Rio Antigo através da fotografia e da caricatura." *Anais: Seminário de História da Cidade e do Urbanismo* 6, no. 3: 1–12.

Velloso, Mônica Pimenta. 1988. *As tradições populares na belle époque carioca*. Rio de Janeiro: FUNARTE.

Velloso, Mônica Pimenta. 1990. "As Tias Baianas Tomam Conta do Pedaço . . . Espaço e Identidade Cultural no Rio de Janeiro." *Revista Estudos Históricos* 3, no. 6: 207–28.

Vianna, Hermano. 1999. *The Mystery of Samba: Popular Music and National Identity in Brazil*. Chapel Hill: University of North Carolina Press.

Wadsworth, James E., and Tamera L. Marko. 2001. "Children of the Patria: Representations of Childhood and Welfare State Ideologies at the 1922 Rio de Janeiro International Centennial Exposition." *Americas* 58, no. 1: 65–90.

Watts, Jonathan. 2015. "Forced Evictions in Rio Favela for 2016 Olympics Trigger Violent Clashes." *Guardian*, June 3, 2015.

Yancy, George. 2008. *Black Bodies, White Gazes: The Continuing Significance of Race*. Lanham, MD: Rowman and Littlefield.

Zenha, Celeste. 2004. "O negócio das 'vistas do Rio de Janeiro': Imagens da cidade imperial e da escravidão." *Revista Estudos Históricos* 2, no. 34: 23–50.

Zilly, Berthold. 1999. "Sertão e Nacionalidade: Formação étnica e civilizatória do Brasil segundo Euclides da Cunha." *Estudos Sociedade e Agricultura* no. 12: 5–45.

INDEX

Note: Page references in *italics* refer to figures.